Time to Head Home by William S. Phillips.
Every plane owes its existence to the test pilots.

The F4-U4 Corsair is a favorite plane of
pilots, model makers and test pilots.

William S. Phillips, a preeminent aviation artist,
portrays this unique fighter in action.

The detail from the above painting that
appears on the cover of this edition is used
by courtesy of The Greenwich Workshop.

D0769966

The altitude flights of Schroeder and Macready ended all questions as to the need for experienced test pilots to break new high ground in flight. From these tests there came the turbosupercharger, special propellers, new and reliable oxygen systems, heated systems for the pilot to both keep warm and keep ice clear of his eyes. Flying in an open cockpit at such heights was both foolhardy and unnecessary, and plans were already being laid down to design ships, intended for extreme altitude flights, to have closed cockpits or cabins. The LePere had never been designed for such experiments, and another point made painfully clear was that were the landing gear retractable, the airplane would have been faster, would have climbed faster, and could have reached greater altitude. Even the wings were now considered inadequate and antiquated, for the LePere was designed to fight at low and medium altitudes in European combat, not produce maximum lift at the highest altitude possible.

From these tests flown by these two men, and one other in which Lieutenant James H. Doolittle (who would become one of the most famous test, racing, and combat pilots in the world) pushed an Army XCO-5 above thirty-seven thousand feet and lost consciousness, racing earthward out of control and recovering barely in time to swing into his landing approach, a vast new experiemental *series* began.

THE BANTAM AIR & SPACE SERIES

To Fly Like the Eagles . . .

It took some 1,800 years for mankind to win mastery of a challenging and life-threatening environment—the sea. In just under seventy years we have won mastery of an even more hostile environment—the air. In doing so, we have realized a dream as old as man—to be able to fly.

The Bantam Air & Space series consists of books that focus on the skills of piloting—from the days when the Wright brothers made history at Kitty Hawk to the era of barnstorming daredevils of the sky, through the explosion of technology, design, and fliers that occurred in World War II, and finally to the cool daring of men who first broke the sound barrier, walked on the moon, and have lived and worked in space stations—always at high risk, always proving the continued need for their presence and skill.

The Air & Space series will be published once a month as mass market books with special illustrations, and with varying lengths and prices. Aviation enthusiasts would be wise to buy each book as it comes out if they are to collect the complete library.

TEST PILOTS:
Riding the Dragon

Martin Strasser Caidin

BANTAM BOOKS
NEW YORK · TORONTO · LONDON · SYDNEY · AUCKLAND

TEST PILOTS

A Bantam Falcon Book / April 1992

ISBN 0-553-29426-1

Published simultaneously in the United States and Canada

Bantam Books are published by Bantam Books, a division of Bantam
Doubleday Dell Publishing Group, Inc. Its trademark, consisting of the
words "Bantam Books" and the portrayal of a rooster, is Registered
in U.S. Patent and Trademark Office and in other countries. Marca
Registrada. Bantam Books, 666 Fifth Avenue, New York, New York
10103.

PRINTED IN THE UNITED STATES OF AMERICA

OPM   0 9 8 7 6 5 4 3 2 1

There's this fellow who's my friend. And one hell of a pilot. And this book is for him.

For *Harold Silver*.

Contents

PART I

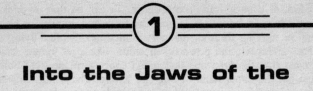

Into the Jaws of the Dragon

Air is thin.

Sometimes.

It's thin if you fall out of your airplane and you don't have a parachute. You can fall out of the damn thing, or jump, or be ejected, but no chute and then this ball eight thousand miles in diameter comes up to flatten out your kidneys, heart, lungs, skull, bones, and skin. Very hard, so that the odds are about a million to one against your ever moving again of your own volition.

Air is thin.

Well, *not always.*

Air is thin only under certain conditions. If you're flying a real hotrock fighter, or a lead sled with wings that's sustained in flight only by meager lift from its wings and the power of a monstrous blowtorch of a jet engine, the air remains thin *only* if your airplane is pointed in a direction that minimizes the terrible blasting effect of air when you're flying sideways. Then that same thin air, so beautifully guided past the aerodynamic shape of your machine, becomes a laughing, shrieking force that can rip your wings from the body of your airplane, or crumple the tail into metallic shards, or decelerate the machine so suddenly and violently the g-forces can mash you into red spinach within your cockpit.

So it all depends on what's happening, at how great a

3

speed, at what altitude (because the air can be thin or thick, depending on how high is *up*), the form and manner of how you're moving through that air. Sometimes, a pilot flying a sleek and swift and powerful machine, like a jet fighter, discovers that the gremlins that infect every airplane ever built just got the upper hand. Things go wrong. The controls mess up and either become useless slop under a man's hands or act as if they've just been set in solid concrete. Engines gasp, blaze, go wildly turbulent, or just plain quit. Anything *can* fail, from mechanical to hydraulic to electrical, and when that happens, a pilot may have to make a decision *instantly* as to whether he'll stay with his ship and fight it for control all the way back to earth, or, a bit more simply, he'll say, "To hell with this!" and he'll leave his airplane.

In the olden times of flight, when supersonic was a dream far in a future that seemed unattainable, bailing out of a stricken airplane usually gave a pilot a high chance of survival. Unless his machine was gyrating violently out of control and g-forces pinned him inside, or his canopy jammed and he was imprisoned helplessly as his craft tumbled earthward, or any one of a dozen critical problems, he had a pretty good shot of getting out, falling free of the metal now become idiotically pilotless, and pulling the D-ring of his parachute so that silk or nylon could fill with rushing air, billow out to its full diameter, and lower him safely, even with a bump or two, to the ground.

But the olden times left us in the late forties and the early fifties, when the first rocket-propelled experimental ships pinched their way through the sound barrier. Pinched rather than punched, because it was still a very dicey affair, and the insurance premiums on the life of a rocket test pilot were insanely high, just as their life expectancy was dismally low. When one of these machines went haywire, tumbling or whirling crazily out of control, the immediate problem wasn't when to pull the D-ring that would release the parachute to lower the pilot safely to ground, but how to get the hell out of that airplane that seemingly had gone mad.

An airplane tumbling or gyrating at high speed is filled with powerful hands that grip a pilot so tightly he can't move. These hands—the violently surging forces of acceleration—can pin a man like a doomed fly against the side of his

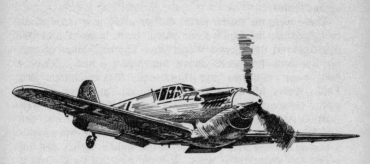

Messerschmitt Me 109

cockpit. After all, when a man weighing two hundred pounds is thrust suddenly to a weight of two thousand pounds or more, and the horizon is a maddened line flashing and tumbling, he really can't move very well when even breathing is difficult. It's much the same as having an elephant sitting on his chest and face. And if he does manage to pull and crawl and drag his way painfully to where he may yet exit his machine, he faces the shrieking monster of wind. Not wind as you or I know it: not wind as we have ever experienced in our lives.

Wind so hysterically violent it is a physical force with flailing knives and battering rams. Wind—the air streaming past the machine—so powerful it makes of a hurricane a balmy breeze, and by comparison even a howling tornado, with all its crushing might and fury, is gentled air. We are talking about wind six, eight, *ten times the speed of a hurricane*. To the man struggling to escape his uncontrollable aircraft, that wind is a solid wall, a battering ram that laughingly traps him within his cockpit. It can snap arms and legs like brittle twigs and do much the same to a man's neck, which, sometimes, is a blessing that saves the man from remaining alive and alert all the way down to the inevitable crunch against earth.

These were the barrier reefs of flight every man faced when he lunged into the speeds made prosaic by the winged machines that followed the Second World War. The beginnings of that air war brought speeds above the three-hundred-miles-per-hour mark—Spitfires and Hurricanes, Messerschmitts and Focke-Wulfs, Mitsubishis and Nakajimas, Yakovlevs and Mikoyan-Gurevich, and those best known in this country, from Buffalo and Wildcat to Hellcat and Corsair, from Airacobra and Warhawk to Lightning and Thunderbolt and Mustang— a parade of powerful propeller-driven fighter planes rushing ever faster through the skies, until the speed of fighters went steadily upwards to four hundred miles per hour and beyond. Then came the first rocket fighters, experimental and dangerous both to their enemy and their own pilots because of balky fuels and wicked flying characteristics. And then the first jets to close out tumultuous months of final battle. Germany rushed into the air with one new design after the other; the famed Messerschmitt Me-262 twinjet fighter, a hundred miles an hour faster than anything with a propeller against which it fought. The Heinkel He-162, the "People's Fighter," a grandiose attempt to build a quick-and-cheap jet that failed to get into combat because it so often broke up in the air in test flights. There were others such as the Arado 234, and experimental machines like the Junkers Ju-287. From the British camp there came the Gloster Meteor twinjet fighter to chase V-1 robot jet bombs, with the Vampire and other models being rushed to readiness to do battle. From the United States, spawned from the clumsy and sodden Bell XP-59A Airacomet, there emerged the spectacularly successful Lockheed P-80 Shooting Star, again with stablemates being readied with alacrity.

Even then, the wicked grasp of wind transformed into steel bars and sledgehammer blows crushed men like toys, snapped their limbs, jerked them violently through the air. There had to be another way to emerge from a stricken machine flying better than five hundred miles per hour, and the engineers came forward with a device that promised survival when there was rarely any chance to live through an emergency.

The ejection seat, a huge catapult built within the cockpit of the fighter. When the time came to abandon a torn and broken aircraft, the pilot grasped the right handles, locked his legs within clamps or stirrups, and pulled a handle or a bar or a switch, little matter which. Beneath the seat, attached to rails along which it would rise, was a powerful twenty-millimeter cannon shell. The pilot pulled the appropriate controls, the canopy above the cockpit tore away (he hoped), and then the cannon shell exploded to hurl the pilot still strapped to his seat away from his machine.

Most of the time, it worked. Much of the time it did not work well. The twenty-millimeter cannon shell sometimes lacked the energy to hurl man-and-seat far enough to clear his aircraft. The seat and pilot might smash into the tail, and that was *that*. Often the sudden explosive acceleration would break legs. Or the cockpit would be so poorly designed that the pilot's legs would be ripped from his body as they slammed into the top of the forward cockpit edge. And then, were he safely to clear his machine, the force of the wind would jerk his legs from their restraints, breaking bones instantly so that they twisted and flailed like billowing rags. Or, just as often, arms would be lashed away from the seat, broken instantly, pivoting in the wind, snapping back and forth like the tongue of an angry snake, so that the man could no longer release his body harness, could not push himself away from his seat, could not pull the D-ring to release his parachute.

The engineers figured a thirty-seven-millimeter cannon shell would be better. It would blow the pilot's seat on its rails faster than before, hurl him higher and farther from his airplane. The restraints were now better, so that there was less chance of arms and legs breaking, so the pilot would remain alive long enough to know he was falling helplessly to his death. But it created a new problem. The acceleration was worse than before.

It broke a man's spine. The punch of the shell was so powerful it jammed the spinal column down into the seat like a berserk hydraulic ram. Not too many pilots survived the terrible pain and physical damage to their bodies; those who survived would live with that pain for the rest of their lives.

Engineers devised new systems one after the other. The first thing to do was to get rid of the powerful thirty-seven-

Boeing B-47

millimeter cannon shell that *exploded*. Far better was a new rocket that would have the same power, or even more, of the cannon shell, but would burn slower, so that the acceleration would be lessened. And by burning longer, it would catapult both man and seat well above and away from his machine. (Some seats, depending upon the design of the fighter or the bomber—in the case of the latter the sleek Boeing B-47 Stratojet—fired seat and pilot *downward* to clear their aircraft.)

Teams of parachute jumpers and skydivers, *and* test pilots, began their acid tests of the new equipment. It worked better than ever before. Men could be hurled with less acceleration and longer propulsion times from their abandoned aircraft. They could even be ejected *through* the canopy if that was needed; the seat rails that went with the seat punched up first, the force of the blazing rocket great enough to smash the canopy and permit pilot and seat to continue on to safety. If the acceleration or other forces were so great, or the pilot were wounded or injured, he could easily lose consciousness from the blows of ejection or being thrust into the hammering winds.

As test pilots are wont to murmur when anticipating such moments, "Piece of cake." Essentially, compared with the "olden days," that was true. The pilot could stay alert just long enough to pull a seat-rest handle, or use both hands to pull a canopy down over his head and face, or he might grasp a ring between his legs and haul up with all his might. Whatever the particular system, it punched the pilot up and away, his departure from his aircraft marked clearly with a blazing spout of flame. He would remain with the seat long enough for his tumbling entry into winds worse than any tornado until he decelerated. Many seats even had fins and strakes so that they became aerodynamically stable as the pilot fell earthward. And if he were unconscious, at a prese-lected altitude above ground, a barometric trigger in the seat would fire.

Beneath the pilot's back and his rump, a strong webbing or belt would snap taut. Seat belt and shoulder harness flew open, and the sudden tightening of the webbing literally shoved the pilot away from his seat. If he were still uncon-scious, automatic systems would haul open his parachute pack, the chute would deploy, and even if still blissfully "out of it," he would drift safely to earth.

Thirty-five years ago this type of ejection seat system was being installed in supersonic jet fighters as fast as their factor-ies could turn them out. The reasoning was stark; pilots ejecting from high-speed jets were being hurt badly, too many were being killed, and the hot jet fighters were swiftly amassing a rotten reputation with their pilots. The new seats changed all that.

But . . . thirty-five years ago another barrier still had to be passed.

The sound barrier was no more. The dreaded wall in the sky *had* been real enough. As new aircraft pushed closer and closer to the speed of sound the air before the planes piled up in the form of shuddering, battering rams. Shock waves as hard as steel streamed from the nose and wings to rip and tear at other parts of the planes. Control forces reversed, strange and terrible and unknown blows ripped into the air-

XS-1

craft. Throughout the world the goal of flying faster than sound was pursued with grim determination. Throughout the world, men died in that attempt. Then in 1947, Chuck Yeager rode the bright orange Bell XS-1 on a long tail of streaming fire "through the Mach," past the speed of sound at his high altitude. Mach 1 had slipped from the impossible to the historical.

Test pilots took up ever-more-powerful fighter planes and experimental aircraft. Wings became swept back to "fool" the air and permit the planes to fly ever faster. Jet engines howled with unprecedented fury, and at first, the new jets went through the speed of sound only by diving under full power.

Then came the latest model in a long line of superb fighter planes turned out by North American Aviation. First the ubiquitous P-51 Mustang that gave "fighter plane" a new meaning with its dazzling speed and tremendous range. The war faded into history, the era of jets was part of the new times, and there appeared the sleek, sweptwing F-86 Sabre. This was the Air Force fighter that could start down in a steepening dive from forty thousand feet and punch past the speed of sound. As great as was the Sabre, it wasn't good enough.

The Air Force wanted a jet fighter that could do two things—go into production *and* fly faster than the speed of sound in level flight.

Out of the North American stable came a new and powerful thoroughbred: the heavy, sleek, F-100 Super Sabre, affectionately and sometimes not so affectionately known to its pilots as the "Lead Sled." You think of a fighter and you conjure up light weight, blazing speed, fire torrents from the engine; agility and swirling motion and deftness in the sky.

The F-100 was a *brute*. It had to do the best job possible with the most powerful engine available at the time, *and it did it*. It flew supersonic in level flight. Despite the bludgeoning weight for its power, it had alacrity enough to be selected by the U.S. Air Force Thunderbirds as their first supersonic fighter for the world-acclaimed jet aerobatic maneuvers they perform with such consummate skill and precision.

All that was, and is, terrific. But there lurked a dragon in the sky. I came to hear of this dragon in a very personal way. Back in the time of those three decades past, I lived and flew with the Thunderbirds in order to write an intimate, detailed, highly personal book on the team and its history. Dick Crane and I flew often in the team's two-seat F-100F; we flew off by ourselves and often we flew formation with the team. If you want to know what it's like to be a part of this superb flying organization, then you've got to get with it both on the ground and in the air. It was sensational.

But there *was* that dragon, invisible, it was true, until the shock waves of supersonic flight became visible, and *then* you might see this great beastie that dwelt in the high sky and glared from the far side of the sonic wall.

A reality of life at the time was that even when the Super Sabre became an operational fighter, even when it was painted in the brilliant red, white, and blue of the Thunderbirds, it was still an airplane under accelerated development and, above all, still being improved in equipment and performance. That meant that no matter what went on in the field, in daily operations, a full team of pilots was still testing the Super Sabre. They didn't go upstairs simply to tickle the fancies of the Lead Sled. Their task was to run not only the exciting moments of tremendous speed, but the tests that test pilots consider necessary humdrum.

New control systems, modified hydraulics, different electrical systems, experimental brakes and flaps, new gun sights, bomb racks, tests for stability and control. Most test flying isn't hero stuff. It's *work*. But unlike the kind of work you find at the end of the morning drive on the highways to office buildings, this office is within the belly of the supersonic beast, and every time you fly, if it's to punch through the wall into supersonic flight or to test a new radio, you place your life on the line.

And there was that dragon that no one had ever survived. Until this time, until the dragon tore loose from its shackles and hurled itself at one man, there was a question no one could answer—but many could imagine.

"I'll tell you right out," the pilots with experience would inform the newcomers wearing their fresh new test-pilot suits, "don't get into trouble when you're on the far side of the Mach. The odds are you won't come home in one piece. That nice airplane you're flying will instantly become a pit bull and he'll sink his teeth into places you wouldn't talk about with your mama."

Early in 1955, George F. Smith was one of the lead inspection test pilots for North American Aviation, and testing the supersonic F-100 was his assignment. If you were an experienced supersonic fighter test pilot in those days, you were better than good. You were among the best of the best. George Smith lived a true pilot's life, a thirty-one-year-old bachelor with a Manhattan Beach apartment only a few minutes from the North American plant at Los Angeles International Airport. Smith, like any veteran test jockey, took every opportunity to impart his own lessons and experience to the new men. The veterans had "the word" to pass on.

And the word from such men was, "If you run into trouble when you're supersonic, do *not*, repeat, do not bail out. Most especially if you're down low. Don't punch out of your airplane because no one believes you'll ever live through that experience to come home. Not in one piece, anyway. Certainly not walking or talking. You may not even be more than a lot of smudge in disassembled pieces. So if you're through the Mach, try to stay with your bird until you decelerate to *below* supersonic."

They had plenty of evidence to back up their advice. Their

examples were clear. The forces of supersonic flight were mighty enough to smash *any* airplane into twisted wreckage while it was still flying. Or as it changed from flying to mindless hurtling.

Just before noon on February 26, 1955, George F. Smith was in the operations flight shack of North American when dispatcher Bob Gallahue motioned to him with a dispatch sheet. "George, we've got Number 659 ready for a test flight. Long as you're here, why don't you take her up?"

George nodded. Sure; why not? Normally when he tested a ship off the line, he took his time preparing to go upstairs. That meant donning a reinforced nylon flight suit and flight boots that would have made a paratrooper happy. But it was just this one flight and George Smith didn't want to go through the whole drill. He was wearing a sport shirt and slacks, not having planned to fly this day. He slipped into his life vest and secured the harness on his parachute, nudged his helmet and oxygen mask over his head and face. He hooked up to the proper connections in the cockpit of the big jet fighter, ran through the prestart check, fired up the powerful jet engine. Satisfied with his instrument readings, he made his radio check and received permission to taxi out and hold short of the active runway. There he went through the pre-takeoff checks. These included, in this airplane, checking out the hydraulic pressures of two systems that boosted his flight control surfaces. Both systems read normally, George called the tower for clearance and moments later sped down the runway to soar into the air.

George kept the afterburner in, a slash of visible flame booming the F-100A swiftly to high altitude. As an inspection test pilot he followed a well-used route for such flights; climb out of the international field, cross the area of Palos Verdes, and swing into a turn toward San Diego. He kept climbing through a cloud overcast that deepened and grew together as he soared upward, and then he was at thirty-five thousand feet.

Piece of cake.

Yet anyone who flew the Super Sabres out of the North American factory always had a thought or two about a man named George Welch. Postwar periods are times of swift memory loss, and few Americans would know the name of

P-40

George Welch. Way back in time, specifically the morning of December 7, 1941, when a powerful armada of Japanese fighters and bombers turned Pearl Harbor into a concussion-racked and flaming junkyard, Welch was one of the few pilots who dashed into the air to fight the Japanese. In fact, he made flights in both an ancient Curtiss P-36 Mohawk and a Curtiss P-40 Tomahawk, and in the face of overwhelming Japanese superiority, George Welch shot down four enemy planes on that disastrous Sunday morning. Welch survived more combat and the entire war, and when the fighting was over and another war in Korea had come and gone, he was flying as a Super Sabre test pilot with North American. Welch, in 1954, came downstairs from high altitude in his F-100. He slipped swiftly into supersonic flight.

As the saying goes, "something happened." The details are still argued, but whatever went wrong in the sky that day, everything came unglued with that airplane as it dove faster than sound. The word is that Welch punched out, or tried to punch out; whatever. He didn't make it. The man who'd come out of a war a terrific fighter pilot and then a test pilot, died. The next word that passed around was that if you bailed out, or punched out, or got out of your airplane at supersonic speed, well, if you were married, then your wife was an instant widow. It was always nagging at the back of a pilot's mind.

The control stick in George Smith's right hand *twitched*. Now, in a propeller-driven airplane flying low in choppy air a twitch, bang, slam, vibration, or whatever is just a part of flying. In level flight seven miles up in a silky jet fighter a twitch is more than enough to bring every muscle in your body to instant rigid attention and open the valves for swift adrenaline flow.

It is *not* supposed to happen. It's bad news. No more piece of cake.

The nose dropped. George Smith had *not* eased the stick forward. He hadn't touched the trim. That was George's immediate thought; the electric trim motor must have shorted out, and one result could be that the huge stabilator at the tail of the fighter was moving to push the airplane into a steepening dive. It was still far from panic time, because when a supersonic fighter in level flight, especially the F-100A, slips into supersonic country, there's a natural tendency for the airplane to nose down slightly. Experienced pilots are ready for it and they're also ready to nudge the trim control slightly to keep the airplane level.

George nudged, but the airplane didn't. It kept nosing over. George pulled back on the control stick. In the F-100A, as in other jet fighters, hydraulic boost gives one man the strength of twelve. So he pulled back gently.

The nose kept going down.

He was fast getting into alarm country. By now George knew something was *very* wrong. He applied strong back pressure on the stick. *It refused to move*. He grasped it with both hands and pulled with all his strength.

The stick might just as well have been embedded in cold, solid concrete. Well, almost. It was worse than that, because "the stick seemed to be moving very slowly away from me," George recalled later, "and the fighter nosing down accordingly." He reasoned later that perhaps the stick *wasn't* moving away from him, because "it doesn't seem possible that the stick would have been moving away; if it had just been frozen, which it was, maybe it would have psychologically felt like it was moving away as I tried to pull it back.''

George was on his way to a dive in a powered bomb. The descent steepened swiftly to twenty degrees. Immediately George thumbed his radio transmit button to call the company radio contact facility, XRT. He told them, quickly and smoothly, he was having hydraulic problems and that he was in a dive and it was getting sort of hairy up there.

By the time he finished his brief report it wasn't a descent anymore. The F-100A was now diving almost vertically and descending like a maddened beast. Another test pilot, Joe Kinkella, monitoring the XRT channel, heard the distress call. Looking around, he spotted the other F-100A whipping earthward like a silver dart. To Kinkella there wasn't a moment to waste. Every second the F-100A was picking up speed and the earth was, in terms of time, *very* close. Kinkella thumbed his transmit button as he stared at the silvery dart and the contrail streaming behind.

"George, bail out! Bail out *now*!''

Geroge Smith needed no words from anyone else to know life was—could be—fleetingly brief. The F-100A was a mad *thing*. By now his dive had gone *through the vertical*. His body began to lift upward from his seat, straining against his harness. He was now starting to pull negative g's, which meant the fighter was now through the vertical and starting to tuck under into an outside loop. That would tear even the tough F-100A to splintered, flaming wreckage.

This was panic time if there ever was going to be such a moment. But there was also not a second to waste. George shouted out a final transmission. *"Controls locked! I'm going straight in!"* That was the last word from him because all he thought of now was getting the hell out of that airplane.

There wasn't even time to think of what every pilot was talking about. *You bail out at supersonic speed, especially at low altitude, and you're a dead sucker . . . that supersonic air will blow you apart.*

There wasn't time to think because George Smith was doing things. His mind and hands were as one. Instantly he stop-cocked his jet engine to kill all thrust. He banged open the speed brake; anything to slow down that ship even a little. His hands moving in a blur of speed, he yanked his

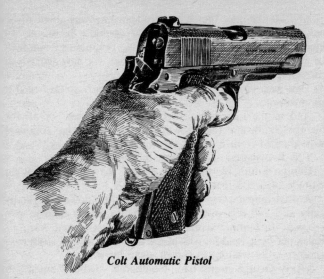

Colt Automatic Pistol

helmet visor down over his face and his right hand yanked hard, upward, on the seat armrest.

A locomotive thundered into the cockpit at full speed as the canopy blew away from the F-100A, whisked out of sight instantly. After all, that airplane was diving nearly 250 miles an hour faster than the muzzle velocity of a .45-caliber bullet from a Colt automatic pistol!

The volcanic roar was so violent, George reacted by instinct to "get away" from the shattering, continuing explosion of sound. His body went forward into a crouch. It was the worst move he could have made. He was now in the worst position for the explosive ejection he hoped would hurl him away from what had become a death ship. His feet were still hard on the rudder pedals instead of being flat and almost directly beneath him.

George shot an incredible, time-almost-stopped glance at his instrument panel. The Mach meter seemed to leap out at him, showing him he was diving at Mach 1.05, well above the speed of sound. He was about to go through the ejection slingshot into what every pilot was convinced was certain death.

And his memory of what was happening was about to be severed. "I don't remember actually pulling the trigger to eject the seat," he recalled laconically. The memory—or lack of it—brought a wry smile to his face. "I saw the Mach meter reading 1.05."

That was all he knew. He woke up in a hospital bed *five days later*.

And in the long run, it certainly appears best of all for George Smith that the incredible violence of what followed was blanked from mind and memory. . . .

The dive started at thirty-five thousand feet.

George Smith blew himself out of the death ship at an altitude of 6,500 feet.

At that moment the F-100A was hurtling downward vertically at 1,140 feet *every second*—better than a mile in five *seconds*. In familiar terms his speed at that instant was 777 miles per hour, and he was in the dense air of low altitude— another killer waiting to snatch away his life.

Likely George Smith hadn't bothered, at that moment, to calculate the numbers. But at his speed, if he had delayed pulling the explosive trigger of his ejection seat by only *two seconds,* he would never have regained consciousness five days later. He would have been *very* dead, because those two seconds were all the time he had left to live.

First he had to haul on that ejection trigger. This blasted him away from the fighter. Then, two more seconds pass until the seat releases its connections and automatically boots the pilot free of the metal structure. All this time, of course, he's decelerating violently, but another two seconds are required for the automatic system to boom the parachute away from his body. In six seconds he would have hurtled downward a distance of 6,840 feet, which was greater than his height when the controlled explosion hurled him from the fighter.

Whatever happened next was erased from George's mind, for as he left the airplane the effect was much the same as if his body had slammed into a steel wall. Instantly the sledgehammer blows striking his body everywhere smashed him unconscious.

No torturer could have done worse to George Smith than this maniacal lifesaving violence. Either the ejection, when his feet were in the wrong position, or slamming into the steel air of supersonic flight, ripped his shoes and socks from his feet. Steel nails tore his clothes to shreds. The howling wind of the dragon—for a human body in supersonic speed *is* in the jaws of the dragon—ripped his helmet from his head. His oxygen mask had been torn violently from his face. Blood smeared from deep cuts on his forehead, chin, and his feet. His body was inhumanly twisted, and he hung in his parachute harness limp and grotesque, a battered and slashed rag doll that seemed lifeless.

He fell with terrible speed, for more than a third of his lifesaving parachute had been blown out of his canopy. And when his chute did open, jerking him to a bone-mauling stop, he was invisible to the world, for he was still in the clouds.

By now George was still alive, and his unconscious state promised a very short time to live. He was well out in the ocean, offshore. He was physically helpless, and being unconscious he could neither get himself free of his parachute harness nor inflate his life vest when finally he would reach water.

Miracles *can* come in bunches. A fishing cruiser, *Balabes*, was in the water nearby with two men, Art Berkell, Mel Simon, and the latter's fifteen-year-old son, Robert. They were there by grace and fortune. The weather was poor for fun fishing; low clouds and intermittent rain. Most boats had long left, but the three aboard the *Balabes* had decided to "stick it out just a bit longer."

No one remembers what fish they may have caught, but they'll never forget a huge explosion nearby that smashed against their boat and pounded the *Balabes* with a roaring shock wave. They dashed to the deck to see water geysering upward, a white foaming explosion soaring into the air only two hundred yards distant. It was the F-100A in its final moment as it tore at supersonic speed into the ocean.

The astonished—and frightened—men in the boat figured they had blundered into a naval target range, and their only thought was to execute the timeworn maneuver of "Let's get the hell out of here!" Then the youngster in the boat stared, pointing up at the sky. "Look!" he cried, and they saw the rag-doll figure hanging loosely from the torn parachute dropping oceanward. Immediately they started at full power to

F-100

where the unconscious Geroge Smith would reach the surface, and as they did so the F-100 with Joe Kinkella in the cockpit hurtled down through the cloud layer and raced low overhead. Kinkella called for rescue from XRT; moments later another pilot, Frank Smith, circled the area in *his* F-100, and then a private aircraft came in low and circled the boat, that pilot also calling in by radio what he was seeing so that rescue boats could get under way immediately.

But George Smith wasn't going to last that long. He came down in a sky of dead calm. That meant he would hit the water like a sackful of rocks and go under immediately, his body further trapped by his parachute folding about and over him. *Another* miracle, this time smaller than the others but just as critical. As George Smith's body splashed down a sudden breeze partially inflated the folding parachute canopy. This was lifesaving, for it helped pull George's face from the water. More small events combined to hang on to George's life. Since he wasn't conscious to manually jerk the lanyards on his life vest for inflation, he had no buoyancy to keep him above the water as the fishing boat raced toward him.

Those "small events" were the air that smashed into George's body, lending unexpected buoyancy to his unconscious form, and some air punched into his torn clothes. All combined to keep his face above water long enough—the time was less than one minute—for the sports fishermen in the *Balabes* to reach George.

Another coincidence; another lifesaving moment. George Smith weighed 215 pounds. He was inert and waterlogged in his clothes and parachute. Getting his unconscious form into the boat was an almost impossible task. An experienced rescue man would have been invaluable.

Once again the odds played in George Smith's favor. During the Second World War, Art Berkell, now an attorney, had been a rescue specialist with the U.S. Navy and had participated in the lifesaving rescues of 275 men. George Smith became number 276. With the others helping, Berkell pulled a knife from his belt, slashed away the canopy from the parachute harness, and the two men and the teenager hauled George into the boat and went to full power, racing for Newport Harbor.

The dice were rolling in incredible fashion. Several miles away was a small flotilla of Coast Goard vessels practicing air-sea rescue and emergency medical procedures. They'd seen the descending parachute and the fastest Coast Guard vessel rushed at full speed to the scene. They intercepted the *Balabes*. No one wasted a moment. They transferred the unconscious and battered form of Smith to the faster Coast Guard ship, which raced to port. Medical technicians gave immediate first aid to George Smith. The captain radioed ahead with a call for help, and by the time they reached dock, an ambulance and doctors were ready and waiting. Another immediate transfer, more emergency medical help, and George Smith was on his way to Hoag Memorial Hospital!

The hospital, in Newport Beach, would be the entire world for the next seven months for George F. Smith.

The unconscious pilot they rushed into the emergency room was more dead than alive. Doctors said flatly he wouldn't live. The doctors really didn't know *what* to do, because no one had ever seen the battered and smashed body of a man cannon-shot into supersonic air before, and they had no way of anticipating the nature of his savage injuries. So it was do whatever was possible and learn the details as you went along.

It was obvious George was in severe shock. His heart beat was barely detectable. Pulse? Hardly any. Blood pressure? So far gone, so low that it failed to register on the monitors. Immediately they jabbed shots into George, fed him one-hundred-percent oxygen, tapped an IV into his arm.

At the time George Smith was blind. His eyeballs had hemorrhaged, the retinas were severely damaged. There was no white to his eyeballs. Everything was bright red from burst blood vessels. The fancy name for "maximum blood-shot eyes," if there is such a term, was subconjunctival hemorrhage.

Virtually every part of his body was terribly cut and bruised. His head, feet, legs, shoulders, and back had been mauled by the blast of the ejection seat blowing him from the fighter. Chafing is an inadequate word for the injuries inflicted from his parachute harness, oxygen bailout bottle, helmet, and other equipment. His lips, ears, and eyelids looked like raw meat, slashed and bruised and torn—they had all fluttered violently from the shock of supersonic air. His face looked as if a bulldozer had run over it several times—grievously puffed and distorted, skin cracked and swollen—and he was hardly recognizable as human from the dark purple of his skin, caused by subsurface bleeding.

When he first smashed into the air, his legs and his arms had flailed wildly, a rag doll in the teeth of a wild animal. His knee joints were cracked and loose; had he been conscious he could never have stood on his legs. The doctors were amazed that his arms and legs weren't broken in dozens of places.

But there wasn't any question about other internal injuries. His stomach had swollen to grotesque proportions, both from air blasted into it and from a lower intestine that had been shaken and pounded like a snake being beaten with clubs (surgery finally saved his life again). Yet the extent of stomach damage was less immediately dangerous than the blows to his liver, which came the closest to ending his life. Constant medical attention, teams working around the clock, kept him alive and began the terribly slow and agonizing return to full consciousness. What kept the doctors nearly frantic was the fact that blood was being slowly absorbed, clotted and dangerous, into his main bloodstream. He developed severe jaundice.

When he regained consciousness, the doctors discovered that in that hell in the sky, rattled in the jaws of the dragon, he'd lost more than his shoes and socks. His wristwatch had vanished. His gloves were gone. And a ring had been snatched cleanly from a finger!

There was more, but it would fill a medical book. George Smith lost sixty-five pounds. Even after full "recovery," a questionable term after seven months, he limped painfully. The doctors told him that if he ever took an alcoholic drink, it would kill him. A small price to pay for remaining alive.

The medical specialists determined that when he crashed into that supersonic airstream, George Smith had been blasted with a deceleration force of *forty gravities*. In a horrifying split second *his weight shot up from 215 to 8,800 pounds*.

George F. Smith gained back weight, went through physical training, and in August of 1955 he stunned the aviation world by passing the examinations, physical and flight, for a commercial pilot license! The man who'd been blind for five days, and had seen through a scarlet haze for weeks afterward, now had twenty-twenty vision.

George F. Smith was back in the world of the living.

There's a wonderful and warm postscript to all this. North American Aviation built supersonic fighters. It also built huge rockets and rocket engines, and the Apollo spacecraft that carried men to the moon.

I had written the novel *Marooned* that Columbia Pictures made into an Oscar-winning film. We worked closely with North American Aviation in making this film, especially at the launch sites of Cape Canaveral Air Force Station in Florida.

I was technical director on this film and I had fun acting in the picture. We did some great scenes with Gregory Peck.

I said *we*. The third actor in these scenes was George F. Smith, test pilot.

We had a ball.

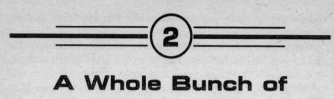

A Whole Bunch of Beginnings

First there were the dreamers. Those who understood no more than their desire to waft gently or with godlike speed through the heavenly air that lay upon the earth. That's all they really had for many generations. An unanswered yearning and often a frustrating rage at the birds soaring overhead with impunity.

Then came the dreamers with set-in-stone belief that the gods lent an attentive ear to their plaintive beseeching and would endow them with the magic of flight if only their faith were strong enough. It was long before the time when men would wish specifically to overcome or to negate gravity, since that was yet a word to be understood, let alone even uttered. In effect, man hadn't yet discovered gravity, so it failed to be included in his efforts to emulate winged creatures that *did* fly. If these souls lacked the pinions to flail wildly and soar, then faith would most certainly have to do, and uncounted numbers of the faithful fell or tumbled on a one-time-only descent from fearful heights off cliffs or other high places. There's no way of knowing how many intrepid adventurers perished in this manner.

A rare few of the more adventuresome, who had plummeted to earth, were fortunate enough to have slammed into bushes or trees and, after breaking assorted bones and scraping off skin, were still alive. Others plunged into less resistant water and, if they didn't drown, also survived. These latter were sought out by those who had yet to test their faith against this unknown force that dashed men wantonly to ground while manifestly allowing birds to fly and, upon questioning the crippled and battered ex-fliers, were told, "This ain't the way to go."

So the dreamers changed their tune. Still they dreamed, but now they bent their energies to imitating those who *could* fly. After all, birds did, and by the millions. Birds large and small, of every color and size and sound; they flew madly, happily, all the seasons long. They flew long distances, vast hordes of these creatures disappearing each year and reappearing at season's turn with astonishing regularity.

Wings! There lay the answer, and as quickly as this brilliant observation sank home, men rushed to assemble wings out of a strange and often dubious potpourri of materials. Thus, in this one fell swoop (a swoop of several generations, it should be noted), the dreamers became the first tinkerers seeking flight. They built wings of feathers, canvas, silk, linen, wood, strings, rope, wires, and leather straps. What would work the best?

If they looked for the first records of man's dreams of flight, they returned to illustrations of mythological beliefs of Greece and Rome, long forgotten but now studied with new interest. If they wished to learn about the first men who had dreamed of actually flying, they could go back more than five thousand years. But there were no pictures, so the hopeful quickly moved forward in time to 1100 B.C. Ah, there it was! Wonderfully preserved, marvelously accurate, obviously true—the tales of Daedalus and Icarus. Great feathery wings, a desperate need to fly, ingenious rationalization, and the stark and gripping drama of the young boy who soared to forbidden heights where the pitiless sun melted the wax that held his pinions to his shoulder blades, causing him to be dashed mercilessly to the earth far below.

The would-be fliers studied the stunning paintings made of the *Winged Victory of Samothrace,* the ancient Greek sculpture from 305 B.C. Those were wings (even if the goddess had somehow lost her head) of great form and power; an interesting combination that likely was the first flight system, mythological or otherwise, where "flying blind" had its ultimate meaning.

And if birds and bats and gods and goddesses could fly, why not larger animals such as the horse? Mythology in those days was the equal of today's encyclopedias; if it existed on canvas or in marble then it was accepted as having some basis in reality. So the winged horse of Grecian Mythology of 1100 B.C., the famed *Puck on Pegasus* sculpture of Coysevox, entered the running for consideration. Fortunately for whatever horse might have been chosen, no one could figure out how to connect wings to the back of the horse, and equestrian flight would have been impossible with wings that were ridiculously small in size against the heft of the animal.

One after the other the mythological wonders passed in the review. If Mythology only had been the impetus for pursuing manned flight (aside from all those creatures flitting overhead), we might not yet be airborne as a civilization. But those anxious to ascend to the high blue took careful note of what historians and men of science thought. The Greek historian Herodotus (484–443 B.C.) predicted that flight was not only possible but inevitable. Then Euclid (300 B.C.) and, immediately after, Archimedes (287–212 B.C.) considered the issues mathematically. Socrates and Plato, show the records, were fascinated by the idea that man would eventually become airborne.

Yet even before these great men of our past gave meaning to the "great question of our times," flight was being attempted by prominent figures. Peasant or king, they were tinkerers all. Indeed, the honor of being the "First Briton to Attempt Human Flight" went to King Bladud. The king fashioned his own design of feathers (borrowing a bit from Daedalus, it was admitted), ranted about magic potions, and climbed to the top of the Temple of Apollo in Trinovantum (now London). Old Bladud must have believed absolutely in his magical powers, for he needed no flight to sustain his prominence. He had been educated in Athens, he was a powerful ruler, he fathered King Lear, and his authority was unquestioned.

Accordingly, he hitched up his feathers, ascended the Temple of Apollo, murmured his incantations, and launched. The chronicler Fabyan lacked the foresight to describe King Bladud as the first on-the-record test pilot, but does report that Bladud fell like a stone, feathers askew, to smash into a church (where we now find Westminster Cathedral) and break his neck and other assorted parts of his anatomy. Much later, after many historians had confirmed the untimely departure from this world of King Bladud, John Taylor in A.D. 1622 wrote:

> Bathe was by *Bladud* to perfection brought,
> By Becromanticke Arts, to flye he fought:
> As from a Towre he thought to fcale the Sky,
> He brake his necke, becaufe he foar'd too high.

But long before Taylor bemoaned in his stately verse the death of the king of Britain in 863 B.C., little-known advances in projecting the future were being recorded with remarkable skill and foresight. In 1250 Roger Bacon wrote one of the most remarkable documents in the history of flight.

> And first of all by the figures of Art itself: There may be made, instruments of Navigation without men to row in them: as huge ships to brook the Sea, only with one man to steer them, which shall sail far more swiftly than if they were full of men. And Chariots that shall move with an unspeakable force, without any living creature to stir them: such as the crooked Chariots are supposed to have been, wherein in olden time they sped to fight, yea in instruments to fly withall, so that one sitting in the middle of the Instrument, and turning about an Engine, by which the wings being artificially composed may beat the air after the manner of a flying bird. . . .
>
> Moreover, instruments may be made wherewith men may walk in the bottom of the Sea or Rivers without bodily danger, which Alexander the Great vied, to the end he might behold the secrets of the seas, as the Ethical Philosopher reporteth: and there have been made not only in times past, but even in our days. And it is certain that there is an instrument to fly with, which I never saw, nor know any man that has seen it, but I know full well by name the learned man that invented the same.

Roger Bacon (1214–1292) was centuries ahead of his time, and throughout his writings he made repeated references to flight by men. He left not a shadow of doubt that he was convinced that man *would* fly. Ah, temerity might have avoided misery for this genius of our past. He so irritated not only the English but also the French, who in the person of Jerome de Ascoli, minister general of the Franciscan order, charged Friar Bacon with spreading heretical doctrines in Paris and other cities. Paris was bad enough, it seemed. The minister general had Bacon clapped in irons, where he spent the next fifteen years in prison, to be released only within a year of his death.

But our issue here is not with saints, angels, devils, prophets, magicians, and the vast ensemble of those looking into the future, but with the individuals who fit the description— as did the hapless Kind Bladud—of the first fliers.

Once again, every one of these men was a test pilot. No one had ever attempted their manner of flight or donned or climbed within their equipment, feathery or stone-laden as it might have been. Yet there is something that grasps at the mind, and it would be wrong not to leave such records without quoting none other than Lord Tennyson (1809–1892), poet laureate of England. Tennyson did not have to wait for men to fly. During his lifetime, and well before his appearance on this world, men were sailing through the skies in balloons. To Tennyson this was but the scantiest harbinger of what was to come, and he created a future for us, in *1842*, that is nothing less than astonishing.

For I dipped into the future, far as human eye could see,
Saw the Vision of the World, and all the wonder that would be,
Saw the heavens fill with commerce, argosies of magic sails,
Pilots of the purple twilight, dropping down with costly bales;
Heard the heavens fill with shouting,
And there rain'd a ghastly dew
From the nations' airy navies grappling in the central blue;
Far along the world-wide whisper of the south wind rushing warm
With the standards of the peoples plunging thro' the thunder storm;
Till the war-drum throbb'd no longer and the battle flags were furl'd
In the Parliament of Man, the *Federation of the World*.

No one will ever know—this may be stated with some certainty—who was actually the first man, or men, to fly. That is, to lift from the surface of the earth in an artificial device that would ascend well above that surface, carrying its pilot and possibly passengers as well. We will never know for certain because historical records, notes, tablets, and other recordings of same are intertwined with mythology and religion and superstition, to say nothing of claims that simply cannot be confirmed. But at least we can refer to what *may* be the first recorded ascension, in China, centuries before the visionary and inventive Europeans ever rose from French soil. If these ancient records are indeed accurate (the recording of the coronation of the Chinese Emperor Fo-kien in A.D. 1306), and a French missionary who reviewed the ancient manuscripts is also accurate and believable in his retelling, then the Chinese at that time lofted skyward in the first balloon flight. The records passed down through the ages record, as well, that the Chinese at that time had created a system of signal devices by which "different-toned trumpets sounded from the tops of high hills and gave notice of impending changes of wind and weather, for use by navigators of dirigible balloons."

Along with these reports there is an engraving of a balloon definitely in the shape of a dirigible, an elongated inflated bag over which has been slung huge nets to support a keel running the length, from one end to the other, of the dirigible, and from this keel no less than *nine* large and ornate baskets were suspended by strong lines, each basket able to carry several passengers. Well; *maybe*.

By 1490 the blazing genius of Leonardo da Vinci was issuing his plans in the form of sketches and detailed notes of machines capable of "mechanical flight." Visionary air screws mark the first mechanical renditions of what would one day become the helicopter, and from da Vinci's talented fingers came the first sketches of parachutes. In this same period the mathematician Giovanni Battista Danti was reported as actually attempting winged flight, but the historical records are mercifully empty of details of such alleged bursts of derring-do. Danti was reported to have attempted his flights in a machine skimpy of description, but definitely over the waters of Lake Trasimeno in Umbria. And from the ramparts of Stirling Castle, John Damian, Abbot of Tungland, was also supposed to have attempted flight in 1507. Again the records report the *attempt,* but unfortunately little else.

But the records become much more specific in the case of Paolo Guidotto, who in 1590 announced his plans to bring da Vinci's mathematical sketches to reality. The historical pages are not certain of just where Guidotti commenced his flight tests, but there is no doubt that he ended up smashing himself against the roof of a house and breaking bones in the process. By 1595, mechanical devices for going aloft seemed still to elude even the most ambitious of those who would fly, but the parachute at least promised some form of controlled movement through the air.

The names began to crowd the pages of aeronautical history, from the tightrope walker Allard who did his best to leap and then fly from a tightrope in an appearance before King Louis XIV (again without record of success, or even survival). By 1709 ideas were changing to mechanics and to science. Gusmao in 1709 actually obtained the patent rights, and a guaranteed monopoly, from the King of Portugal. Frustratingly slim is the record of Marquis de Bacqueville's attempt, in 1742, to fly a winged craft across the river Seine in Paris. By 1766 Cavendish and Black were conducting scientific experiments with hydrogen for "aerostation vehicles," which we know today as being the first balloons of their type and lifting power. At Giessen in 1781, Blanchard appeared with his winged "Flying Machine," and once again the records are maddeningly empty *of results.*

But there's no question that prophets were following in the footsteps of the earliest forecasters that man absolutely would fly. The Jesuit priest Francisco de Lana in 1670 published a mathematical work that even today would stand strongly on its presentations of aerial navigation, for Lana also produced a series of design proposals for such machines as a "vacuum balloon: to consist of four copper globes, each about 25 feet in diameter, and from which all air had been removed." Since air has weight, reasoned Lana, the vacuum of the balloons must cause an ascent. He designed a vessel in which four globes would support by separate lines a man-carrying

basket and, once aloft, would move before the wind by ma-
nipulation of a triangular sail.

It is remarkable how these men of science viewed the future. Lana plunged into design but also poured out his heart
and soul in prophecy, and he saw manned flight as an abomi-
nation that ultimately would be forbidden. He warned sternly
that,

> God will not suffer such an invention to take effect, by
> reason of the disturbance it would cause to the Civil Gov-
> ernment of Men. No City can be secure against such an
> attack. Ships may at any time be placed directly over it,
> and descending, may discharge Souldiers. The same would
> happen to private Houses and Ships of the Sea.
>
> It may over-set them, kill their men, burn their ships
> by artificial fire-works and fire-balls. Thus they may do
> not only to Ships but to great Buildings, Castles, Cities,
> with such security that they which cast these things down
> from a height out of Gun-shot, cannot on the other side
> be offended by those from below.

Whew!

But by now we were getting into *real* hardware. The term
"test pilot" had yet to be invented, but there is no question
that to us, those attempting to fly in their experimental devices *were* test pilots. The logic is simple enough. They
would launch themselves into the air in untried machines,
attempting at the same time to swiftly gain such skill in their
antics that they would fly safely and under control to return
smoothly (or at least with a chance of survival) back to earth.
In 1675 Besnier of France, a locksmith by trade, built a crude
(in today's view you might substitute "suicidal" for crude)
device with which he hoped to glide through the air under
control. The framework bristled with small "planes"—experimental airfoils, or wings—which the "flier" would operate
with frantic nonstop motions of his arms and legs, a sort of
hysterical swimming through the air in order to sustain lift.
Besnier claimed he flew, or glided, as the case might be. He
rushed off the edge of a high roof—his own house—and

paddled madly through the air, crossing over a barn (or a river, depending upon which eyewitness you heard), and then thumped down successfully on the roof of another building.

The issue has always been clouded in serious doubt, but of the next step there's no question. A traveling showman watched Besnier, was fascinated with his attempts and appreciative of what success could bring in the way of fame and fortune, and he bought the "apparatus" from Besnier.

The first time he flew—or tried to fly—he experienced the awful truth of gravity. Off he went from a rooftop, and down he plummeted to his death.

Well, if man couldn't fly in machines he built, certainly he could fly while lashed to, or hanging fiercely to or from, huge man-carrying kites (which are still flown today). This wasn't considered *flying* as such, but that's begging the description of going aloft and returning successfully. It fits within the category of free-drifting balloons, which, if they would fall within a tighter description of a kite, would be attached to the ground by a secure line. Both ascend, one by the force of the wind, the other as an aerostat because the entire package is lighter than the atmosphere surrounding it, and it seeks a level of balance by climbing to where air pressure is reduced, and then levels off.

A group of scientists in England, notably such men as Cavendish, Black, Priestley, and Cavallo, ushered in a new age and a meaningful portent of flight by developing the formulas that would enable men to use hydrogen gas in sealed balloons. What was hailed as the law of aerostatics was clearly a harbinger of manned balloon flight, for with hydrogen (and other gases, even those as simple as heated air) the problem came down to basics. If the weight of the balloon filled with hydrogen were less than the air in which it was released, it would rise, and if the force of aerostatics were sufficiently great, it didn't matter if the basket beneath that balloon were filled with rocks, pigs—or men. To all balloonists of the future, there must be a hallowed niche for Henry Cavendish. He pioneered in the use of hydrogen by identifying it as a gas, a substance, distinct from any other. He worked out the principles of the relative densities of air and hydrogen, and then, eager to move from calculation to actuality, built balloons with hydrogen sealed in their bladders and sent them soaring into the skies. Thus was built the solid foundation of what has since then been known as "lighter-than-air" buoyancy and lifting power, and what Cavendish perfected in 1766 remains as vital today as it was so long ago.

Ascent into the sky, if not yet flight by aircraft as we would describe them today, rushed upon the world with sensational flights in France. The Year That Will Never Be Forgotten is 1783, when more than 300,000 people flocked to different sites in Paris, France, to be witness to the astonishing moments of history when unquestioned flight would begin. The Montgolfier brothers and their contemporaries swept the imagination of the world, reaping honors and acclaim. It seems fitting that this was the same year that the Treaty of Paris was signed, a document also known as the Peace Treaty, between the fledgling United States of America and Great Britain. As the American Revolution came to its long-sought close, France swept upward with its daring adventurers who were forever enshrined in history as "the men who rode the clouds in the first practical vehicles of the air."

It seems especially fitting that the first minister of the United States, none other than Benjamin Franklin, was among the highly impressed observers of events and lost no time in notifying George Washington that there was now proven a "Discovery of Great Importance . . . which may possibly give a new turn to human affairs."

At Annonay in Paris, on June 5, 1783, the Montgolfiers carried out the first flights in public, to be recorded as an official event, with their balloons lifted by air heated from fires stoked beneath the great bag that soon billowed, tugging at its rope restraints, and then rose to a tumultuous roar from the crowd.

On August 27, 1783, another ascent took place, this time from the Champs de Mars, and recognized as the first inflammable air balloon released from this site. Less than a month later, on September 19, 1783, the records listed officially "The First Ascent with Living Animals at Versailles," in the Montgolfier balloon.

And then, on November 21, 1783, it was time to advance from the Versailles occasion with its passenger load of a sheep, a rooster, and a duck, and commit to true manned flight. Five hundred thousand of the awed and faithful came to the garden of the Château de la Mouette in Paris. At two o'clock that afternoon, Pilatre de Rozier and the Marquis d'Arlandes lifted up in their Montgolfier balloon. A half-million voices cried out encouragement as the two adventurers rose in stately ascent to three hundred feet. They waved to the crowd and the roars from below seemed strong enough to sustain the balloon in flight. The wind carried the balloon to the south, and for twenty minutes the great balloon drifted across the land, to descend safely in a field five miles distant.

The new age was *here*. Soon balloons would be ascending from dozens of countries. Crews and passengers in the many flights made would be counted in the hundreds and then in the thousands. As swiftly as people clambered into baskets to be taken aloft, the inventors, joined by impatient mechanics and the inevitable "tinkerers," were hard at work to go beyond the simple uplift and drifting freely before the wind.

There must be more control. This was the new cry of the aeronauts. They built paddles, huge air screws, propellers turned by human power, every device imaginable that might lend a directional force and some control to the aerostats.

And as grand as these balloon voyages into and even above the clouds might be, it was obvious to those who studied the growing science and technology of flight that at its very best the balloon—even transformed into the first blimps and early dirigibles with engines spinning propellers—would be sorely limited in speed and control.

The race for the airplane was on.

3

Wood, Linen, Glue, Ropes, Wires, Gas and Guts

There's a substantial difference between ballooning beneath a swollen gasbag, or even within a powered blimp or, at some time in the past, luxuriating on the promenade deck of a huge dirigible, and *flying* in a machine with wings that will fall out of the sky unless the pilot uses wit and knowledge to keep that thing airborne under control.

The first difference, of course, is that there aren't any more great dirigibles. Or even lesser ones, for that matter. The days of the great airships, magnificent behemoths nearly a thousand feet long and able to cruise almost anywhere in the world, are gone. Finished. Way behind us. Even with their enormous metal structures and the safety of helium rather than the tricky, super-sensitive hydrogen gas that turned the *Hindenburg* into a monstrous barbecue in New Jersey skies, the helium super-airships, from the *Shenandoah* to the *Akron* and the *Macon*, have all gone the way of the dodo.

And, of course, the blimps. Gasbags held in shape and form by the internal pushing of their helium bags, sufficiently stout to suspend a gondola and engine(s) beneath, and to lumber ponderously about the sky in the manner of some distressed hippo that's swallowed a freight-car load of CO_2 bottles, and can't quite make up its mind as to where to bloat-float. The blimps, of course, have their purpose in life. Back in wartime days (that's World War II, kids) they were great for lumbering over convoys at sea, searching for nasty Nazis in submarines, and then hopefully dumping bombs on the subs just visible beneath the surface. Today the blimps are employed to haul radar antenna about the skies in what is basically a fruitless search to catch drug-running airplanes; fruitless because the drug runners make certain to fly where the blimp's radar doesn't reach, or when someone aboard the blimp has a case of Montezuma's revenge and they *must* get back to earth and a tile-walled bathroom. What the blimps do best of all is to exist for its pilots to have great fun. They either paint advertising slogans on their sides or mount electric signs that flash and dazzle. Then lumbering is the best way to go because it gives the people below time to read the flowing light signals imploring the onlookers to *Buy!* Sometimes the blimps hover above expensively touted football games so their long lenses can look down on the gridiron to prevent a surrealistic TV-screen view that turns Grandma green.

And then there are the balloons of today. There are the super-balloons, multimillion-dollar, technologically wonderful, scientifically designed helium wonders, beneath which are suspended pressurized compartments with all the comforts of home and hearth so that affluent adventurers (not for the poor folk, certainly) can venture about the world setting marvelous records. In recent times these silvered onion shapes and double onion shapes have crossed the Atlantic Ocean and the Pacific Ocean, and by the time this page sees print, we may be hosting the first men (and perhaps women, but they'd better be *very* friendly in the limited confines of their cabins) to fly around the entire planet nonstop. In a gasbag. That's a lot of doing, and obviously it's not for the madding crowd. Just those who've got the long green *and* the spirit of adventure and challenge to have a whack at something no one has ever done before.

Finally, the hot-air balloons. These are the great guffaws and ramparts of fun, pleasure, adventure, and challenge for many tens of thousands of people the world over. Blasting heated air from propane burners into colorful gasbags of round, onion, square, oblong, rectangular, diamond, crescent, or any other shape you like, including rolled-up newspapers, beer bottles, Coke machines, cows, dogs—name it and the balloon builders will create it to your order—soaring in great races and competitions, the hot-air balloons are the spice of wafting flight.

And there end the comparisons needed to separate the wheat from the airborne chaff. There are a number of means that we can use to distinguish the basic differences between the winged aircraft and all others that loft the clouds and high blue. An airplane (and this includes those optical illusions with sound effects that we call helicopters) is a machine of negative buoyancy. Either it is producing lift from its airfoils while above the ground, or it becomes a helpless pawn in waiting gravity that will soon enough bring its flight to an end, no matter what the pilot wishes.

The balloon, all fun and whooping laughter, is a vehicle of positive buoyancy. It *floats*. It has lift because, due to heated air or helium or other lifting gas, it weighs less than all the air it displaces and moves upward to a point where it achieves equilibrium with the surrounding medium. That's what balloons and submarines have in common. At first blush this seems an inordinate comparison, but it is most apt. A submarine is a positive buoyancy vehicle that floats in a liquid medium, just as the balloon floats in its gaseous medium. Make the submarine too heavy, or fill its tanks with water instead of air, and the word "flotation" loses all meaning and the submarine—ah, you guessed it: *it sinks*. So it must always maintain a positive lifting force in its surrounding medium.

If you're flying a balloon, you're going along for the ride. It's much the same as sprawling in an inflated rubber tube or a raft in water. You float, and you drift before the currents, whether they be air or water. And those currents can become violent, whether from a thunderstorm's winds or the raging white water of rapids in a river. You can try to get out of the way in the rubber tube by paddling to the nearest shore for safe haven, and depending upon the clutch and fury of the angry water into which you've just plunged, you may or may not make it. But ordinarily, in placid water, no matter what may go wrong, you're still floating. You can let go, ignore the rest of the world, and do your dumb-and-happy thing. If it's the balloon that has your immediate attention, because the air is angry and full of snarling blows that toss you about and threaten to dash your gasbag at great speed into cliffs or trees or high towers, your only escape is to vent your lifting force and get down to the ground with as few bruises as possible to your person.

There it is. In brief, you are not in command of your destiny. You throw the dice with the gods of weather and chance.

All flying is like that, really. It is not an occupation that in past decades could be called safe. The scientific answers to the myriad problems and consequences of flight were not yet available to the earliest pilots. While there was no question that a balloon of positive buoyancy would lift from the ground when its fetters were released, in the first flying *machines* there was no guarantee that they would leave the ground at all, no matter how swift their passage as they raced along, trying for takeoff speed, and if they did become airborne, there was even less guarantee that they could be controlled safely, or would not be swatted from the sky by structural failure, a dying engine, an airsick pilot, or weather too furious for the machine to fly in.

Through a period of many years, when our industrial giants were determined to sell as many personal aircraft as possible, the big gimmick in advertising was "you fly this airplane just like you drive your car."

It made great advertising copy and many people believed what they read. Those same people, who flew like they drove, were also very quickly, very dead.

Imagine, then, the first attempts to produce a winged machine that was heavier than air, that was structurally sound, that had enough power to fly safely, or even that had wings of such a shape (neither camber nor chord nor center of gravity were terms familiar to the earliest designers and would-be pilots) that they would sustain the lift necessary for continued flying, especially if the airplane assumed "unusual attitudes" in the air like standing on a wing, or rolling inverted, or trying to climb straight up (or straight down, for that matter). More than the airplane had to be sound, for the early engines were some of the most dangerous, fire-prone, failure-seeking devices of terror ever created by the mind of man. They spattered burning grease and oil over machine and man, they spat flame from their exhausts or almost any part of their engines, they spun propellers that quite often splintered suddenly, as if struck by an ax, and they carried fuel of such a nature that a single spark could set everything ablaze. And in the early machines with cloth wings—linen or canvas or even silk—a dope was used to seal the material, keep it from stretching or pulling too tight from wind and rain. And that dope material (think of it as a varnish) was of a chemical nature wonderfully suited to burning swiftly and violently.

The air, the sky above, was more of a mystery than we might ever conceive. It was a dangerous reef that no man had ever charted, and no man truly understood. It was filled with winds that despite their invisibility could tear apart any flying machine ever made. It possessed an uncanny knack of covering all the visible earth with fog to the pilot overhead. It could create clouds of stupendous energy, width, and height, furious in their nature, possessed of evil demons we know now as updrafts and downdrafts. Roll clouds, rotor clouds, lightning, microbursts, downbursts, turbulence, jet streams, fog, rain, drizzle, sleet, snow, hail, haze—to say nothing of birds!—filled the apparently empty expanse known as the sky. And the only way to know of these thronging threats was to get up there and plunge into the unknown.

There is another point to consider if you are ever to understand what the early flying machines were really like. *They were fragile,* in many cases almost lacelike, built of thin wooden slats and struts, of fabric that would rend and tear and tip and flap and burn. Their metal parts often consisted of materials that could be bent by the fingers of a man and, when subjected to vibration, wind, and other forces, often failed in flight, so that what was an airplane one moment would become disintegrating wreckage the next.

Even the means of controlling an airplane was a mystery of gargantuan proportions. What is commonplace today with rudder, elevator, aileron, slat, slot, stabilator, spoiler, flat, and other such devices was unheard of by our aeronautical pioneers. Flight is a probing and danger-sharing adventure that demands slow progress with a high price; often the only path to new and necessary knowledge is failure and death.

An essential ingredient missing from the early days was the "power package"—the engine to carry the first machines into the air. What was available was usually monstrously heavy and oversized, and produced pitiful power despite being so large and cumbersome. The people constructing the first airplanes (and *everything* was done by hand) knew they had to keep their machines as lightweight as possible. Obviously, the lighter the device, the less lift was required from the wings to keep it aloft and the greater the chance for successful sustained flight. And the lighter the machine, the less power was necessary to get it airborne and keep it going. The power requirements of the first airplanes were simple enough. The pilot started the engine, prayed it would run at full power after starting, and then he just let it run. No throttle to increase or decrease power. Just full bore. Let 'er rip and *go*! No mixture control to change the air-fuel ratio as the airplane flew higher, for in those early flights the pilots were more than content to *stay* low. Closer to the ground was a comforting blanket to them. And certainly they didn't have a carburetor-heat control, for the formation of ice in carburetors was still unknown, let alone understood. In short, they kept everything as simple as possible.

Then there was the matter of inherent stability, which, in many cases, perhaps most, was a grisly joke. Many early designers believed that once the machine became airborne, keeping it stabilized, that is, wings essentially level and the aircraft proceeding in a straight line, was a function of dihedral. From the fuselage outward, the wings extended not at a perfect right angle, but were inclined upward. Anyone who had even a modicum of knowledge about the wing, the airfoil, realized that the wing produced lift *upward*. So if the airplane were to be upset—tilted to one side—by a wind gust, then it would continue its bank until it simply fell out of control. Ah, but dihedral could be used for built-in stability. The concept was simple enough and it made sense. With the wings angled upward, the force of lift was inclined slightly toward the center of the airplane instead of straight up.

Now it was tipped to one side by a wind gust. The upper wing, the one that was higher, exerted its lifting force farther from the vertical. It was no longer working full-time against the downward force of gravity. But the wing that was lower

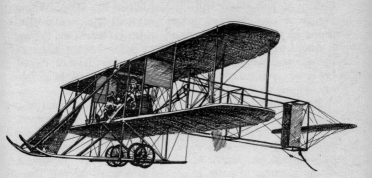

Wright Flyer

was now level with the ground, and *its* lifting force was being exerted straight up. So the wing that had been lowered was now providing more upward lift than before, and since it exerted more lift than the opposite wing, it would force the airplane back to an even keel. Tests with gliders proved that the concept *worked*.

But it worked only to a very limited extent, because it required an extremely well-balanced craft flying (or gliding) in smooth air. The calmer the air, the better the system worked. Once the air became turbulent from winds, from convective currents rising from heated ground, or other such disturbances, often the ability of dihedral to provide the *only* leveling force, vanished, or could not compensate fast enough, and you had an "upset" airplane. Unless the pilot had some means of control—being able to rock the plane from side to side so that he could always return to level flight—*controlled flight* was patently impossible.

That, in fact, was the problem even the Wright brothers, as late as 1902, only a year before the first successful controlled flight of a powered, heavier-than-air machine, considered to be virtually unsolvable. The year before they made history at Kill Devil Hill on December 17, 1903, Wilbur Wright was so frustrated at their incessant failures at control in the air that he shouted angrily to his brother, Orville, that it would be at least a hundred years before man would ever fly. He was wrong by ninety-nine years, as history shows, but it was a stroke of intuitive genius that changed the prophesy, as we shall see very soon.

The first airplanes—which, until the Wright brothers built and flew the Wright Flyer, were all unsuccessful in sustained, controlled, flight—counted on dihedral and the ability of the pilot to move his body from side to side, or forward and backward in the manner of a bobweight, to alter the balance of the machine in order to control it through the air! There were no other controls for banking or turning. The pilot had a stick (or wheel or rod) that moved an elevator up or down to produce climbing or descending flight of the machine. He also had the rudder, the vertical control surface that moved from side to side, for turns.

At this point, coordinated control systems were still in the future, and using the rudder to turn an airplane didn't work quite the way it did for a boat—to the consternation of the builders and the pilots (most often the same person). If you are flying a machine in level flight and you push down fully on the left rudder pedal, which swings the rudder fully to one side, the airplane doesn't really *turn*. It *yaws,* a sort of sloppy slide of the nose of the airplane to one side, so that the airplane now is flying askew—it basically continues flying in the same direction as it was flying before, but the entire machine is flying while the nose is *not* pointing in the direction the airplane is moving.

The trick is to use both rudder and ailerons, the small control surfaces near the far end of the wing along its trailing edge, for a coordinated turn. To achieve this, the pilot brings in, let's say, left rudder. Either simultaneously, or immediately after he starts his rudder movement, he moves the control stick to the left. This lowers the right aileron (aileron is from the French and means, literally, little wing) and raises the left aileron. This coordinated movement causes the airplane to bank to one side, but it is still fully coordinated because the control forces of the wings and the tail are balanced.

The airplane now begins a smooth and coordinated turn to the left, as the pilot intended. It isn't the rudder that's turning the airplane, nor is it the ailerons. The airplane is banked at an angle to the horizon. The lifting force of the wings is also now being directed at an angle from the horizon. If the lifting force is now to the left, and the use of rudder and ailerons is keeping the airplane properly balanced, that wing-lifting force will carry the machine smoothly to its turn.

There's one more effect to consider and it calls for keeping in mind that an airplane in a bank no longer exerts its wing-lifting force directly upward—against the downward pull of gravity. That means that when it flew in level flight, and was balanced, lifting force against gravity, and the power (or thrust) of the engine against the drag of the machine moving through the air (which can be, and is, formidable), everything was where it belonged, and the airplane flew on steadily. But now that we've shifted the lifting force partially to the side, some of the lift is spent on bringing the airplane through its turn, and what's available to counter the direct downward pull of gravity is diminished. So if you reduce a lifting force in one direction (against gravity), then the "downward pull" of gravity dominates, and the airplane will descend.

For the fully coordinated turn, then, the pilot must compensate for this loss of lift to sustain height either by using his elevators in the tail to raise the nose slightly (so that the wing exerts more lift and holds altitude, but also slows down the airplane in terms of speed) or by increasing the power of his engine. That's fine and dandy *now,* with all these years of experience behind us. But in these fledgling times when the facts of flight were still largely a mystery, ailerons were in some distant future, and most engines didn't even have a throttle, none of the above would apply.

Today we accept the shape of the wing as commonly as we do the tires on our automobiles. Not so when simply getting airborne was an adventure in itself. Many of the experimenters of yore knew enough to shape the wing in terms of size and extensions from the sides of their airplanes, but just how the curvature of the wing affected flight was a mystery. That curvature and the thickness of a wing is critical to lift, control, and even to flight itself. To their great discomfiture they attempted flight with wings neatly curved and shaped around their *edges,* but flat as a sheet of plywood. Engine power and speed got them started, even to the point where they lifted from the ground and staggered into the air. But not for long, for these were "flights" all too often measured in seconds.

Finally, there were the twins of trouble—drag of the machine through the air, and structural integrity. Drag is obvious to anyone who works with moving an object through the air. The more resistance to movement, the greater the drag. The greater the drag, the greater the turbulent whirling of the airflow, and the more power you need to stay airborne. Excessive drag—and in early days the drag was often far greater in terms of force than the power of the engine and propeller to keep it airborne—meant that the airplane would either not fly at all, or if it became airborne through catapult or other "slingshot launches," it came down with the usual disastrous results.

And last, and initially very much least, structural integrity. A nice phrase that obscures the simple fact that many of the early machines *lacked* structural integrity. Standing on the ground, an airplane might appear stout enough. Then it took off. In the air, the wings now had to provide a lifting force that would overcome gravity. The greater the lifting force (such as with increased speed or the weight of the machine) the closer the machine came to the strength of the wings being no longer able to stay where they were placed—safely and securely on the airplane. It doesn't require an accountant to work the numbers. If the wing is strong enough to sustain a load of 1,000 pounds, and you take it into the air and load up that wing to 1,300 or perhaps 2,000 pounds, the wing will fail. *It breaks.* And when it does, it usually brakes in violent fashion, tearing loose from the airplane or folding up and over the fuselage, so that in a moment of ripping wood and tearing fabric your airplane is now a collapsed pile of wreckage falling back to earth.

That's why we needed so many adventurous airmen in those days. Almost as fast as the men climbed aboard these machines, they were either killed or messily tangled in wreckage. A pilot's life in the early days might have been something on the order of an airborne "Yo-ho-ho and off we go," but it was also distressingly brief.

The shift from hopeful dreaming, the longing to become airborne in a controllable, reliable machine swung from designs on paper, and models, to the first aircraft built full-size, for flight with men, just short of the midnineteenth century. In 1843, Sir George Cayley, who was swiftly gaining fame in England as the "Father of British Aeronautics," presented an astonishing design he was convinced would open the air age. His "First Heavier-than-Air Flying Machine Design" certainly was ingenious in concept, but in reality it was a complex monstrosity that would have received applause from Rube Goldberg. It featured two *circular* wings, one on each side of a fuselage (at the bow of which was a prominent, carved bird's head), to provide lift for flight, while two huge propellers spun about by a cumbersome steam engine moved the contraption through the air. Heavy canvas was set up to protect the steam engine (and ostensibly also to keep the pilot from being scalded). Cayley also designed a "broad horizontal rudder, or tail," for control (which today would be called an elevator), as well as a diminutive vertical rudder for turning control.

The complexity of the design, and the staggering problems it presented in structural integrity, is what surely saved the lives of whatever men were chosen to take aloft this monstrosity. What saved their lives as the first test pilots (for they would have to learn what to do and how to do it from the first moment of flight) is the simple fact that the huge device never made it off the ground.

In his book on the Wright brothers, *Kill Devil Hill,* Harry Combs captured the essence of the problems facing Cayley:

The first man to have made significant headway in the *theory* of successful flight was, in their [the Wrights'] judgement, Sir George Cayley, a wealthy Englishman who perceived, early in the nineteenth century, that adopting the wing-flapping method of flight used by birds *might* be a fruitless avenue. Cayley suggested that there were really two separate problems of flight: to sustain a machine in the air, and to propel it. If Cayley's ideas were sound, then pursuit of a flapping wing machine was destined to fail. What surprised Orville and Wilbur Wright was that, despite these conjectures, Cayley had wasted his energies in trying to develop a machine that would fly by flapping its manmade wings.

Nevertheless, Cayley did in fact carry the theory of aerial flight forward. Much of his work was bent toward gathering realistic data about airfoils, rather than simply assembling the "build-it-yourself" materials to attempt flight. As early as 1804, Cayley constructed an ingenious whirling-arm mechanism. It was spun by a weighted cord so that an attached wing section would race about a closed circle, and in the process be subjected to the wind of its own movement. Cayley could also modify his airfoil sections, test which design exerted more lift than another, and he learned very quickly that the angle at which the leading edge of a wing attacks the air is a critical factor in producing lift. This one crude experiment—crude but magnificent in its simplicity and especially its findings—must be considered a critical breakthrough in designing the wing shapes that would finally bring flight.

So at least Cayley *tried* intelligently, at great effort and huge expense. At about the same time there appeared on the scene—in newspapers throughout the world—what was described in glowing terms as a "gigantic enterprise for flight," the new Aerial Transit Company in England that would first organize and then provide "regularly scheduled" flights for people and mail "to all countries."

This surrealistic derring-do came on the scene in 1842 as the brainchild of William Samuel Henson. If nothing else, the publicity of Henson brought thousands of people to believe in aerial travel, notwithstanding that Henson had yet to get both feet off the ground at one time. What he proposed for 1842 was on a scale that might well be compared with the Apollo program of the United States that landed six astronaut crews on the surface of the moon *and* brought them home safely.

Henson paraded his program in the form of speeches, sketches, and business proposals, and displayed a huge monoplane (the first such recorded design with a single instead of double wings) powered with a steam engine driving two huge six-bladed propellers.

If Henson had intended to be fanciful, he could have done no better with his serious design. His craft had a wingspan of 150 feet (!) and from its aft fuselage there sprouted a huge horizontal tail that was worthy of a sailing ship. Into his design went a vertical rudder of astonishing fragility, as well as "lateral rudders" (elevators).

His propeller blades (twelve in all) were mounted to the rear of the cabin. One can imagine the power needed to turn twelve huge blades in all, as well as carrying "Passengers, Troops, and Government Despatches" from England to China and India, as well as the weight of all the water from the steam boiler. In fact, the flights from England to China were to be accomplished in no less than twenty-four hours. Henson and his cohorts applied for a patent that was "simple in principle and . . . perfect in all the ingredients required for complete and permanent success."

And he was going to do all this with a steam engine that produced, if it worked perfectly, *thirty horsepower*! That kind of energy could barely have moved the monster aerial carriage out of the indentations its weight would have made in a grass field.

Henson spent his fortune, along with those of several partners, to build models to prove that his full-size machine would work. The model itself was as large as a modern-day aircraft, with a wingspan of forty feet. The group gathered on a grassy field on Bala Down in England, choosing nighttime because of its cooler air and the absence of onlookers who hooted and guffawed merrily at these "crazy inventors."

They should have accepted the derision rather than the nighttime moisture and a heavy dew. As moisture collected on the wings of the model the silk covering shrank steadily through the night, and by the time Henson was ready for the test flight, the wings had both shrunk and warped to uselessness. That was enough. Henson kissed off England, sailed to Texas, and vanished from sight.

As the Wright brothers themselves were to emphasize many years later, Henson's great "Aerial Steam Carriage" would never have flown, even if it had three hundred or perhaps three thousand horsepower. It was fragile beyond belief, a butterflylike contraption of enormous size, and it would always have been cursed by the propellers Henson chose. Those propellers were incapable of producing *thrust*— the energy needed to move from a standstill to flying speed. They would have whirled merrily, all right, but their flat surfaces would do little else. They were the same propellers that aeronauts were turning furiously to propel swollen gas-bags through the air—with something less than success.

The time was at hand, largely due to the tremendous acclaim and popularity of balloon flights throughout the world, for the age of true flight to commence. There had been enough people in the air at altitudes low and high, on journeys brief and extended, through weather fair and foul, to have advanced understanding of the characteristics of the ocean of air in which we lived and, finally, were moving. Keeping pace with aerostatic adventuring and advancement were many other fields of science, engineering, and technology, all aiding the still-stumbling but aspiring aviators.

Employing the best of the new technologies, one design after the other appeared on the scene, so many for a while that they seemed to be jostling one another for the favor of both the public and the scientific world. Parachuting from balloons had sprung up as a new daredevil pursuit to capture public fancy, and at times the parachute descents were entirely unplanned as a balloon bag collapsed *into* itself, and its upper netting captured the bag to hold it in the form of a rounded canopy—a "super parachute."

In every sense the men (and some women) rising to new heights and braving the elements were not simply pioneers, as most historical tomes judge them, they were pilots, and they were test pilots. They flew into more unknowns than they did familiar territory. They encountered unforecast bitter temperatures at extreme heights. They often passed out, and some died, from the lack of oxygen at high altitude. Every one of these lessons learned became the foundation for men who would one day fly on wings into these same aerial territories and conditions.

Two events of 1847 stand out. One was another proposal that contained within its design a strikingly novel approach. Werner Siemens, an officer in the German army fascinated with ballooning, and a brilliant, self-taught master at aerial navigation, issued his proposal for the first rocket-propelled aircraft. He used the word "rocket," but more accurately the rocket was to fire individual packets of gunpowder, the explosive force of each blast imparting breathless acceleration to the bathtublike fuselage and cockpit. Siemens had also studied aeronautical design more than his contemporaries realized; his proposal included warped wings, which one day would become reality in designs throughout the world.

That same year a balloon ascent and horrifying near disaster captured the attention of the world. Just about everything that happened on this flight could have pinned test-pilot wings on the men involved. On July 6, 1847, Henry Tracey Coxwell, his close friend Richard Gypson, and two unidentified friends ascended in a balloon basket from Vauxhall Gardens, London. It was not to be an ordinary flight, for the balloon rose into a sky threatening with dark clouds and rain, yet these foolish but very brave men continued the flight with full load of fireworks in their basket!

The angry sky kept its promise and soon the balloon shot up into a wild thunderstorm, through which it kept rising with frightening speed, smacked about by turbulence that hurled the basket violently from side to side. Lightning blazed all about them and finally a bolt seared into the top of the balloon. By now they were at seven thousand feet and hanging on for dear life, Coxwell straddling and grasping hand holds in the hoop above the basket. He looked up, dismayed to see gas blowing away through the balloon neck. He hadn't had time to shout a warning when abruptly the huge bag collapsed upon itself and fell like a boulder downward through the still-raging thunderstorm.

Some men think and act swiftly in the most dire of emergencies, and Coxwell proved to be one of those men. Immediately he yanked a knife from his belt and cut the neckline keeping the balloon bag open. Of a sudden the failing balloon blossomed out in the form of a huge parachute, the descent slowed, and all four men returned to earth with a thump that shook them up but had them grinning madly with their unexpected survival.

Mixed in with balloons and steam engines and rockets were strange prehelicopter designs (that hopped and strutted and jumped up and down, usually to disintegrate from their own flimsy construction) and, for a while the darling of the pilots-to-be, the *ornithopter*.

If the birds flew by flapping their wings, why couldn't man do the same? Dozens of excited designers and builders rushed to build their flapping contraptions that would use arm and leg power (and prayer power) to leap into the air and frighten the feathered creatures about them. Dr. W. Miller of London built, in 1843, the renowned Miller Ornithopter, a shoulder-braced, foot-on-cable design that became renowned not for its ability to fly (it couldn't) but for its elegant construction. After all, anything with wings of oiled silk and hollow cane construction could not have been the product of any old commoner. Miller enjoyed brief fame for his design, but after it was noted that his feet continued to remain planted on solid ground, he was quickly forgotten.

To some men the only way to reach the coveted man-carrying airplane was to experiment first with scaled-down models. But the moment you move from a successful small model to a large aircraft, you change *everything*. It's more than a simple multiplication of size and performance. New problems appear with exponential speed.

Another oddball design came along in the form of the Letur "parachute flying machine." Letur was a brave man and a test pilot in every sense of the word. He would descend in a parachute carried beneath a balloon, and on the way down, flap vigorously with huge paddles to perform what may possibly be regarded as the world's first known aerobatics. In 1854, beneath the balloon of his friend Adams, he rose from Cremorne Gardens in London. At altitude, he shouted to Adams to be cut free. Adams obliged and Letur was on his way down, astounding onlookers with swinging gyrations, turns, and other maneuvers of his "parachute flying machine."

He made a spectacular landing—smashing into trees that refused to get out of his way. The impact killed him on the spot.

And there was the "magnificent imitation of that great flying creature, the albatross." The Brittany sea captain Jean-Marie Le Bris, completed his artificial albatross in 1857 of lightweight wood, steel wiring, canton flannel, and cords, the whole contraption configured to flap the albatross-shaped wings that spread twenty-three feet to each side of a canoe selected as the fuselage. On a sunny morning, at Trefeuntec, he tied a long rope to a horse-driven cart. Then he shouted to the cart driver to gallop off at full speed while Le Bris furiously worked the albatross wings. To everyone's amazement the speed of the running horse pulled the artificial albatross into the air. But as quickly as it started, the flight-to-be ended. You never know from where your troubles will come. The line from the cart to the albatross whipped wildly for a moment, whirled about the car driver, and hauled him, screaming hysterically, into the air, the shrieking driving the horse ever faster. The astonished Le Bris released the tow-line, the cart driver tumbled to the ground, and the horse continued running, now dragging the hapless cartman behind him. No one is sure what happened to that distressed fellow, but Le Bris cried, "Enough!"

The science of flight, despite the false starts, *was* making headway, and one achievement alone began to draw closer the long-sought triumph of successful powered winged flight. As each inventor or scientist created new designs or confirmed new knowledge, what they learned spread to other aspirants the world over.

Airplanes were not yet flying, but they had a froglike agility that seemed to infect designers and builders everywhere. If they did not fly, they at last hopped, much in the manner of the Le Bris albatross and its ill-fated brief surge into the air. In 1849 George Cayley built a triplane glider, a machine of such paperlike fragility it seemed it must fall apart just from its own tenuous structure. Because it was too fragile for a man to attempt flight, Cayley convinced a young boy to climb into the glider seat and be pushed down a convenient hill. To everyone's delight and astonishment the glider sailed into the wind and continued to fly. If it did not soar upward, it at least maintained a fair balance in its path and landed without harming the lad.

Indeed, four years later, Cayley was ready with a stronger and larger glider for the same type of flight. If we are to accept the tale related many years later by Cayley's grand-daughter, the scientist tried to convince his coachman to test the "new and improved model." The coachman agreed, but with great reluctance, and doubtless no one was more stunned than he as he sped down a hill, the wings grasped the air, and he floated across a low valley, finally to stumble into rising ground where he stopped in a cloud of churning dust.

Emerging from the terrifying machine, beating dust from his clothes, he confronted his employer and tormentor. "I wish to give notice!" he cried. "I was hired to drive, and not to fly!"

To this unnamed coachmen goes a singularly unusual niche in history as the first test pilot to quit a job he had held for only moments!

Experiments burgeoned throughout the world and it becomes impossible to keep a record of who did what first, simply because there were so many tests of new devices that were never given public notice. Thus, we will only recount experiments of which we have specific knowledge.

In 1857, a French naval officer, Felix Du Temple, flew a large model aircraft with an engine mounted at its nose, its wings at angles that Cayley had recorded in his notebooks. Its flight balance was remarkably stable (but so were the conditions when it was tested). Nevertheless, the first model with a clockwork power system did fly, and a later and larger version, propelled by a steam engine, left the ground successfully *under its own power*. Another great step forward had been taken. Du Temple's success was critical. The question was no longer whether the machines could fly. Rather the problem was one of size and the power needed to carry a man, even though man and aircraft would have to operate within an enormous cloud of unknowns as to control and reliability. But that could all come later.

Du Temple kept trying and went for the full-sized airplane. Here the specific details are lost, and dispute enters. But as the history tomes record the event, the new hot-air engine-powered aircraft, with a young man aboard and the engine running full blast, was started down a ramp inclined along a hill. Did it fly? No one knows for sure, but it *hopped*. It left the ground. Did it do so mainly because of the momentum imparted by running down the ramp rather than from the propeller thrust and lift from its wings? The answer is shrouded.

There was a moment in time when the aeronautically

minded stopped what they were doing to focus their attention on an international event, as scientists and engineers convened in England to found the Aeronautical Society of Great Britain. Here, at this gathering in 1866, a marine engineer by the name of F. H. Wenham astounded all who heard of, or read his words.

Wenham had seriously studied aerodynamics—the science of the forces of flight. He presented a paper at this first society meeting that changed forever the hopes of aspiring inventors and aviators. Wenham took the theories and concepts of flight, most of which were disastrously inadequate, and gave them true substance. What he proved, above everything else, was that when you cambered a wing—slightly arching the wing with its rounded surface on top of the airfoil—you drastically improved the flow of air over that surface in such a way as to produce an amazing amount of lifting force. He also established, to the astonishment and delight of listeners who strained to rush home to redesign their works, that if you moved such an airfoil into the wind, at a slight upward angle (the leading edge being higher than the trailing edge), then it was the forward part of the wing where the greatest lifting force was attained. It was a quantum leap in understanding, and it presaged an explosion of new designs and successes. But Wenham had more to say. Most designs to date featured wings that were long from leading to trailing edge, but comparatively stubby—their span was much too short by Wenham's standards. If you built a long and narrow wing, he told his entranced audience, you would further increase the lift and stability of an aircraft.

These incredibly brilliant insights produced a problem obvious to his audience of experienced inventors. The idea of the long and narrow wing (what today we call the high-aspect ratio wing) was great in theory, but it also brought with it severe problems of structural integrity. Wenham nodded to the questions thrown at him. There was another means, he explained, of achieving the same effect. You could keep the wings comparatively short, but you would obtain your desired lift only if you built two sets of wings, one atop the other to gain doubled lift.

The biplane—in this moment of theory, at least—was born. *And it worked.* (Not yet, but the time was drawing near.)

New designs came thick and fast, and by no means were the wild concepts gone from their hops and jumps and inevitable collapse and crashes. The flapping wing designers remained unflappable in their determination, even if at high monetary cost and continued loss of life.

If the flapping-wing ornithopters didn't work, how could they kill anyone? Easy enough when a man was struck in the neck or his head by a heavy blade slicing against his temple or his throat, but far more dramatic when height was at issue. In 1874 a Belgian, de Groof, shut down his shoemaker's shop to work full-time on his weird but wonderful contraption known as the "Beating-Wing Flyer," a combination of parachute sail and glider. It was so startling in appearance it seemed the work of a madman, and neither the Belgians nor the French gave permission for flight tests in their respective countries. De Groof hied off to London where he contracted with a balloonist named Simmons to haul him aloft. On June 29, 1874, suspended from the balloon, he shouted with triumph as his device worked perfectly. A second flight was made as quickly as possible and at one thousand feet de Groof cast himself free from the balloon.

Therein lies the difference between support from above and the support of your equipment. The "Beating-Wing Flyer" fell in wild gyrations, the wings tore apart, the connecting mechanisms tore loose, and the hapless de Groof fell with arms and legs flailing in terror until his brief downward flight terminated with his body smashing lifelessly on the ground.

Scratch one more test pilot.

There's no doubt but that well before the Wright brothers flew at Kill Devil Hill in North America, the French inventor Clément F. Ader *flew*. Why no worldwide acclaim, then? There's a world of difference between flying and flying *successfully*. Ader produced a new monoplane design of weird but essentially streamlined shape that also applied proper proportion of power to weight. His Eole aircraft rested on skids and had all the appearance of a bird caricature. Yet it had forty horsepower from a steam engine to drive a machine of only 1,100 pounds, and with a long wing spanning forty-six feet, it had great promise of success.

But now the point must be made again. None of these

people knew how to fly. Their machines, no matter how well designed and powered, lacked suitable controls because no one really knew what it took to attain that control in flight. This requirement was so basic—and so lacking—that there seemed almost a worldwide conspiracy on the part of inventors simply to ignore the problem. The existing feeling was: "Just get me off the ground and into the sky and I'll know what I need to do as soon as I get there." Talk about your famous last words!

Ader's Eole flew, all right, and even on its first test flight. On October 9, 1890, the machine lifted from the grounds of the Château d'Armainvilliers to the shouts and huzzahs of friends assembled secretly for the test. Amazed, they watched as the Eole rumbled through the air (Ader later claimed it flew for a distance of 150 feet, but this is disputed). What is not in doubt is that the Eole didn't land. It came down in a crash that churned the Eole into instant wreckage.

Ader survived and built his second Eole, and this time, in 1891, he prevailed upon the French army at Satory to let him use their level grounds for his test. Again he soared into the air, and again he lost control during his flight, and again he came down with a resounding crash, tearing off a wing and further damaging Eole II.

That finished the Eole series, and Ader designed a third and new ship, this time known as the Avion. It resembled a leathery flying dinosaur of ill proportions of wings to body, and rested on four tiny wheels. His steam engine now powered two four-bladed propellers, neither of which had any really effective thrust (or he might have had much greater success). At any rate, he was ready in August of 1897, this time with solid backing from the French army. On the first test of August 18 it hopped into the air from its creaky little wheels, but then plopped down again after only a few feet. On the next trial two days later, the wind blew fiercely and Ader was cautioned to wait for calmer air. He refused, knowing full well that the strong wind blowing across his wings gave him a free dividend in lifting force. It was like doubling his engine power. Quickly he turned into the wind and was released. The wind was so strong the Avion almost leaped into the air.

It was not a wise decision. Ader went aloft but had no

control in the rolling turbulence and the winds smacked him from the air like a board slapping a bird. Avion was so much crumpled wreckage and that was the end of *that*. But at least Ader lived through it all. Three crashes out of three and he survived. A neat trick, plus the fact that Ader lived another twenty-eight years, long enough to see the entire world take to the air in successful flight.

One of the most promising inventors, Alphonse Penaud, was also one of the most tragic in the history of aviation. Penaud was a gifted inventor and a work-crazy tinkerer. He designed and built model airplanes, helicopters, gliders, and ornithopters that performed with amazing reliability. Once again the warning is sounded: these were *models*.

Yet his ideas were virtually on a par with that genius F. H. Wenham. Penaud patented a number of revolutionary concepts for aircraft, the most important of which was a single control column that would in a single motion operate both the elevators and the rudder. Clearly he had an intrinsic grasp of the problems of control in flight, a staggering breakthrough for its time. With a thorough understanding of the forces and problems of drag, he also patented his mechanism for retracting the landing gear of any airplane after takeoff to streamline and increase the flight efficiency of the machine. Continuing his clear understanding of drag and streamlining, he proposed a smooth glass canopy for the pilot, and he showed foresight by "burying" the engine within the fuselage and using a system of gears to turn two propellers.

Penaud's concepts were so advanced that instead of bringing him acclaim and recognition, they instead produced a whirlwind of hoots and denouncements. He was ridiculed as an irresponsible dreamer, for what good were all these marvelous ideas if Penaud did not have an engine that could even bring them to testing in flight? There was, of course, no response to such argument at a time when engines were woefully inadequate and presented a tremendous obstacle to gaining the means even to attempt flight by a machine heavier than air.

Penaud was brilliant *and* brittle. He failed to withstand the barrage of condemnation, and overcome with both rage and depression from his vast audience of critics, he shot himself through his head.

It is strange to accept that *had* there been an engine, Penaud likely would have lived on to become one of the most recognized names in aviation.

Scratch one more test pilot who never had the chance to fly.

Then there was the eccentric, wealthy, inventor genius Sir Hiram Maxim, the gutsy American scientist who for his own reasons discarded his American citizenship and sailed off to England. Maxim had an enormous personal fortune with which to dally, and dally he did in a kingly and pretentious manner. He had, after all, invented the machine gun that forever carried his name and efficiently dispatched from this life several hundred thousand unfortunates on the battlefield, earning his fortune in the process. This enabled Maxim to do virtually what he wished, and on his newly acquired sprawling estate in Kent he had his engineers build for him a half mile of special railroad track.

This must be one of the weirdest episodes in the history of aviation, for Maxim was possessed not of the desire to fly, but essentially to make his point and flaunt that confirmation in the face of friends and critics alike. He designed, and had his personal staff build to his specifications, a gargantuan flying machine. Two huge steam boilers at full heat produced no less than 360 horsepower (a power rating unheard of in those days) to direct power to gigantic propellers. Everything about the Maxim aeroplane was of gigantic proportion. From one tip to the other the wing spanned 110 feet, and was so huge it measured more than four thousand square feet on its surface. According to Maxim, he didn't *really* care if his monster flew; he wanted only to prove that it could and would fly. And that was a lot of doing for an ungainly but strangely workable machine that weighed seven thousand pounds!

This must be the only true case ever of the ''test pilot who never was and never wanted to be.'' Maxim mounted his giant on a tracked running gear to guide it along the rails; this running gear alone weighed three thousand pounds and was absolute deadweight for the aircraft. If the Maxim intended to fly, the running gear had to be dropped as the machine went aloft (a system that was copied many years later by designers and engineers the world over and is still in use today).

Many people derided Maxim's machine as a "gargantuan bluff of gargantuan proportions." Maxim, already wealthy from brilliant inventions, sneered contemptuously at these hooters and then ignored them.

In the first test Maxim checked to see that the guardrail to keep the machine from flying was *not* attached. For this test was one of sturdiness and power rather than flight. Maxim had removed most of the wings; he had stub wings and his framework and engines and the ship *couldn't* fly. They fired up the benzine fuel for the steam engines, the propellers clattered with a shattering roar; eighteen feet in diameter, they shot the machine forward as the clamps were cut free. The test was made for another reason; Maxim's structure was made of steel tubing, and as steam was released from the engines it fed into the tubing where it was condensed back to liquid and sent back to the engine to be used again. It was ingenious, *and it worked*. The Maxim groaned forward, picked up speed into a wind of ten miles per hour—and proved its designer wrong! The giant craft, missing most of its wing surface, lifted smoothly from the track and sailed beautifully onward for a distance that has never been specified. *But it was flying*. However, Maxim wanted that sort of nonsense ended immediately. He was not as stubborn or as foolish as many believed him to be when he said actual flight was *not* his goal, for he understood fully that if the craft reached any appreciable height, he would be encased within a monster over which he lacked any control.

One year after this preliminary test, Maxim was ready for the "big one," but this time, with its wings fully extended, he personally made sure the guardrails were properly in place to prevent flight higher than six inches above the track. They fired up the engines, steam hissed and roared, the propellers whirled with great speed, and the Maxim sped down its track with startling speed and acceleration.

The entire system worked so well, and so much lift was generated, that the Maxim broke free of its guardrails and began true flight. Men shouted with surprise and exultation, but at that moment, when the huge craft was about to achieve true, unquestioned free flight, Maxim immediately shut off the engine. Once again, he had acted with great insight, for the monster aircraft lacked any landing gear, and had it become airborne, the odds were it would have smashed to splintering wreckage upon returning to the ground.

That was enough for Maxim. He announced triumphantly that "Propulsion and lifting are solved problems; the rest is a matter of time." And with that he was done with flight and swept off in a cloud of success that left observers stunned and confused. Maxim refused to have his machine rebuilt and had all evidence of his tests disposed of.

Would the Maxim have flown successfully? To the extent that Sir Hiram Maxim permitted it to fly, it was an astonishing success. But for whatever reason, it did *not* achieve free flight, under control, and land safely; thus, it is forever confined to being one more great curiosity in the history of aviation.

During and immediately after the "Great Maxim Mystery," inventors concentrated on another system of flight— gliders that could fly for hundreds of feet through the air and under control. These were the last great experiments before true aircraft flight, and the chief actor in this endeavor was the German inventor—and true test pilot—Otto Lilienthal. From the onset of glider building in 1891, he stated his purpose: he wished to become a pilot skilled in controlling his glider in flight. That way, when the proper engines of light weight and greater power became available, he would already be a pilot proficient in *flight,* and he would take the world by storm. Lilienthal was no idle dreamer. He was also a true pioneer in that he accepted nothing he was told or that he had read from other men; he tested everything himself.

By 1891 he had amassed sufficient data from the experiments of other men. Every step in aviation really takes place in this manner; everyone stands on the shoulders of those who've gone before them, and Lilienthal was now into building its first gliders. They were designed with consummate care. He chose the single-wing monoplane, and unlike so many before him, he selected carefully the best of the best and he built his gliders with cambered wings. Their lifting force was excellent, and he wisely used a fixed tail assembly that offered directional control.

All machines built for flight are compromises; in Lilienthal's case the need was for both sturdiness *and* an absolute minimum of weight. The German inventor-pilot also wanted tried-and-true systems for the most part, so many of his gliders were of identical size and shape, with a set wingspan of twenty-three feet. Lilienthal had worked out the formula carefully. He now had a wing surface of 150 square feet to support the combined weight of the glider, 44 pounds, and his own body, 176 pounds. This would enable him to glide from a hilltop, fifty to seventy-five feet above the ground.

Without movable controls, he used shifting CG (Center of Gravity) for control. He squeezed into a fuselage opening, grasping holding bars, and ran forward to fly. Going downhill into the wind, he would reach flying speed quickly, and as the hill fell away beneath him Lilienthal was gliding beautifully through the air. To go up or down he shifted his body weight forward or backward. To bank to one side or the other or to correct for wind gusts, he moved his body from side to side. As thorough as was this arrangement, it left many people breathless, for Lilienthal dangled precipitously from his fragile craft while airborne, and every landing had to be a perfect running-legs touchdown or he could easily break his legs.

At first he flew perhaps sixty to eighty feet. Gaining experience as a glider pilot—for he was now the foremost aviator in the world—he began leaving from the summit of higher hills and into stronger winds. He flew faster and farther, marking his successful flights at three hundred feet, then six hundred feet, and finally up to a thousand feet from start to finish. Launching from low hills near Berlin, Lilienthal and his mechanic (who appears to have been ignored by most historians as the second-most-experienced pilot in the world at the time, and while the world remembers the name of Lilienthal, who knows who was Hugo Eilitz?) made hundreds of flights, and then Lilienthal increased his own flights to more than two-thousand-foot glides.

Lilienthal left no question as to his goals. "To fly is everything!" he shouted to his compatriots. "To contrive a Flying Machine is nothing; to construct one is something; to control it in flight is to reach the heights!"

It was advice that soon would be taken most seriously by two bicycle mechanics in Ohio. . . .

In 1896 Lilienthal was glide-testing biplane gliders. He moved to different launching sites, always searching for the better hill and the best winds. His flights in the biplane, with its added lift and strength, convinced him that he was ready for powered flight. The momentous challenge had arrived. Now he built his own motor weighing ninety pounds and burning carbonic acid gas (but delivering a pitiful 2.5 horsepower) and installed the motor in the glider biplane. What abruptly stands out, almost garishly, is that Lilienthal modified the glider with wing tips that *flapped* up or down. He would use this system, he told Eilitz, to change the lift of one wing or another as he desired, and therefore have the ability to control banks and turns. To operate his rudder, Lilienthal built a crude but ingenious system of operating the rudder by moving his head left or right. A band was fashioned to go about his head, with a line running back to the rudder. Before flying the powered machine, he ran his final glider tests with the new control equipment.

On August 9, 1896, the day before he planned to fly the powered and new biplane *aircraft* (which the glider had become with the addition of his engine), Lilienthal decided suddenly to make a last gliding flight in one of his standard machines. This was at Stollen, where he had flown many times.

Lilienthal, as he had done so often, launched from his hilltop into blustery winds. They were much stronger and more turbulent than he had anticipated. A wind gust suddenly pitched the nose at a high angle. Lift burbled away from his wings as the glider hung on a stall, and to recover, Lilienthal swung his body desperately to get the nose down. *Too steeply*.

From a height of fifty feet the glider plunged almost straight down into the ground, crushing the structure and smashing Lilienthal with terrible force against the earth. Hugo Eilitz rushed to his side. The great pioneer lay helpless, his spine broken. He was unable even to speak.

The next day, Otto Lilienthal, *pilot*, died.

Neither Eilitz, his mechanic, nor Otto's brother, Gustav, had the heart to continue the experiments. The biplane with its small engine was ready for flight. Gustav Lilienthal had it moved into the corner of a storage shed, and there it remained, never to fly.

We were getting closer and closer to that shining goal of controlled flight and safe landing in a powered heavier-than-air machine, extending from the feathery structure of Lilienthal to the monster of Maxim. Twists of fate and human stubbornness still defied man's attempts to grasp the holy grail of true flight, but by now a growing swarm of hopefuls was running full tilt toward that flight.

It was fish-or-cut-bait time, and newcomers rushed to the forefront, seeking the elusive goal. Percy Pilcher was a Scot with the same burning desire as those about him, and he followed the exploits of Lilienthal with undisguised admiration. He was also wise for his age and utterly honest in his goals, as well as recognizing that he needed as much information as he could get if success were to become his in the air. He built a glider with the hopeful name of the *Bat,* and studying his fragile contraption carefully, he hit upon the idea of going to the best source in the world to be taught. Off Pilcher went to Germany to meet with Otto Lilienthal. Impressed by the Scot's frankness and enthusiasm, Lilienthal spent hours answering questions and offering sage advice, and then, in a gesture of admirable and invaluable aid to the younger man, he allowed Pilcher to fly his own biplane glider. The excited Pilcher sailed in wild enthusiasm across the valley used by Lilienthal, embraced his new German friend, and rushed home to resume his own work.

He could hardly believe the news that came so shockingly from Germany. The great Lilienthal was dead, and all his work had been ended once and for all by a grieved family. Pilcher doubled his efforts with his *Bat.* They were far from successful, but by now Pilcher had the knowledge to add a tailplane so strongly recommended by the German inventor. One after the other he built new and better machines, flying the *Beetle* and the *Gull,* but with less than resounding success. Then came his *Hawk,* in which he replaced leg power on the ground for fixed wheels. The *Hawk* was built in the fashion of a bird's outstretched wings, but it employed the cambered wing and the Lilienthal tail, and Pilcher flew his latest machine for a distance well over seven hundred feet. He was ready to install an engine in his craft and "go for the big one."

But nowhere in the world could he find an engine light enough, and with sufficient power, to lift him from the ground and sustain him in controlled flight. Undaunted, he worked for a full year, well into 1898, developing and building a small engine that would turn its propeller with a total (miserable) of *four* horsepower. Pilcher was convinced it would do the job.

Before he was ready to attempt powered flight, Pilcher attended a meeting of the Aeronautical Society in London, where he spent long hours with a fascinating Australian, Lawrence Hargrave. To Pilcher's astonishment, he learned that Hargrave was a brilliant engineer and mechanic, was dedicated to aeronautical research, and two years before this meeting (early in 1899), Hargrave had built the world's first rotary engine. In a drastic department from accepted designs, the Hargrave engine ran on compressed air, the crankshaft remained locked in position, and the engine cylinders rotated about the crankshaft.

Six years before this meeting, Hargrave had also developed his own box-kite design of cellular arrangement. Yet it was a kite that could be flown as a glider or even as a powered airplane. With Hargrave's full cooperation, Pilcher borrowed two box kites from the Australian, flew them successfully, and spent day and night modifying a machine of his own into a triplane glider.

By September of 1899 Pilcher was champing at the bit to make flight tests. He could be the first man in the world to succeed where so many others had failed. He notified friends and official observers of two tests he would make, one in the glider just completed, and the more important flight in the *Hawk* that had already proven so promising.

Sometimes the gods on high have a very warped sense of humor. With the two machines ready, a small crowd had assembled for the tests when the skies darkened ominously, lightning sizzled, and a downpour drenched machines and crowd. Pilcher, already keenly aware of incipient problems, at once canceled the triplane test. He could not know without a serious study of his craft how much warping of the wings had occurred, or how much shrinkage and weakening had taken place with the wing covering. Wisely, he announced that as soon as the rain ended he would fly his *Hawk*.

The gods smiled (although some felt it was more a smirk) and the rain ended. With a fresh breeze at hand, Pilcher climbed into his proven *Hawk*. He launched beautifully, the glider flying with perfect control as it reached thirty feet above the surface.

Everyone heard a sudden *crack!* Everything happened in horrifying swiftness; the sound was the failure of a tail-assembly brace. It snapped in two, the tail section tore away; the *Hawk*, without this arrow stability, flipped wildly through the air, tumbling like a broken toy, and smashed against the ground.

Percy Pilcher was dead.

Several years earlier another aviation pioneer—a highly accomplished engineer and scientist—had appeared on the scene, and tossed his own hat into the ring to gain history's seat as the first to fly in that still-elusive powered machine. The problem, already recognized by so many, was to find a light enough power source that was compatible with the necessities of weight and thrust. Octave Chanute entered the "competition" well into his later years, unlike his contemporaries, who were for the most part young and lusty men filled with excitement and pioneering spirit. In this respect Chanute was a contemporary of Sir Hiram Maxim in that both men were recognized scientists. Chanute, indeed, was often hailed as a "great scientist" who had spent forty years in bridge and railroad engineering, was vice-president of the Association for the Advancement of Science, president of the American Society of Civil Engineers, and also president of the Western Society of Engineers. He was a doctor of science of Illinois University.

As he grew older Chanute turned from his honors and laurels in heavy engineering and lifted his eyes to the skies. Otto Lilienthal's gliding flights enthralled him, and his own examinations of the German's gliders convinced him he could improve upon and outdo anything else being tested in the world. With such convictions in mind he threw his talents into a detailed scientific study of flight. He also wrote scientific articles on aeronautics, turning out so many (treasured by other would-be airmen) that they were gathered up into book form and published in 1894 as *Progress in Flying Machines*. To historians even today the Chanute collection is regarded as the first solid foundation and reliable record of attempts to fly, the problems facing engineers, and possible solutions for all concerned. It ranks as one of the classics of historical aeronautics.

Chanute expended enormous effort and a personal fortune in moving from the written page to flight. He used his skill in engineering and truss construction to bring innovation design to his gliders, and from the outset it should be emphasized that in several years of tests with different models, types, and sizes of manned gliders, Chanute's pilots made more than two thousand gliding flights—without a single accident!

Yet Chanute fell prey to one of the deadliest blind alleys in building the first successful flying (not gliding) machine, for which the gliders were a necessary step along the way. He sought that elusive grail—elusive because it was then impossible to solve, and it remains impossible today—of *automatic stability*. The concept was so inviting, and its possibilities so limitless, that doubtless it virtually hypnotized Chanute. To him, a glider should fly with inherent stability— that is, if it tipped to one side or moved in any way out of its intended line of flight, its wings and lifting force would *always* return the craft to stable flight. This was a quicksand of defeat for uncounted inventors and first-time flyers, and it snared Chanute as well, despite his overwhelming success in his glider tests.

Aided by Augustus M. Herring and William Avery—of the pair, Herring became one of the most accomplished gliding pilots in the world—Chanute began to make new designs. All of his airfoils were cambered, so that from the outset he had good lifting effect from his experimental machines. He worked at first in a Chicago laboratory, designing and refining wing and structures. Then he and his assistants went off to the rolling sand dunes thirty miles east of Chicago on the edge of Lake Michigan. A full staff went with them, including other scientists and mechanics. In the next two years they test-flew not only Chanute gliders, but others based on Lilienthal designs (and built by Herring).

Chanute learned quickly from Herring's skilled flights that hang gliding was a risky business, and the pilot had to be a virtuoso in the speed and accuracy of shifting his body weight to keep his machine from falling out of control. More and more, Chanute emphasized automatic stability, a dead end he never seemed to recognize. Instead of opting for controllable (movable) surfaces of his wings, he even built a glider with twelve wings, arranged in pairs. It was a nice effort to increase automatic stability, but it was also self-defeating. The many wings, stacked one atop the other, produced turbulent airflow and drag in their aftermath (which Chanute had failed to anticipate), and worsened the basic instability of the design. When it did fly, it was like trying to glide smoothly in a huge cream puff, and was quickly abandoned in favor of a model with five wings as well as another pair of wings aft of the main assembly. Chanute hoped that Herring would be able to use the rear planes for steering, but success again eluded them.

One after the other the Chanute designs moved from cumbersome stacked-wing arrangements, finally settling on two new designs—a triplane and a biplane glider. The most effective of these was a beautiful biplane with a tail assembly set well aft of the two main wings. The pilot hung from a truss directly beneath the main lower wing, much in the manner of the Lilienthal and other gliders, but that tailplane so far back of the wings gave the biplane marvelous "arrow stability," which had been needed so desperately in almost every glider built by every inventor in the world. The Chanute biplane had 135 square feet of wing, weighed but twenty-three pounds, and with its superbly cambered wings could easily carry a 170-pound man at forty miles per hour through the air as it glided downward from the top of the sand dunes.

By 1897, in the second summer of their flight tests, Chanute was moving remarkably close to truly dependable designs. As gliders, they flew beautifully, just so long as the pilot didn't try to fly in turbulent wind conditions, and then the sought-for "inherent stability" evaporated as quickly as a fine mist under a hot sun. Chanute experimented with "swerving wings" that were intended to increase in-flight control, but just how these worked, and what improvement they may have been, seems a mystery to this day. But there was no question about another improvement. After watching Herring clinging for his life to the glider frame in every flight, Chanute built his next glider with a seat beneath the bottom wing so that his test pilot could *sit* and apply all his attention to *flying* instead of becoming a hapless soft bag dropping from the sky.

The new tests proved that the Chanute gliders were still effective and outstanding in their design and construction. But now Chanute seemed up against a solid wall preventing further development. His pilot, Herring, was almost frantic to fly with engine power, and at every opportunity belabored his employer to "get with it." Chanute demurred. More improvement was needed first in "automatic stability."

The division between the two men grew rapidly. Herring was weary of repeating so many tests over and over again and not seeing what he considered to be the only proper next step. Unable to resolve their differences, the team finally split, Chanute back to his drafting board (he would later spend much time with Orville and Wilbur Wright, both in study and on the sands of Kitty Hawk), and Augustus Herring in pursuit of an engine. Herring used Chanute's basic design to build yet a new model biplane, featured a twin tail (another innovation), a wheeled undercarriage, a seat, and finally, an engine.

Once again the weakness of the power source held off the future. Herring had his engine, but it ran on the power of compressed air, and it lacked the capacity to spin the two fat, curving propellers Herring had mounted fore and aft of the engine. Nevertheless, he gave it his all. In 1898, claimed Herring, he was able to take off from the ground on the glider's wheels, which certainly qualified the machine as an airplane. What happened next became shrouded in argument and lack of proof. Herring claimed he had flown for "a few seconds." No verification was ever provided, and Herring's claims, at times very loud and angry, were dismissed.

Herring deepened into a bitterness that seemed to follow him for the rest of his life and, many years later, was well described by Harry Combs in his epochal work *Kill Devil*

Hill as "the perennial thorn in the budding aviation industry's side." After his stint with and unhappy separation from Chanute, Herring worked briefly for Professor Samuel Pierpont Langley, established the Herring-Curtiss Company, watched his business collapse in bankruptcy, later resurrected the same company in 1918, and then filed a wild barrage of lawsuits against Glenn Curtiss and many other aviation pioneers, all the while reasserting that it was he rather than the Wright brothers who had made the first fully successful powered and controlled flight. For five years his lawsuit against Curtiss and others rambled through the courts until, in 1923, the court ruled against Herring. He appealed, and while that argument was still pending in 1926, he died of a stroke. In this same year the state of New York dissolved the controversial Herring-Curtiss Company.

(This proved a harbinger in the aviation industry, the appalling explosion of lawsuits and countersuits that have bedeviled aviation since its inception. With Herring dead, everyone concluded that the issue was buried forever. Not so. Two years after Herring died, while his heirs continued the original appeal, the appelate division of the Supreme Court of New York State reversed the decision of the lower court! At that time the issue, snarled in legal tape, seemed unresolvable. The appeal that won came in 1928; by that time Glenn Curtiss had left aviation in a dark mood and with many unfavorable remarks about Herring, his heirs, and seemingly almost anyone who had dragged him down from flight into legal entanglements. He chose instead of aviation to work in real estate, mainly in Florida. Two years after the Herring estate's appeal was granted, Glenn Curtiss died, and the whole messy affair came, it seems, to naught.)

As history would finally sort out all the competition, there remained two major forces in the lead to gain the coveted goal of being the first to conquer the air. In the eye of science, the public, and the government the one man far ahead of everyone else was Professor Samuel Pierpont Langley, whose "calling cards" were overwhelming, for he was recognized as a spectacularly successful and brilliant astronomer, physicist, engineer, and scientist, *and* was the secretary of the Smithsonian Institution.

Langley put a massive effort into manned flight, beginning his experiments in 1886. The next year he built a succession of flying models he dubbed "aerodromes." For his exploits with these models, he has been called the first man to "demonstrate the practicability of mechanical flight."

But as history would show—and history is unforgiving of failure—the elegance of that statement ended up being more poetic than practical.

Yet for a while it seemed that Langley really would surmount the final barriers. In May and November of 1896 he brought his years of tests to unquestionably successful flights of model aircraft with a tandem-wing design, powered by a 1.5-horsepower steam engine. The wings spanned thirteen feet, the model was sixteen feet in length, and the steam engine spun two propellers. Launched by catapult from a houseboat on the Potomac River, the model flew smoothly for a distance of 3,200 feet, a highwater mark in anyone's book. When the engine exhausted its fuel, the model descended gently to the river's surface. Langley gathered up his model, made necessary repairs, and went for another try. Again the model flew beautifully, covering 3,200 feet at a speed of twenty to twenty-five miles per hour. Alexander Graham Bell was one of the witnesses to the latter flight and declared: "Its motion was so steady that I think a glass of water on its surface would have remained unspilled."

Later that year, on November 28, 1896, Langley flew another model from the houseboat catapult. This time the model flew at thirty miles per hour for the unprecedented distance of 4,200 feet.

Langley was battering down the door to manned flight. If his models were increased in size and power, declared his supporters, they would carry a man successfully through the air.

But to everyone's astonishment and dismay, Langley seemed satisfied to follow in the footsteps of Sir Hiram Maxim. He was convinced he had solved, in terms of science, all the mechanical problems of flight—and abandoned his work in favor of his duties at the Smithsonian Institution!

Little known to the public was the fact that Langley had been driven to this "hiatus in research" by observers who felt he was "playing with useless toys" rather than accepting the full challenge of the man-carrying machine. Because of newspaper and other criticism, Langley's attempts to secure the money with which to continue his experiments met with failure. Building the man-sized aerodrome called for the expenditure of tens of thousands of dollars, which Langley did not have and could not secure. His role in the pursuit of manned flight might have ended right then and there, except for the onset of what has always been a tremendous boost to flight: *war*.

Five years after the Spanish-American War of 1898, President McKinley was of the opinion that aircraft would play a commanding role in future wars. Balloons had already been used in great numbers in Europe; indeed, they had made possible a series of marvelous escapes from a besieged Paris and, in addition to other battles and wars, had played a critical role in the American Civil War.

At first Langley accepted the president's urging to make a "last great demonstration" of his flying machine, this time with a pilot at the controls, with something less than full belief. But McKinley had that Last Great Poker Hand to play. He ordered the War Department through its Board of Ordnance to deliver fifty thousand dollars to the good professor to get on with his mechanical works.

Overnight, from fiscal obscurity, Professor Langley was the darling of Washington and a figure of growing heroic stature to the nation. Aviation enthusiasts the world over watched with intense interest as Langley, with a slim and bespectacled assistant, Charles M. Manly, prepared for the great event. But once again enthusiasm stumbled against the same high wall that had bedeviled so many men before them: the lightweight engine with sufficient power to sustain flight. Langley had ordered an internal combustion engine just for this purpose; its maker was to deliver to him an engine not to weigh more than a hundred pounds and be capable of twelve horsepower. Ah, the promises that are broken! No engine ever came forth.

If there is an unsung hero in all this, it is Charles M. Manly. Not only for the Langley aerodrome project, but for *all* of aviation the world over. In one of the most incredible and ingenious accomplishments of all time, Manly closeted himself in his workshop and did the impossible. He built his own engine, and of his own design.

It didn't meet the specifications of one hundred pounds and twelve horsepower. Manly built a radial aircraft engine that weighed 125 pounds, but it produced the unheard-of energy of fifty-two horsepower! And it was able to spin the cumbersome twin propellers of the aerodrome at 950 revolutions per minute. At long last the final obstacle was overcome.

Well, *almost*. The airplane still had to fly successfully and to alight successfully. Langley had more than enough money to hire all the help he needed, to purchase all the materials he needed, and to build anything he wanted. It was no secret that President McKinley backed him so completely that more funds would be available should Langley prove successful.

On October 7, 1903, the full-size man-carrying tandem-winged aerodrome, with more than enough power to spare, was ready for the first flight trial. And the same man who virtually overnight created the world's best and most powerful aircraft engine would be its test pilot. Dashing in white canvas shoes and light clothing, wearing a life preserver and automobile goggles over his glasses, Manly climbed aboard the aerodrome, poised on its catapult to be hurled into the air. Two boats waited nearby, one filled with members of the Smithsonian, the other with newsmen crowding every available space. If ever there was a countdown for a launch, *this* was it. The engine roared noisily, Manly braced himself, Langley held his hand aloft and then signaled to a waiting axman—yes, a man with an ax. The ax went up and came down to sever the restraining cable of the catapult, and the huge aircraft surged forward faster and faster.

And dumped right into the river.

Seems the great scientist didn't know how to build a catapult that worked. Major M. M. Macomb of the army's artillery corps, present as an official observer, reported: "The trial was unsuccessful because the front guy post caught in its support on the launching car and was not released in time to give free flight, as was intended, but, on the contrary, caused the machine to be dragged downward, bending the guy post and making the machine plunge into the water about fifty yards in front of the houseboat. The engine was uninjured and the frame only slightly damaged, but the four wings and rudder were practically destroyed by the first plunge and subsequent towing back to the houseboat. This accident necessitated the removal of the houseboat to Washington for the more convenient repair of damages."

Hope springs eternal. Langley, Manly, and a large crew worked day and night to overcome the stigma of the ludicrous accident. At least Manly now had some flying time—a few seconds' worth, anyway—and he wouldn't be caught by any sudden lunge of the catapult. Two months later the second aerodrome was completed and ready for flight, a tug hauled the houseboat back into the river, and a crowd much larger than before gathered for the great event.

Not that Langley had been supported fully by his peers. Indeed, many of his closest friends and scientific fellows thought he was traveling swiftly around the bend and ought to get out while the getting was still good. Langley was now seventy years old and his personal physician was furious with him. The press enjoyed every moment, a small minority wishing Langley well, the large majority having a field day at his expense.

December 8, 1903. The houseboat rested across the Potomac River, near Anacostia. Tugboats and smaller vessels filled with army officials, museum staff, and newsmen bobbed about in the water as launch time drew near. They wait for hours as everything is readied. The wind springs up, strong and with growing gusts, and by the time Langley is ready the sun is just above the horizon.

Finally, it is 4:45 P.M. A newsman reports the sun has just set. The wind is from the north. Manly takes his seat, adjusts his goggles, starts the engine. It kicks in perfectly and its roar echoes across the water. Twin propellers spin perfectly. Langley signals, the ax comes down, the catapult is freed, and the launching sled rushes forward. The aerodrome is off the sled and it's flying!

No, it isn't!

A terrific sound of splintering, tearing wood and fabric bursts from the airplane. By the time it leaves the catapult rails it is breaking in half. The rear wings twist and rend violently and crumple. For bare seconds, the stricken machine hangs in the air, nose pointed upward, propellers thrashing, and then . . . it reverses direction.

And flops like a stricken, broken bird backward into the river.

But what about the pilot with his precious few seconds of powered flight (mostly thrashing about madly as he fell)?

Manly's life was now in great danger. Plunged underwater, he was horrified to discover that his life preserver was caught in the tangled wreckage. He fought desperately to break free. *He couldn't!* His frenzied attempts to save his life gave him strength he'd never known and he tore his life preserver in two. He thrashed, lungs almost bursting to reach the surface.

His head crashed into something solid. How could that be when . . . He wildly thrust aside chunks of floating ice, sucking in deep lungfuls of air. He half turned in the freezing water and stared in mixed disbelief and horror as the houseboat, which had been sailing into the wind, bore down on him like a slow but relentless juggernaut.

Manly shouted for the boat to stop; it came on like a floating locomotive. An observer in a nearby rowboat heard and saw Manly and pulled furiously on his oars to reach the stricken airman. With only seconds to spare before he would be crushed by the houseboat, a hand grasped Manly and hauled him to safety. The huge bulk of the houseboat rumbled by.

The great Langley demonstration was over.

Manly went on to other pursuits.

A reporter for the *Washington Post* had written of the first attempt and failure: "Manly looked down and smiled. Then his face hardened as he braced himself for the flight, which might have in store for him fame or death. The propeller wheels, a foot from his head, whirred around him one thousand times to the minute. A man fired two skyrockets. There came an answering 'toot, toot' from the tugs. A mechanic stooped, cut the cable holding the catapult; there was a roaring, grinding noise—and the Langley airship tumbled over the edge of the houseboat and disappeared in the river, sixteen feet below. It simply slid into the water like a handful of mortar."

And this reporter was *kind* to Langley. Newspapers

throughout the country tore Langley to shreds. The gentlest of these remarks were "fiasco," "complete failure," and "foolishness."

And that was for the *first* failure. After the second debacle, as Harry Combs put it so well, "Manned flight was, in the general consensus of editors as well as congressman, stupidity that had about as much chance of success as perpetual motion."

It sometimes takes the vantage of hindsight to place everything in its proper perspective. Other claims to the contrary, the Langley aerodrome, even with the finest and most powerful engine of its type in the world, would never have flown from its clumsy catapult on the Potomac. Even the best scientists of that day still believed that what a *model* could do, a full-sized manned machine could do, if only it were magnified several times in size and power. In truth, again quoting Harry Combs, "Langley's *Aerodrome* was in reality a travesty of aerodynamic design and . . . despite its excellent engine, the machine could not possibly fly."

The press castigated Langley, Congress lambasted the army (and President McKinley) for wasting the taxpayers' money on idiocy, and the public hooted and jeered. The aerodrome episodes on the Potomac had thrown back public or government belief in true manned flight by uncounted years.

Which is why, nine days later, the nation, and the world, refused to believe what had really happened on the sands of Kill Devil Hill on the coast of North Carolina.

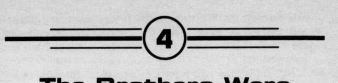

The Brothers Were Wright

Neil Armstrong, the first man to walk on the moon, and long before Project Apollo was even an idea, was one of the leading experimental test pilots of the United States, flying devilish experimental jet fighters and dangerous rocket aircraft from the Air Force Flight Test Center in the California desert. I knew Neil Armstrong then, as I knew many of our leading test pilots also flying from the broiling desert surface. He is a close friend of Harry Combs, whose energy and great persistence brought about the book *Kill Devil Hill*, the most revealing and detailed ever written on the two men who accomplished what had been, until their epochal first flights on December 17, 1903, "the impossible."

There is a rather special angle in Neil Armstrong's foreword to Combs's book, and although Armstrong speaks well about the story that Combs told, he also permits us a look at the Wrights as only one of the greatest test pilots of all time might see them. The details he emphasizes are not so much technical or even scientific, but rather allow us to see Orville and Wilbur Wright as human beings, and thus give one a glimpse of why Harry Combs became so determined to record for all of us a story that, despite all its previous tellings lacked that personal understanding.

It was a convivial bunch of riders. Dismounting to let their horses graze, they joked at the events of the morning ride through the Wyoming hills. It was warm and bright, and the grassy bank along the crystal-clear tributary of the North Platte was a perfect spot for lunch and relaxed conversation.

Inevitably, the talk turned to airplanes. Inevitably, because these men were drawn together by a common interest in progress aeronautical. Each had dedicated his career to aviation, and each had made his mark.

It was not clear how or why talk turned to Wilbur and Orville Wright; nor was it surprising, considering the nature of the group. It was surprising that they were unable to agree on certain major facts relating to the brothers' lives.

To one of those assembled, Harry Combs, the point was not insignificant: everyone knew of the Wrights; few recalled the essence of their lives and achievements. This spark of interest continued to glow. In *Kill Devil Hill,* Harry Combs relates how, in time and circumstance, it kindled a flame that grew into a consuming blaze of fascination. He became addicted to discovering the key to the Wrights' success. He retraced their path, both technically and geographically, and, along the way, he grew to know them as people.

The brothers were not easy to know, in person or in retrospect. But their ability and their integrity were impressive by the standards of their day or our own. They were both imaginative and pragmatic. They were doers with dreams.

Throughout all of human history, men have envied the flight of the birds. Perhaps no desire better exemplifies our natural predilection toward freedom. The Wrights, too, admired the gull and hawk. Although their inspiration probably stemmed more from the accomplishments of men, they acknowledged the importance of the contributions of the feathered fliers. Five years after his first powered flight, when receiving an award from a French aviation society, Wilbur said, ''I sometimes think that the desire to fly after the fashion of birds is an ideal handed down to us by our ancestors who, in their grueling travels across trackless lands in prehistoric times, looked enviously on the birds soaring freely through space, at full speed, above all obstacles, on the infinite highway of the air.''

Their access ramp to that ''highway of the air'' was Kill Devil Hill, a sandy knoll on the lonely windswept Carolina beach. And it was at Kill Devil Hill that Harry Combs began his quest to unravel the mystery of the birth of flight.

The author is an airman. He writes from the vantage point of one who has known the exhilaration and terror of flight.

Harry Combs also has a deep respect for, and broad knowledge of, history. By historians' standards, the written records of the Wright activities are excellent. Additionally, some of the relatives, friends and observers of the brothers were available to personally confirm (or deny) the accuracy of the various accounts of their lives and work.

It is said that history is like a mirror; it can only look back. Undoubtedly true, but there is great value in pausing to look back, for only with an appreciation of where we've been can we hope to understand where we are heading.

Kill Devil Hill is a story of synergism and serendipity, of sense and sensitivity. More important, it is an airman's careful analysis of one of the most dramatic achievements in the human experience.

There is, of course, a most specific reason for emphasizing the words of Neil Armstrong. There are innumerable accounts of the Wright Brothers, and there are also innumerable conflicts and contradictions throughout many of these. Fortunately, I was provided access to all the documentation gathered over many years by Combs, who in his aviation career ran a flying school, designed, built, and raced his own airplanes, flew as a fighter pilot and a transport pilot, flew civilian and military, became the president of Gates-Learjet and many other firms, and would one day be soaring cross-country at fifty-one thousand feet in a Learjet, and the next day be winding his way slowly down through the valleys of Arizona and Colorado. In short, the airman's airman.

While this book is not a history of aviation per se, I have felt compelled to retain an historical perspective. Again and again I have emphasized that in these earliest days of flying, every pilot was a test pilot because he had no other choice. That includes, of course, the Wrights, who, like some of the leading exponents of flight before them, made hundreds of flights in gliders of their own design and construction so that they would be as capable as possible to *fly* their machine once it left the ground under its own power. The short hops, thumps, wallowing, sagging, and other miseries of attempted powered flight before the Wrights all came to naught, and afforded their pilots not a nickel's worth of *flying* experience.

In the classic history of flight from its beginnings to 1930, *The World in the Air,* published by G. P. Putnam's Sons, the information is both detailed and on a grand scale. The contributing authors and editors of this stupendous two-volume work give due credit to just about every man who struggled to fly. And there could hardly be a more fitting tribute than was given to the events at Kill Devil Hill in 1903. Their accolades begin with the heading: "Birth of New Age— Wrights in the Air." Immediately afterward is their stunning conclusion: "Man's victory over the elements after 5,000 years."

That wraps it up well, indeed.

The story of the Wright brothers immerses us in a multitude of engineering challenges, perseverance, and slowly gathered skill in *piloting.* At the risk of repetition, it must be emphasized that the first men to fly had to be pilots—test pilots—sufficiently skillful to survive a virtual no-man's-land of constant danger and the threat of fatal impact with the ground.

Harry Combs put that particular issue under a bright new spotlight. "Interestingly," he wrote in *Kill Devil Hill,* "in recent years a number of highly trained and experienced airplane designers and builders have attempted to construct and fly 'authentic' replicas of the original *Kitty Hawk Flyer.* None of the reproductions ever flew successfully. Missing were the precise conditions at Kill Devil Hill that chilly December day in 1903, but so was the most essential factor of all: the unique genius of the Wright brothers themselves."

Keep that thought in mind. . . .

• • •

The Wrights were fully aware of what their predecessors had attempted, how they tried to fly, why they failed, and why they *must* fail no matter how many more times they would try to achieve the powered flight they sought so desperately. They became close friends with Octave Chanute, they studied the papers and records of all those pioneers you have already met in these pages. They scoured the scientific studies and conclusions of the men who were considered the greatest scientific minds in all the world. And therein lies the secret to the one decision, more than all the others combined, that finally brought them their own stunning success.

For, almost all the time that they were designing wings, testing wing shapes in a marvelous wind tunnel of their own design and manufacture, studying the conclusions of the great scientists, they were always bedeviled with a problem that refused to be solved.

The Wrights had no choice but to conclude, after their own exhaustive investigations, that the right questions had never been asked.

These two brothers had never received high-school diplomas. They earned their keep by printing and selling a small newspaper in Dayton, Ohio: they came from a family with strong religious convictions, dominated by their father, a towering figure of the local church.

If we try to trace the interest of the two brothers (out of five children, of whom Orville and Wilbur were the youngest) in aviation, we run smack into a dead end. Yet it makes great copy to report that their interest in aviation began when Wilbur was eleven and his younger brother seven, and their father brought them a toy helicopter for amusement.

The Wrights themselves contribute to this yearning desire to *create* significant moments, and it has become history embedded in cement that this was the "start" of their devotion to aviation. But that is patently nonsense, because there wasn't any aviation in those early days, if you except the balloons that were proliferating throughout the world. There was no aeronautical science except in remote pages and speeches with closed groups. Everything else was fancy, and hardly much different to the two young Wrights as thundering from the earth to reach the moon. Even the brothers finally put *that* matter to rest when they recalled: "A toy so delicate lasted but a short time in the hands of small boys, but its memory was abiding."

The transformation began with sport—the sport of flying kites. Even this was a hobby, but they went at it with an excitement and experimentation that *did* whet their appetite for things that could fly, even if on a long tether to the ground. Then the kites, too, fell into the background. There was work to do! If you were the male sons of a minister then by God you worked for your keep. Nevertheless, in between the start of a toy flying machine of bamboo, cork, and paper, and even building some of their own helicopter models and flying kites, the foundation was laid down in their minds.

But they did not remain for long in one place. Their family moved from Dayton, Ohio, to Richmond, Indiana, and then in 1884 trekked back to their home at 7 Hawthorn Street in Dayton.

If there are other signs to distinguish these two young men from the world about them, it was their highly individualistic manner of doing things. Wilbur, for example, *did* complete high school requirements (in Richmond) but disdained going through the ordeal of an "official" graduation. Instead, he bent his efforts to new studies in Greek and trigonometry. Orville, much more spirited, threw himself into algebra and later Latin. Consider those subjects of trigonometry, arithmetic, algebra; consider what roles they would play in later years when the Wrights turned their attention to what every engineer, inventor, tinkerer, mechanic, and scientist had *failed* to do. And it is difficult to reconcile their determined studies, especially in the case of Orville, for he was in his own way an unrepentant hell-raiser who had even been rejected from school in sixth grade. For the rest of the year he held this matter secret from his parents and simply never bothered returning to school.

At school year's end the dam broke. All thumping hell went with it and the school officials insisted he repeat the entire sixth grade. Orville refused and shouted he would *never* return to that class. Taken aback, the school officials thought themselves clever and said Orville could go to seventh grade, but he must, he absolutely must, meet all school standards.

Perhaps with a deep inner conviction or an impish smirk

t standing his ground, Orville stormed into seventh grade,
hammered at his studies, and at the end of the year was
he outstanding student in mathematics for the entire city of
Dayton!

On the other hand, Wilbur eased away from those scientific
and mechanical interests that so fascinated his brother and
prepared to enter the ministry, a move that delighted his
father, Bishop Wright. It was not to be, and the terrible pain
Wilbur Wright was soon to endure is one of the driving
moves that eventually brought him to things aeronautical.

By March of 1885 Wilbur was ready to enroll in Yale
Divinity School with his final goal of entering the ministry.
But before he could commit himself, he was playing a game
of *shinny* on skates, with friends. At 140 pounds, Wilbur,
although light, was wiry and excelled in sports. His plans
ended with this game, as a shaft of hardwood smashed into
his mouth. He was hurled to the ground, blood literally exploding from his face, now a garish pulp. Writhing in pain,
he fought to understand what had happened, for the pain
overwhelmed him. His lips were shredded, gums ripped and
torn, and many teeth shattered. Fortunately an army surgeon
watching from a nearby veterans' home witnessed the accident and rushed to Wilbur's aid. The youngster returned
home in agony, face heavily bandaged, his world in his eigh-
teenth year as badly torn and mangled as his mouth and face.

For months afterward Wilbur lived with unremitting pain,
enduring forced loneliness to spare his family the sight of his
suffering, returning again and again to doctors for surgery,
for work on his bones that were healing so slowly, and preparing at this young age for false teeth to replace those exploded from his mouth. Forgoing all hope for the ministry,
he surrounded himself with and delved deeply into his books.
It is difficult in this brief passage really to relive or to reenact
for the reader the long and terrible months for Wilbur Wright.
The accident had other grievous effects; he developed heart
palpitations and doctors gave his family the grim news that
his heart had been damaged in the accident. Then an intestinal
disorder struck. With pain assailing him from all sides, his
world a shrunken enclave of suffering, he decended into a
melancholy state in which he was convinced his heart would
soon fail him completely.

For four years Wilbur lived in this self-imposed isolation, hurting within and without. And nothing the irrepressible Orville could do brought Wilbur upward from his lonely well. Orville had turned to a sudden fascination with printing. He delved into every nook and cranny of printing, taught himself the operation of presses, rebuilt old machinery, adding his own and superior innovations, and as time passed, what started as a hobby became a livelihood. He began to churn out small newspapers, handbills, pamphlets, posters, doing all sorts of printing that produced appreciable income for the family. More important for our interest was the pattern of hands-on innovation; Orville created new equipment that was superior to anything available on the commercial market. The key here is that creative innovation, the assault on problems for which no answers could be found in books.

Wilbur wanted nothing to do with this frenetic and financially successful endeavor. Then, as happens so many times in life, the pain and anguish of another stirred response deep within the bastion of defenses Wilbur had erected. His mother developed major pulmonary problems. She weakened steadily and soon was completely bedridden. Suddenly it was Wilbur by her side. Each day it was the face-battered Wilbur who lifted his mother from her upstairs bed and brought her down to the house parlor where she could at least share the daily life of her family. According to Bishop Wright, without this unflagging tenderness, Susan Koerner Wright would have succumbed years before her final days. Wilbur had given his mother the gift of at least two years beyond that time when her doctors said the end was at hand.

The passing of Susan Wright also brought on a special change in Wilbur. Suddenly he showed interest in the growing printing business of his younger brother. They tackled "insoluble" problems together and came up with new machinery that amazed press engineers.

And here was another key to what was coming. Wilbur's suggestions, worked out in exhaustive detail, were at first ridiculed by professionals and experienced hands. No matter his ideas worked and their printing presses turned out products faster and better than anyone had ever dreamed. Together they developed one new press in particular that was studied by the foreman of a major printing company. He stared in disbelief at the contraption the two young men had created. It whirred and hummed and clanked noisily and ran with a speed and smoothness that had the foreman blinking incredulously. This good worthy finally slipped off a jacket, lay flat on the floor, and slowly worked his way beneath the press to study every detail of its operation. When he completed his inspection, he wriggled free of the press, dusted himself off, grabbed his jacket, and glared at the brothers. "I still don't understand *why* it works," he muttered.

There is that key. What other men, professional and experienced, said could not be done, the Wright brothers *did*—and better than anyone thought was possible. They were now a *team*.

So it was evident to both of them that new, giant commercial presses would soon outperform their own equipment, and they would forever remain small and isolated in this business. On to other challenges! And on to the next critical step that would lead to flying the world's first successful airplane.

In 1892, Orville bought a new "Safety Bicycle" that had shaken the cycling world by having both wheels of the same size. The Columbia company turned it out with pneumatic tires, it rode with marvelous smoothness and efficiency, and it absolutely fascinated Orville. In swift order, the printing business was pushed from his mind and he hurled himself into learning everything he could about bicycles. Accompanied by Wilbur, who was reduced by stomach pains and his weakened heart to spectator status, Orville rushed into cycling competitions and meets. But he was far more than a skilled competitor.

Together he and Wilbur had become, as Harry Combs put it so well, "superlative mechanics" with bicycles. The next step was almost a foregone conclusion. Friends showed interest in whatever new designs the brothers produced. The Wrights also had enough money to invest in their own business, and West Third Street in Dayton quickly became a mecca for cycling enthusiasts. And the Wright brothers were up to their ears in what they loved most and did best— working out problems, producing new designs, and building with their own hands.

At first they hesitated about throwing so much money into their own designs, but an avalanche of business soon changed that, and the Wright bicycles were snatched up as fast as the brothers could produce them. They also created new full-pressure balloon tires, they designed new widened forks and frames, and their machines were the rage of Dayton. Orville had little sympathy for delays and problems he felt were the result of ignorance and ineptitude. One such example was a clumsy accounting machine in their office. He hated the detestable thing, tore it apart, and in quick order invented a new and vastly superior accounting machine. He took a new look at the noisy and distressingly unreliable typewriters of their company, disemboweled several, and soon produced a new model that amazed his workers with its smooth operation and reliability.

Then came *the* day. It was September of 1894 and *McClure's* magazine published a great spread on Otto Lilienthal and his gliding flights and experiments. The story and pictures excited the brothers as any new device, invention or endeavor always stimulated them. But contrary to what has been written so often, Wilbur and Orville did not hurl themselves into challenging the possibilities of flight. The Lilienthal story was to bake slowly in their minds, waiting for the right moment to emerge.

Such connections, in their own rarely visible or recognized manner, make history. Two years after first reading of Lilienthal, Orville Wright lay near death from typhoid fever. Doctors gave him a fifty-fifty chance to survive. Orville survived his bout with typhoid fever, and it is his convalescence period that deserves our attention. For as he emerged from his feverish struggle for life his interest in new events brought his mind upward from its fog. The news of the day, what great events had happened, what was promising—these were the things Orville wanted to know.

Lilienthal's death was *the* news of the day. Wilbur sat by Orville's bedside, reading to him the latest newspaper stories of what had happened in Germany. Again a signal was sounded for the future. The newspaper reports were so obviously ridiculous that they attracted the attention of the brothers. Even *The New York Times* was clumsy and hapless on almost every reporting account. "The apparatus worked well for a few minutes," wrote the *Times* newsman.

Wilbur snorted with disdain. The brothers shared their sarcasm. If anybody had ever flown for "a few minutes," the world would have been stood on its ear with amazement. Then Wilbur hooted in derision as he read that Lilienthal had flown "quite a distance, when suddenly the machinery of the apparatus got out of order, and man and machine fell to the ground."

To the Wrights this was appalling stupidity. On its face the report was absurd, and this very absurdity led them to discuss what might *really* have happened. Their exchanges led to arguments, a pastime they had always loved. But the nature of their argument led them to attempt to pierce the story behind the scenes, to learn more about Lilienthal and how he came to attempt to fly, and, likely unknowing the significance of the event, they began their own journey into the realm of flight.

Pursuing as much information as was available, Wilbur concluded that no matter how brilliant Lilienthal had been, it was obvious that the German inventor-pilot had been traveling a dead-end road. To Orville, Wilbur said with disdain, the Lilienthal wing was deficient in design and lift. It lacked proper size proportional to the performance it must provide in the air, and its lack of proper directional control was absolutely unacceptable to any hopes for true flight.

From then on, as soon as Orville left his bed, the grand search accelerated. The brothers attacked every publication in their local libraries to search out whatever was available by and about men attempting to fly. The *lack* of reliable information was to them astounding. Even the most learned and experienced inventors seemed to be stumbling about blindly. Despairing of obtaining locally what they sought with such effort, Wilbur, on May 30, 1899, sent off to the Smithsonian the following letter:

> I believe that simple flight at least is possible to man and that the experiments and investigations of a large number of independent workers will result in the accumulation of information and knowledge and skill which will finally lead to accomplished flight. . . . I am about to begin a systematic study of the subject in preparation for practical work to which I expect to devote what time I can spare from my regular business. I wish to obtain such papers as

the Smithsonian Institution has published on this subject, and if possible a list of other works in print in the English language. I am an enthusiast, but not a crank in the sense that I have some pet theories as to the proper construction of a flying machine. I wish to avail myself of all that is already known and then if possible add my mite to help on the future worker who will attain final success. I do not know the terms on which you send out your publications but if you will inform me of the cost I will remit the price.

Three days later the package was on its way to Wilbur, and when it arrived, the Wrights were exposed to such classic (and some not so classic) works as *Progress in Flying Machines* (Chanute, 1894); *Experiments in Aerodynamics* (Langley, 1891); *The Aeronautical Annual for 1895, 1896, 1897* (Smithsonian, 1985–87); as well as four pamphlets issued directly by the Smithsonian—*Empire of the Air* (Mouillard, No. 903); *The Problems of Flying and Practical Experiments in Soaring* (Lilienthal, No. 938); *Story of Experiments in Mechanical Flight* (Langley, No. 1134); and *On Soaring Flight* (Huffaker, No. 1135).

The Wrights were soon engaged in their own direct studies of birds flying and soaring, especially along the eastern seaboard, where offshore winds and high dunes provided not only steady lift but powerful updrafts. They found the Frenchman Mouillard to have provided the most thorough examinations of the flight characteristics of birds, but it is at this point that their own enthusiasm sagged as they delved ever deeper into the history and struggles, and the repeated failures, of those who had already challenged the skies. For the first time they comprehended that to fly successfully they must master an enormously complex set of answers to equally complex questions, many of which still had to be asked!

There were many great men of science who had attempted to conquer the air, aside from those we have already met in these pages. Alexander Graham Bell, once favored as the lead contestant in the battle for controlled flight, operated on a par with his contemporaries of the day—*failure*. And here was none other than Thomas Edison, that genius of invention, keen of eye for the future of science and what man could accomplish, who had been entranced with the possibility of manned flight since childhood. Never one, even as a youth, not to attempt dangerous experiments, but also wise in the way of possible consequences, Edison once fed birdseed to a close friend, sent him to an upper-story window of his house, and from the safety of the ground below shouted, "Jump! You can fly!"

History mercifully does not record the subsequent events. Except that in later years, despite urging by the U.S. government, Edison refused huge sums of money to perfect the manned flying machine. Unless and until someone produced an engine of no more than forty pounds weight, that produced at least fifty horsepower, manned flight was "absolutely impossible," according to Edison.

Obviously, the brothers were to prove even the great Edison absolutely wrong.

Wilbur and Orville contacted Octave Chanute, and his response began a close personal and professional friendship between them. In the years to come, Chanute would often join the Wrights on the North Carolina sands, and they were ever grateful for his advice and assistance.

But through it all the brothers could not escape from the growing realization that *all* the greats of aviation to date had run down the wrong track to achieve manned flight. Wilbur, as a start, and from the outset of their relationship, told Chanute in no uncertain terms that the Lilienthal gliding tests proved very little beyond the *gliding* flights. Furthermore, the Lilienthal observations contained another disastrous error. All you needed to do, emphasized Wilbur, was to study buzzards in soaring flight. When a wing dropped because of an air current, all the bird had to do was twist (or warp) his lower wing. Increased pressure increased lift and the buzzard was instantly restored to equilibrium.

In the years following their study of aeronautics and flight, the Wrights built a superb wind tunnel to test hundreds of wing shapes and designs. They used their native genius and mechanical skills to weld wood and wire and cloth into gliders that flew better, and under better control. Their gliders could be flown as kites first to test lift and control and later enlarged to carry a man through the air.

It was easy to gloss over the *years* of intensive and exhaus-

tive tests, the failures that had to be explained and then elimi-
nated from their designs, the expense and effort. Suffice to
say that nothing the Wrights did was haphazard. They attacked their problems on a hard scientific basis. They knew
what they had to do to make the single great breakthrough—
to control the machine *in flight,* to turn left or right, to fly
upward or downward, and to do so instantly. This was the
issue most argued by all the other aspirants of flight who
championed automatic stability.

They argued that no man could possibly react quickly
enough to changes in pressure, balance, lift, and other factors
to safely fly an airplane. Without automatic stability from
wing dihedral, man just could not fly. This was not the consensus of a few but of every scientist and inventor the
Wrights studied.

This was their dilemma. *Either everybody else in the world
was right and the Wrights were wrong—or the Wright Brothers had to accept that every great scientific mind in the world
was wrong, and they were the only ones on the right path.*

It was an incredible, epochal conclusion, but finally the
Wrights had no choice: they agreed they had to dismiss virtually everything ever written on manned flight.

Wilbur later spoke of their situation in 1899: "There was
no flying art in the proper sense of the word, but only a
flying problem. Thousands of men had thought about flying
machines, and a few had even built machines which they
called flying machines, but these machines were guilty of
almost everything except flying. Thousands of pages had been
written on the so-called science of flying, but for the most
part the ideas set forth, like the designs for machines, were
mere speculations and probably ninety percent was false.
Consequently, those who tried to study the science of aerodynamics knew not what to believe and what not to believe."

The holy grail sought by the Wrights was to change the
angle at which one or both of their wings attacked the air.
If they could change these angles, and do so quickly and
with reliable response, they would be changing both the lift
and the *direction of lifting force,* and a man could then *fly*
his machine under excellent control. A bird could warp its
wings, as Wilbur had stressed again and again. And then
Wilbur had a stroke of genius.

As Orville described the moment:

> Wilbur . . . demonstrated the method by means of a small pasteboard box, which had two of the opposite ends removed. By holding the top forward corner and the rear lower corner of one end of the box between his thumb and forefinger and the rear upper corner and the lower forward corner of the other end of the box in like manner, and by pressing the corners together the upper and lower surface of the box were given a heliocoidal twist, presenting the top and bottom surfaces of the box at different angles on the right and left sides. From this it was apparent that the wings of a machine of the Chanute double-deck type, with the fore-and-aft trussing removed, could be warped in like manner, so that in flying the wings on the right and left sides could be warped so as to present their surfaces to the air at different angles of incidence and thus secure unequal lifts on the two sides.

Or, as we would say in our current idiom, *right on!*

But by the summer of 1901, with intensive hard work behind them, building and flying gliders that failed to produce the lift they had calculated, they found it necessary to force themselves to continue their work. They returned to Elizabeth City (on their way to Kitty Hawk) in July of 1901, only to be caught in a devastating hurricane with winds screaming at 107 miles per hour and spawning killer tornadoes. This was the time to hang on tightly; several days later the storm abated. They hied off to the sands, built their workshed and glider storage shed, and were immediately inundated by vast swarms of mosquitoes that "came in a mighty cloud, almost darkening the sun." The attacks nearly drove them mad, but again they hung on grimly until fresh winds blew away their tormentors. When all was done, they assembled their glider with a 22-foot wingspan and a wing area of 290 square feet, weighing in at just under one hundred pounds.

It was time to fly into a welcome stiff wind. Wilbur settled himself in the prone position on the glider (to reduce drag from sitting up, which would have reduced the glider's effectiveness), their assistants grasped the wing tips and started running down the sand dune used for their launching point.

When they cast the glider loose, it plopped senselessly into the sand. It had not really flown an inch. Wilbur gloomily studied his machine, decided it was nose heavy, helped the men return it up the dune, settled himself farther back on the wing, and off they went again.

With the same miserable results.

Five more times they tried, and five more times their glider settled like a duck with a load of buckshot in its belly. Jaws set grimly, Wilbur and Orville kept making changes.

On the ninth launch from the sand, they were stunned to see the glider continuing through the air. It flew for three hundred feet, and they rushed to congratulate Wilbur. They found a grim visage awaiting them. Wilbur had had fits with the controls. They didn't work properly. He had struggled simply to remain airborne. Again they made changes and launched the tenth flight.

The wind had abated, yet the glider lifted into its gentle path. Moving at barely twelve miles an hour, it began to rise. Wilbur fought the controls to stay close to the sand for safety, but still the glider soared until it was the height of a three-story building.

Abruptly, terrifyingly, the glider slowed in midair. Its speed dropped alarmingly, and both brothers knew that Wilbur's life hung on a string. *This was the same situation in which Lilienthal had flown and had been killed.* The glider was stalling! Losing all its lift and poised to plunge out of control into the ground.

Nothing Wilbur did with the controls worked; he had full pressure on the elevator, but the glider hung perilously in the air. Desperately, he hauled his body as far forward as he could. Orville and their assistant ran madly to reach the glider when it struck sand and then they stopped, amazed, as the glider settled in a gentle, floating motion back to the ground.

This time Wilbur's broad grin told them everything; they had encountered the dreaded killer stall and overcome it. It was the forward horizontal elevator that pushed them through the barrier. As the glider lost speed the forward elevator *stalled first.* Without lift at the foremost part of the glider, the nose fell. As the nose fell the wings regained lift to support the machine in the air.

Their design, partly by brilliant engineering, but also, according to the Wrights, as much a "happy accident of design," had brought them through the dreaded moments. Orville wanted to quit for the day and review their progress and make still more improvements to the glider. Wilbur refused, and that afternoon he was back in the air making one test after another.

Finally, with every second in the air giving him more skill and confidence, the glider seemed to lose all control despite every attempt at correction by Wilbur. Body position and full-down elevator meant nothing. Wilbur had become overconfident; his speed had dropped dangerously and now the wind was pushing the glider backward! Again everyone braced themselves for the grinding crash—and again, to their amazement, the glider floated gently to the sand.

The forward position of the elevator was *everything*. Later, Orville concluded that their problems arose from the fact that "in the first case the center of pressure was in front of the center of gravity and thus pushed up the front edge; in the second case, they were in coincidence, and the surface in equilibrium; while in the third case the center of pressure had reached a point even behind the center of gravity, and there was therefore a downward [force]. . . . This point having been definitely settled, we proceeded to truss down the ribs of the whole machine so as to reduce the depth of curvature."

More tests, more changes, more flights. By the next year the size of their glider had reached a wing area of more than three hundred square feet. The modified wings worked superbly, and control was now within the instant reach of the pilot. At times Wilbur skimmed the sands; on other flights he took up the machine to once perilous heights.

By now Wilbur was measuring his flight time in minutes rather than seconds. Octave Chanute was present for the successful glider trials, and it was he who took pictures, thus giving us a legacy we might otherwise never have had.

They now moved from flights in a straight line to turns in the air—and almost killed Wilbur. They still had no vertical rudder, and instead of turning when Wilbur warped the wing surfaces, the glider slid in a sickening yaw. The lower (or inside the turn) wing moved slower, so it lost lift first. But the outer wing, moving faster and faster in the turn, exerted so much lift it was starting to roll the glider. It is a killer trap for the unwary; in this case the wary were facing the *unknown* despite all their caution.

And they could not solve the problem that summer of 1901. Wilbur later wrote: "When we left Kitty Hawk at the end of 1901, we doubted that we would ever resume our experiments . . . When we looked at the time and money we had expended, and considered the progress made and the distance yet to go, we considered our experiments a failure."

They returned to Ohio, Wilbur's face bruised and swollen from plowing headlong into the ground more than once.

Their dilemma, not yet understood, was that while they had achieved two-direction control—that is, in two axes—safe and controlled flight is impossible without control in *three* axes.

The Wrights were back on their sand dunes in August of 1902, with a larger, heavier and modified glider—this time with two fixed vertical fins, behind the main wings. Their purpose was to instantly create a drag force whenever the machine entered a slip during an attempted turn. This would stop the wild swing and would also force down the nose, and the glider would continue in a constant turn.

They hoped.

They began testing the glider in early September. Tentative and careful flights, each one a bit longer than the former, and trying out the new controls. The "great event" they struggled to reach almost ended in one wild flight when Wilbur, working the new control system (but still lacking any real experience with *flying*), lost control and plunged to the ground. He and the glider miraculously escaped unscathed, and Wilbur doggedly returned to his tests, making twenty-five flight glides before the day ended. Then they took time off to modify their cantankerous machine. Orville drooped the wing tips to combat the effect of winds striking the glider from the sides, and then he, too, flew with the machine. Longer and higher until it was obvious he was a "natural flier," grinning with his swoops and glides—until those moments when the glider "got away from him" and took off on its own to smack abruptly into the ground, covering Orville with sand and shaking him up thoroughly.

On the last flight of the day Orville lost control completely.

The glider smashed into a dune, wooden ribs and spars snapping like twigs, cloth covering ripping from one end of the machine to the other. Orville lay tangled in the terrible wreckage, a machine almost destroyed, and then he extricated himself from the debris and climbed out without a scratch.

They rebuilt the glider. Several days later, again testing, they were astonished to find the glider whirling crazily toward the ground; they were in a tailspin without knowing it, and without understanding what had happened except that they had completely lost control. Later they would figure out the answer. One wing was without lift, the other was producing lift, and the only thing the glider could do was to drop earthward while turning (spinning) as fast as it could go.

The problem lay in those fixed vertical fins. If they could be turned, when the wing warped, it would solve the problem of excessive force being applied to the glider in a turn. Quickly they removed the double fins and installed a single fin that could turn. When the pilot used the hip cradle on the wing, securing his body as well as allowing him to warp the wings, the rudder at the same time would turn. *If* this arrangement worked, they might be able to get past the unexplained and violent loss of control that drove them to distraction.

October 8 was the first day for the tests with the new controls, at first all straight ahead to check out the basic stability of the glider and its modifications. Two days later Wilbur was flying more than three hundred feet in a single glide, but he was banking and turning with marvelous control! He was flying as a pilot should fly, knowing what to expect, anticipating actions and reactions, flirting with the winds, sensing the motions of his mechanical device.

The world's first real flier had discovered the reality of his dream.

In the next fourteen days they made more than four hundred flights, climbing, gliding, turning left and right, and landing perfectly. Before they left for Ohio late in 1902, they were in the air as long as twenty-six seconds on a single glide and covering more than six hundred feet and exceeding thirty miles an hour. What was critical now wasn't time or distance. It was replication of the incredibly successful test flights and the now sure mastery of their glider.

•　•　•

Consider:

In the spring of 1903, the Wrights were ready to install an engine in a new glider. They knew nothing of the Manly engine installed in the Langley glider. Had they had such an engine, they would have astounded all the world with a flight that would continue as long as they had fuel. But they did not have that engine, and nothing could be found to meet their needs.

So the Wrights designed their own engine. The mechanic who ran the bicycle shop, Charles Taylor, found the brothers pointing at him, and then heard the words. *Build the engine.* No drawings. No plans. They *talked* about what they needed, and Taylor built it piece by piece, and when he was done, they'd hoped for eight horsepower and found out that they'd done better than they'd believed possible. The finished engine gave them twelve horses.

They didn't have any propellers. None to speak of, anyway. They'd already discarded every propeller known as clumsy and horribly inefficient. Well, if you don't have propellers, design them. The Wrights did just that, *and then they carved their propellers by hand.* They needed two propellers that would produce thrust at just around 1,100 revolutions per minute. They carefully designed their propellers to turn inward toward each other. This would cancel undesired torque.

The efficiency of those propellers was astounding. Years later, when men would fly with engines five times as powerful as the Wright engine built by Taylor, the effective thrust of the Wright Flyer with only twelve horsepower would prove to be superior to all the others! But they didn't know that in the early months of 1903, and so they cut and whittled and shaved to their own exacting specifications.

By October of 1903 they were back at Kill Devil Hill, and the disassembled parts of their new machinery arrived in bits and pieces. In this waiting time they continued gliding practice. Time in the air was increased to more than forty seconds on repeated flights. They continued learning the hard way— through unexpected crashes and hard slams into the ground.

By November their camp was short on food, bereft of creature comforts, and everyone was suffering from the bitter cold. Yet November 15 saw the machine assembled for its test. With a man aboard it would weigh over seven hundred pounds. Would all the screws and connections hold together?

They did not. With the engine running, everything shook loose. This forced them to shut down and tighten each fitting with exacting care.

November 19: their propeller shafts arrived at camp, even as the water in the ponds about them was freezing over to ice.

December 12: they made their first attempt at flight.

The previous days had been brutally frustrating. One problem after another bedeviled them, even some so simple as the bicycle sprockets that repeatedly slipped from the propeller shafts. That problem was solved by melting tire cement over the whole system so as to seal it tightly.

December 14: Wilbur attempted the first flight in the airplane. It did not go well. As the Flyer left its guide track Wilbur pulled up the nose in order to build up speed. He was too fast and too sharp. The Flyer lofted, then fell off at an angle, hitting hard and breaking several wooden structural members. However, damage was slight, and best of all, Wilbur was uninjured.

December 16: a gale sprang up during the night; in the morning the Wrights stared miserably at an angrily boiling surf. The wind was howling at over thirty miles an hour, creating a steady mix of salt-spray air and driven sand. Everyone spent that day and most of the night wondering if another hurricane was on the way.

December 17: Orville was at the controls, the engine clattering, propellers spinning. It was a dangerous moment to attempt flight in an airplane that had never flown before. Wilbur's previous attempts had not been considered true flight. Now, with winds whistling around their ears at twenty-seven miles per hour, it was brave indeed to launch.

The holding cable was released, the Flyer shot down its track on the starting trolley and rose into the air. Its flight path was erratic; Orville was overcontrolling! Yet it flew for at least a hundred feet before a final dash toward the ground. Orville corrected on the controls and it was another twenty feet before the Flyer again touched sand, cracking a landing skid in the process.

No matter! *Orville Wright had flown!*

He flew against a wind of twenty-seven miles per hour, lofted across a distance of 120 feet under control (erratic as it was), and had remained airborne for twelve seconds. Even as he climbed from the airplane and it was started back toward its takeoff trolley, both brothers knew what was wrong. Their controls were too sensitive. They were overcontrolling because they really had no choice. Common sense dictated ending the tests then and there, for overcontrol in that thundering wind was an invitation to disaster.

Predictably they refused to quit. The weather was terrible and might worsen. But now they at least understood their problem. They repaired the skid and by 11:20 A.M. Wilbur was lying on the wing signaling that he was ready to go. He flew a distance of 175 feet. They were elated but far from satisfied.

Orville made the third attempt, and again he ran into severe problems of overcontrolling. With less time at the controls than his brother, the simple fact was that Orville didn't know how to fly.

Exactly at noon, Wilbur was ready for the fourth attempt at powered flight. The wind had picked up and the situation was more dangerous than before. Sixty feet of track lay before Wilbur when he cut loose. The Flyer rushed ahead. Forty feet from its start it lifted into the air.

The Flyer bucked and pinched wildly, Wilbur fighting for control every foot of the way. Then he was a hundred feet from his start, and even if it was erratic, he still had control!

Two hundred feet!

The Flyer lunged wildly; Wilbur fought it back. The wind screamed and a powerful gust hurled the Flyer downward. Wilbur was fast as a striking snake on the controls; he held her off above the sand and eased to slightly higher altitude.

Three hundred feet and he was still flying, and miraculously, the violent winds abated.

Four hundred feet!

Five hundred!

Six hundred!

Men shouted with wild joy. Still the Flyer went on!

Seven hundred feet!

Wilbur worked the controls as he had never done before. *Eight hundred feet!*

He could have gone on but for a conspiracy of the elements: a dune rose before him, the winds suddenly shoved the Flyer earthward. Wilbur fought to clear the dune—it was clear sailing beyond. But the winds owned him now. The machine lunged for sand, struck hard, cracked wooden members, and stopped. Wilbur killed the engine.

He was quietly delirious.

History was theirs.

The conquest of the air was real.

Wilbur had flown for fifty-nine seconds of powered flight. From start to landing he had covered a distance of 852 feet.

But if you computed the distance through the air, considering the Flyer's airspeed, and the howling winds, and everything else, his flight was actually more than half a mile.

But that didn't matter now. Fifty-nine seconds and 852 feet, taking off under its own power, controlled in flight by a man, and landing at an elevation at least as high as the starting point.

It had happened.

There's a marvelous postscript to the moment that would soon launch an explosion of flight throughout the world.

Two months before the epochal day of December 17, 1903, Simon Newcomb, considered the leading scientist of the United States, and the sole American scientist since the days of Benjamin Franklin to become an associate of the Institute of France, wrote an article for the newspaper the *Independent* . . . in which he said that by "unassailable logic" human flight was absolutely impossible.

Adventure and Disaster—It's Time to Fly!

So epochal an event as the first successful manned, powered flight would be expected to bring dazzling honors and awards. But it was not to be. The ridicule that raked Langley and other would-be fliers had already established public opinion against flying. The first flights at Kitty Hawk also suffered from a vast isolation from the rest of the country, and newspaper editors the land over snorted with disbelief and disdain over the news from the cold and windlashed Carolina shore. Finally, early in January of 1904, a disbelieving Wilbur Wright issued his own statement to the Associated Press. It received less print space than a story of a dog run over by a horse-drawn carriage.

Apathy, indifference, disbelief, and a numbing silence was the general response to the achievement of the Wrights, the many photographs of their accomplishment notwithstanding. This inevitably drove the Wrights far from any close association with either the American press or the public, and they resumed their test flying in 1904 from a cow pasture near their Ohio home, using a catapult. Without the strong winds of Kitty Hawk, their machine now needed this extra assist to gain flying speed.

As they flew with their greatly improved machine they

yielded to a natural desire to at least be recognized for what they had done. They decided on another attempt and brought a great many newsmen to their lonely pasture just outside of Dayton. The gods of chance have strange ways. Winds were blustery and dangerous, and their engine would not start. The reporters showered sneers and ridicule on the Wrights, judged them as either crazy or quacks bent on publicity. They then stalked off.

The brothers tried once more, the following day. A few hardy reporters, apparently with nothing else to do, showed up.

This time the engine ran smoothly, and the reporters watched with sudden new interest as a heavy weight fell and the catapult shot the airplane forward. Just as it left its launching track, the engine failed. Powerless, heavy, lacking flying speed, the machine flopped to the uneven ground of the pasture.

That was the end of that. These few members of the press who had lingered went away, shaking their heads and promising never to come back.

Yet by September, the advances in the machine were so great, and piloting experience had gained so much, that Wilbur was making new record-breaking flights. He flew in circular patterns about the Ohio pasture, demonstrating his magnificent control and the reliability of their machine. By November of 1904, Wilbur had advanced to circling their "airfield" through four complete turns, flying a distance of over three miles, and remaining in the air for more than five minutes.

And they flew in virtual isolation.

Came 1905 and their progress proved astonishing.

Barely eighteen months before, their greatest achievement was that last flight at Kitty Hawk of 852 feet over the ground for a total flight time of fifty-nine seconds. One year later they were flying circular patterns in repeated circuits over three miles and for more than five minutes. And why not longer flights from Point A to Point B?

There were no airports in the nation. There weren't any facilities to service a flying machine when it finally landed. Fuel, repairs, and other necessities were nonexistent. As well as they were doing, their air paths were still restricted.

In January of 1905 they offered their designs to the War

Department, citing the value of aerial reconnaissance and especially the potential promised by new engines. They tried not once, but three times, and each time the U.S. government kissed them off without so much as even taking a look at their aircraft or asking a single question. Even the U.S. Patent Office, which had filed their patents for their glider design years before, now began to balk at what it considered preposterous claims of powered flight!

Then, by the end of 1905, the ability and performance of the Wright biplanes erased all doubts that man had embarked with full capability into the endless oceans of the air. They were able to fly, and keep flying, limited only by the amount of fuel they could carry! On October 5, 1905, Wilbur flew nonstop for more than thirty-eight minutes and covered a ground distance of more than twenty-four miles. It was also a striking testimonial to their engine design, their propellers of unmatched thrust and efficiency, and the very structure of their machines, which now were subject to repeated stresses and strains of flying and landing. Both men had become as expert as was possible within the limitations of their aircraft and the flight time available.

What is astonishing is that a world that had struggled to gain the secrets of flight for some fifty-five centuries now paid virtually no attention to what had been accomplished by the Wrights. They had filed patent papers. They were observed flying in Ohio by hundreds of people—a streetcar line ran past their pasture airfield and local people gathered to watch the astounding sight of an airplane whizzing through the air with a flier aboard. But to the nation at large, the Wrights remained in a sort of mystic limbo.

By 1906 a cold anger settled in with the two brothers. They were fully aware that those still wanting to fly would utilize what the Wrights had developed so successfully, and with the American government showing all the interest of a stone, the brothers took a path of virtually absolute silence. During the year 1906, when they could have made further enormous strides, they did not bother to build a single new model of their aircraft, gripping testimonial to the frigidity of the public and the isolation forced upon them. The Wrights carried out their policy of secrecy to the point of not flying for two and a half years.

It is still incredible to realize the huge and bottomless pits into which dreams can fall.

The Wrights stirred themselves in 1907. Essentially, their attitude now was to hell with the U.S. government. They had had enough ridicule and rebuffs; they also knew the potential of what they had done, and they turned their backs to the United States and set off for Europe with their airplane in a huge wooden crate.

Still no success. Still this confounding stillborn miasma in which they were foundering. They asked $250,000 for their airplane, the *only* proven flying machine in the world. But by now sensitive to the machinations of governments and industry, they also made it a part of their agreement that they must be paid *before* they would demonstrate their aircraft in flight.

Again disbelief and the cold shoulder. They left their crated airplane in Le Havre and, disconsolate and angrier than before, returned to the United States. Their situation may be compared to someone who has gone to the moon and back, with witnesses and photographs to confirm every aspect of that soaring adventure, is willing to repeat the performance— and is tossed out of every door he enters!

But it wasn't *all* silence, as it turned out. In France, where manned flight had always been a glittering goal—and always just beyond reach—Captain Ferdinand Ferber of the French army received exciting news about the Wrights, from none other than Octave Chanute, who had been with the brothers at Kitty Hawk. In one of those sardonic twists of fate, it turned out that Ferber had been trying to build and fly gliders based on the Lilienthal design. No luck; he floundered and plopped about his local hillsides. Then came the Chanute letters with details of the Wright biplane gliders, and Ferber ashcanned the Lilienthal designs and rushed a Wright design to completion.

To his dismay, the Wright-design gliders also floundered and flopped. In disgust, Ferber gave up, but he was also convinced the Wright brothers were no closer to flying than he was. Now, it turns out that Chanute, in his elder years, had never sent complete information to Ferber, and getting a racehorse to compete with only three legs really doesn't cut it. So once more the name of the Wrights in terms of flying success was given the heave-ho.

Chanute made up for scant information when he lectured in Paris in April of 1903 at the French Aero Club. Here he performed an enormous disservice to the Wright brothers by lavishing detailed information of the Wright control system of their highly successful gliders. The French audience hung on every word. The Wrights were operating rudder and wing-warping controls simultaneously? They looked at one another with astonishment. *Mon dieu!* They fairly trampled one another rushing back to their workshops.

Chanute had unknowingly set off a bomb of explosive growth and development, for he had literally handed to the French (and several aspiring pilots of other European countries) an architectural layout for successful flight.

Yet, despite isolated successes, the ghost of misinformation never ceased haunting the Wrights. Robert Esnault-Pelterie and a friend Ernest Archdeacon, both wealthy, pooled their resources to get Léon Levavasseur, also an accomplished engineer, to build a copy of the 1902 Wright glider. Whatever data they had was again lacking in some critical details, and even by 1904, their version of the 1902 Wright biplane glider turned in another case of floundering and flopping. These Frenchmen then uttered whatever was their national equivalent of "eech!" and judged Chanute either as overly charmed by the Wrights or an old man who couldn't tie his shoelaces anymore.

But good news overwhelms bad, and it was seized quickly by Louis Bleriot, who would have made a marvelous actor in a movie with a sinister storyline. Energetic to almost vibratory levels, hawk-nosed, and grimly intent, he paid close attention to what had transpired with the three French engineers who copied what Chanute told them was the Wright design. He accepted their failure not at face value, but with reservations. Being an engineer himself, Bleriot was all too familiar with oral rather than blueprint presentations and knew very well how a single bit of missing data could wreck an entire project.

He had followed a second attempt of Esnault-Pelterie, who, upon deciding that the warping wing control of the Wrights was inherently dangerous, had brought him to invent the aileron—the little wing at the outer trailing edges of the wing. He built a new ship of his own design with "independent horizontal rudders" on his glider and tested it in 1904. The ailerons worked very well indeed, but the glider of Esnault-Pelterie hardly worked at all. It sagged in flight, wobbled, staggered—and belly-flopped on every flight attempt.

(Little did Esnault-Pelterie realize he was thirty-six years behind the times. In 1868 Matthew Boulton in England had designed, and registered his design, for the aileron!)

Bleriot joined up with a group of French inventors and would-be pilots, including Archdeacon and Gabriel Voisin. They built gliders on floats and had these towed aloft by speedboats. They met at first with mixed success, still relying on "automatic stability" rather than "manned flyability." Somehow they survived the inherent weaknesses of relying on marked dihedral to keep them safely balanced in the air.

Another name entered the competition in the form of Alberto Santos-Dumont. A Brazilian living in France and the pilot of successful small dirigibles that had already made him famous in Europe, he built a flying box kite powered by an Antoinette engine. The airplane looked like something built by a demented child. Santos-Dumont sat within the main box-kite cell, and far ahead of this unit, on long structural members, he placed another and smaller box kite for flight controls. The airplane would give every impression of flying backward through the air. *If* it flew, of course.

Well, it flew, and the little Brazilian became the first man in Europe to qualify as an airplane pilot. *Very* wisely, for his first flight he had his cumbersome machine carried aloft beneath a balloon. Then he cut loose and fell earthward. But the wings grasped lift, and the fifty-horsepower engine (a miracle for its time) banged and snorted into life and Santos-Dumont made a beautiful descent and landing. That didn't qualify him as making a proper flight from takeoff, but the brief foray into the air gave him invaluable piloting experience. Two months later on October 23, 1906, he lifted off from the Bagatelle Flying Field and at twenty-five miles per hour flew a distance under control for two hundred feet. The next month he managed a flight of seven hundred feet.

All Europe thrilled to these exploits, yet remained unaware that the very best Santos-Dumont was able to do was still

150 feet short of the day the Wright brothers first flew in 1903!

One after the other, more and more inventors and hopeful pilots joined the growing ranks of the air-minded in Europe. In 1907 Henri Farman flew his Voisin biplane a half mile at better than fifty miles per hour. Esnault-Pelterie built a sleek monoplane with two wheels in tandem beneath the fuselage, and a wheel at each wing tip (to keep from "digging in" as the wind bounced him about on the ground), but what really distinguished this REP ship was the fact that it had a tractor engine (pulling, instead of pushing, like the Wright design), and it was a monoplane without external bracing wires. The airplane was sorely lacking in pilot controllability, but it flew and it gave great promise of this design for the future.

Leon Delagrange was both an accomplished inventor *and* sculptor. He flew a large biplane with wings so wide and a box-kite tail assembly so large he resembled a formation of sheets in the air, but—and it's a great and lusty but—in 1907 he flew successfully. In a list that would grow with alarming pace, he took aloft the first passenger and then took the first woman into the air. By 1910, in an flying exercise in Bordeaux, he died in a crash.

The Hungarian-born Trajan Vuia fascinated all France with his man-carrying glider flights, then captured their admiration when he built—and flew—a "giant child's toy" in his "Flying Tricycle," which looked like a bat made of a wooden erector set and crumpled linen sheets in the form of bat wings. Riding along on pneumatic tires, it lofted skyward on a liquid air motor (whatever that was) and clattered through the air. The flight was successful, barely so, as the shaking and jittery motion of the *Bat* threatened to tear the machine apart. In a move of great insight, fledgling test pilot Vuia accepted the plaudits of the watching crowd, and apparently vowed never to take his weird assembly into the air again.

Another wheeled contraption outdid—if that was possible—the Vuia *Bat* in the competition for sheer clumsiness and incompetence of design. Karl Jatho of Germany somehow managed to attach together a weird mangling of wires and wooden braces covered with fabric, mounted a nine-horsepower motor and propeller in this deformed kite shape, placed it on four wheels above which reared naked-looking stilts attached to the lower wing of the powered kite. In November of 1903 he actually beat his machine into the air and on one flight reputedly covered a distance of two hundred feet. He gained less than historical fame by virtue of eyewitnesses to the event, who reported it not so much as a flight but a clattering, jerking, up-and-down, bang-on-the-ground-and-go-up-again passage for its short and hazardous journey.

What spurred on these new pilots was a combination of factors. Along with lightweight and more powerful engines, continuing rumors that the Wrights *had* flown at least promised that even some of the worst machines ever built could be dragged, even if groaning in protest and sagging from structural hernias, through the air for a modicum of flight success. And then, with this power, gliders-cum-airplanes that would otherwise never have flown because of their clumsiness, poor control, and staggering forces of drag, were able to be hauled aloft as though by an invisible chain lifted by favoring gods.

One such contraption was a triplane generously described in the historical flight records as a "peculiar model," and built by a Danish and a French flying team. Ellehammer and Cornu assembled their decidedly weird triplane, with a seat for the pilot and large bicycle wheels beneath, and a forward-mounted engine with a tractor propeller, the latter being recognized later as one of the worst propeller designs ever to be used for flight. It looked like a paddle-bladed propeller that had failed miserably aboard an extinct dirigible balloon. Never mind; the damned thing flew, and in January of 1908, with the gods favorable to these daring mortals, Ellehammer actually managed a flight of some six hundred feet across the Danish isle of Sindholm.

Once again there were instances where Europe went completely bananas over flights in France and other countries, hailing them as the greatest feats since man ever yearned to fly—blissfully ignoring that whatever they were doing, the Wrights had far exceeded them years before. In January of 1908 Henri Farman flew more than 3,600 feet in a challenge that called for a takeoff, a flight of 1,800 feet, a turn, and return to the takeoff point. For this feat he won a prize of fifty thousand francs. Europe went mad with excitement and praise.

But, now, gentle reader, compare the 3,600 feet flown by Farman with only one turn in his flight, to the flight more than two years before, by Wilbur Wright—when he flew for more than thirty-eight minutes and made dozens of turns and complete circles over a measured course of twenty-four miles.

England was moving into the air with its leading aviators counting among their ranks S. F. Cody, A. V. Roe, J. W. Dunne, and others whose names would one day become household words. Cody was clearly the wildest of the bunch. Born in the United States, he had a chuckling sense of humor, and once in England, he dressed as an Arizona sheriff, clanking spurs and all. Despite his longhorn mannerisms he was a brilliant designer and proved an excellent flier. In October of 1908 he built and flew his own biplane, flew it for the War Office, and received clear honors when they designated the machine as the British Army Aeroplane No. 1. He had greatly mixed success with his own designs, including a biplane glider without a tail and with sweptback wings. It was his way of trying to attain that elusive goal of automatic stability. The machine might have worked, but it needed more power than any engine Cody could obtain. He kept experimenting and flying until 1913 when he joined the growing list of new pilots who died in their machines.

If Cody was flamboyant, the former merchant marine officer A. V. Roe was considered downright dangerous (but who could have forecast that "Avro" would become one of the most famous, and most powerful, aircraft companies in the world in years to follow!). Roe flew biplanes and triplanes. He was tremendously excited about flying and threw himself into every new flight as though it was a personal challenge. He also lived under a lucky star, for he crashed so many times in England, frightening uncounted numbers of people and terrifying horses and cattle, that he was brought to prosecution as a menace to public safety!

Flying was at last taking off (no pun intended) in the United States as well, and there, too, the fliers' names became household words.

Included is one name that had been around for a long time but still remained closeted from public view—until 1908. In February of that year the U.S. Army emerged from its dark hole of unimagination and took a hard look at the Wright biplane and, to the astonishment and delight of the Wright brothers, delivered to Wilbur and Orville a bid acceptance to build an aircraft designed to army specifications. If the Wrights were to succeed, the machine must carry two men in seats, it must take off under its own power, fly at least ten miles nonstop at an average speed of forty miles an hour, and must carry enough fuel to cruise a range of 125 miles. There was one more requirement: the machine must be capable of being transported by a mule-driven wagon. At first this last item seemed ludicrous. On a second look, considering the rarity of level fields and the backwoods areas that must be used, *and* the terrible roads of the day, it was a necessity.

It was an opening of floodgates for the Wrights. Their first problem, however, was to get back into the air so as to hone their rusty flying skills. Neither man had been airborne for more than two years. Even as they planned their return to Kitty Hawk with their 1905 model and busied themselves with the design work for the army machine, further opportunities appeared with news from France. A syndicate in that country, watching with amazement as pilots hurled themselves into the air, judged properly that aviation was here to stay and purchased the French patent rights to the Wright design for the unheard-of sum of one hundred thousand dollars. This meant that Wilbur must leave soon for France to demonstrate his machine and teach others to fly, while Orville remained in the States to complete the new military craft and demonstrate it to the U.S. Army.

At first, Wilbur was greeted with the same derision and scorn he had known before in both his own country and in France. The public laughed. The press wrote scathingly of Wilbur Wright, making great fun with the fact that his machine was of 1905 vintage and had lain in a crate for several years—while the French, they stressed, had leaped far ahead of anything the amateurish American bicycle mechanics had ever even hoped to accomplish.

Then Wilbur quietly assembled his machine in a shed at Le Mans, France, at a racetrack. The skids brought on more hoots and catcalls. Wilbur ignored it all, climbed aboard as a huge crowd assembled. He fired up the engine, this time seated comfortably rather than lying prone. The two unusual propellers of a design utterly strange to the watching crowd—including many French and other European inventors and pilots—whirled away. Everyone waited for the ungainly-appearing machine to lift from its launching track and then fall like a shotgun-blasted pheasant to the ground.

The onlookers were stunned into silence. Stunned, and shocked, for the bird didn't wallow at all. The Wright machine soared smoothly into the air and flew with the speed and grace of an eagle and the nimbleness of a sparrow.

The date, epochal in the history of European flight, was August 8, 1908. Little need in these pages to list all the accolades that burst in the skies of France to shower down in a blizzard of praise and wonder over Wilbur Wright and his airplane, for we could fill all the pages of this book with the quotes that began with stark and attention-grabbing headlines in a dozen or more languages. It all came together as the startled observers, forced first into open mouthed silence, realized what they were seeing, and began to shout with joy and cries of encouragement as Wilbur wheeled and turned and soared with "impossible" ease and absolute control. These same pilots had flown, all right, but their machines were clumsy, and only by the more powerful engines they had available were they able to drag themselves into the air, with every moment of flight a constant threat at returning unbidden to earth.

The headlines spelled out MARVELOUS! SENSATIONAL! INCREDIBLE!

Far more to the point was the public announcement from none other than the highly feted Frenchman, Delagrange. Overcome by what he had seen in Wilbur's amazing flights, he announced to his fellow pilots, *and* to the press, "We're beaten. Compared to this American, we don't even exist."

In the days and weeks following, Wilbur Wright set one record after another. The huzzahs grew louder, all Europe rushed to watch the miraculous flying machine and its quiet, even shy, pilot.

Then came another telling remark, this time from Bleriot, the designer-pilot who insisted the monoplane was inherently superior to any possible biplane design. Gesturing to the Wright biplane, Bleriot stated that there was no question anymore: the Wright aircraft was so far advanced over anything in Europe that any comparisons were odious.

And from an English contemporary, Major B.F.S. Baden-Powell, came the statement that attracted more attention in military and political circles than it did to the public. "That Wilbur Wright is in possession of a power which controls the fate of nations is beyond dispute."

Suddenly the army contract being attended to by Orville Wright gained unexpected prominence: the word "military" had transformed the phrase "which controls the fate of nations." Heads of state the world over turned their attention sharply to everything Orville was doing. And what Orville was doing was spectacular. His new two-seater flew like a dream, and in the initial flight tests, the machine, lightly loaded with only Orville aboard, turned in an astounding performance. On almost every flight he set a speed, endurance, range, or altitude record, and on the next flight following he would break additional records. And while Wilbur was being hailed as the "Paul Revere of the New Age" for his European exploits, Orville was sticking it where it hurt to all his former critics, and gaining a nation's adulation for his superior airmanship and performance. He made his first "official" government flight at Fort Myer on September 4, 1908. The next day he was aloft for four minutes, and the crowd, expecting a few short hops, "went crazy" over the circular flight. Five days later he set a new world endurance record by thundering overhead for an hour and five minutes.

On that same day he was given the accolade of taking up the "First Passenger in Official Flight" when Lieutenant F. P. Lahm flew in the new Wright machine (the army did not know that in the months earlier, Orville had made a two-person test flight with his mechanic, Charley Furnas). On September 12, with a different army officer aboard, he increased his time aloft to one hour and fourteen minutes.

Then tragedy struck. On September 17, with Lieutenant Thomas Selfridge aboard (Selfridge was a brilliant young officer and aircraft designer who had designed the first Curtiss airplane, the *Red Wing*), they flew at seventy-five feet when one of the propeller blades smacked into a stay wire. The weakened blade snapped off; immediately the plane staggered out of control. It plunged to the ground and the impact hurled the two men through the crumbling wreckage to the ground. Selfridge never regained consciousness; he was the first aircraft passenger to be killed (Selfridge Air Force Base is named in his honor). Orville took severe injuries, two ribs were broken and his left thigh badly fractured, and he had been cut and bruised across most of his body.

Ten months later he showed up again at Fort Myer with another plane he had built while convalescing! This time he completed his tests, surpassing all requirements of the army, and with Wilbur now at his side, watching everything he did, Orville met the final test requirements on July 30, 1909, with Lieutenant Benjamin D. Foulois aboard, by flying ten miles in fourteen minutes, averaging 42.6 miles per hour. That extra fillip of speed earned the Wrights a bonus of five thousand dollars to their Army contract.

The victory was especially gratifying to Wilbur. As he stood on the ground, stopwatch in hand, timing the skillful flying of his younger brother, he knew that back in Europe dozens of aviators were trying desperately to surpass Wilbur's last European-tour flight. On that occasion he had stayed aloft (in their original 1905 model) for two hours and twenty minutes, and covered a ground distance of seventy-seven miles. (It would be eight months before that record fell, and in the interim Paul Tissandier, one of the greats of the pioneers, did his best in a Wright biplane to beat Wilbur's record—and was killed in the attempt.)

The public avidly followed all news of records and record-breaking flights, and few attempts would enchant the world audience more than the first attempt to cross the English Channel by airplane. For a while the public didn't know which way to turn and watch and listen. The first airplane flights were already under way in Romania, Sweden, Austria, Canada, Russia, Portugal, Turkey, and other lands, and airplanes were flying faster and higher than before in America, France, Italy, Germany, and wherever a challenge was to be met.

Wilbur Wright had returned from Europe to be with his brother after completing his record-breaking endurance flight on the last day of 1908. Before he left, newsmen pressed him for a few words. The inimitable Wilbur smiled at the anxious crowd. "I only know," he said slowly and quietly, "of one bird, the parrot, that can talk, and it doesn't fly very high."

On his return to America, Wilbur found a choice moment and place for all the country to know beyond all question what their machines could do. He assembled his biplane on Governors Island in New York Harbor, the newspapers announced that Wilbur would be flying, and several million people looked to the sky as Wilbur gave them their very first sight of an airplane in flight. He took off from Governors Island and flew north along the Hudson River to Grant's Tomb, and then returned south for a smooth landing.

What Wilbur accomplished in America had its equal in Europe with the "Challenge of the Channel." The *Daily Mail* of London offered a prize of some five thousand dollars to the first man to fly successfully across the Channel. Hubert Latham, who claimed nationality in both France and England, announced he'd take a crack at it. He was famous for wild flights, for being a chain-smoker and a skilled pilot—as well as for having an irrepressible death wish. Latham feared he had terminal tuberculosis. "Why wait to die slowly? Who wants a lingering death?" he told his friends. "Far better to go out in a blaze of glory doing something that's wonderful." He crashed—again and again and again. On July 19, 1909 he took his crack at the Channel crossing, flying a slender and fragile Antoinette monoplane with advanced flap-type ailerons and a powerful (for its time) fifty-horsepower engine.

About a third of the way across the Channel the powerful engine quit cold. Latham drifted downward and dropped smoothly into the water. If the Antoinette could no longer fly, it made a wonderful raft, and the French destroyer that pulled alongside to rescue him found the pilot relaxed and calmly smoking a cigarette.

(Latham's feared tuberculosis seemed to improve with every smashup. No matter what he did, no matter how foolhardy or crazy, he survived *every* crash. Oh, he died when still a young man—gored by a wounded buffalo in Africa!)

With Latham's airplane in the drink, Louis Bleriot came forward to try his hand at the challenge, and he chose his own monoplane for the event. While all this was going on,

Orville Wright was setting records in the army trials in the United States, so that the world kept shifting its attention back and forth between America and the French-English countryside. On the night of July 24, 1909, Bleriot awakened at 2:30 A.M. He had earlier burned his foot and pain kept him awake. He hobbled on a crutch to his automobile and drove to the field at Les Baraques, near Calais. A strong wind earlier in the night had slackened. His plane was in a tent and he ordered it brought out immediately. For the next half hour he fidgeted, hobbling about his flyweight machine, looking at the sky, until suddenly he climbed into the seat. It was 3:30 A.M. and night flying was considered then to be completely crazy. No matter; Bleriot went aloft to circle the field several times. His twenty-five-horsepower Anzani engine had a nasty overheating problem, but not in the cool night air. Bleriot landed. "Fill the machine with fuel," he ordered his mechanic. "In ten minutes I shall be on my way to England."

At 4:35 A.M. he took off. His astonished friends and helpers watched him fly out of sight. They'd never heard the orders to the mechanic and assumed Bleriot was up for another test hop. Then they realized he was *really* on his way and shouts of joy and encouragement filled the air. Bleriot had taken off in the proverbial nick of time, for within minutes the wind had picked up so greatly that takeoff would have been too dangerous.

If ever there was a test for a pilot, this was it. Bleriot launched in predawn grayness toward England in his tiny eggbeater of a machine with a balky engine, a wing-warping system, and absolute faith in himself. He sat amidships his spindly winged steed just aft of bracing wires. No windscreen, so both propeller and airstream blasted into his face, bringing with them every passing bug. More to the point of piloting, Bleriot did not have a single instrument of any kind in his machine! He flew entirely by feel and judgment. As it turned out, two events saved the flight. At one point the engine began to overheat and threatened to quit in the next few moments. Bleriot would quickly follow the path of Latham—down into the Channel. But he flew into a rainshower and the water cascading against and over his engine cooled the Anzani to normal operating temperature!

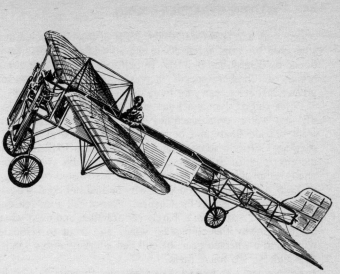

Bleriot Monoplane

On he went, wet to the skin and absolutely delighted with his good fortune.

But a crosswind had sprung up and Bleriot was being pushed to the north of his course. "I was alone, isolated, lost in the middle of the foamy sea, seeing nothing on the horizon, not even a boat." Then he did see several ships, judged that they were headed for English ports, and steered in the same direction as they were moving. Finally, "I was happy to catch sight of . . . a gray line which detached itself from the sea. . . . It was the English coast."

Within days, in addition to winning the prize money for his epochal flight, Bleriot was deluged with orders for copies of his little monoplane. More than one hundred aircraft were ordered, with customers literally forcing their money into his hands.

And so went the first decade of the air age, every man a test pilot, every flight an adventure, every new record a mark to be toppled. There was glory, and there was death. There were wonderful new designs. There was also a horde of machines ugly and spiteful in flight. Most of these stumbled and staggered for brief moments in the air and then were abandoned by disgruntled builders. But altitude records kept going higher and higher, speeds increased, and planes flew for greater distances, carrying more and more passengers.

Pilots rigged their machines onto pontoons and floats and the first water-borne machines came into being. They then went beyond floats and built flying boats, such as the outstanding Curtiss machine that was in the air in 1912. Bleriot, the champion of the Channel, built an incredible, weird, ungainly ellipsoidal-wing floatplane and first tested his design in 1906. Other pilots wondered why he had not used a floatplane to venture across the Channel. Bleriot had good reason. The machine was clumsy, barely controllable, and even when he threw away the ellipsoidal wings and went to standard wings and a wheeled gear, he still had a turkey on his hands. And turkeys are lousy fliers.

Everywhere one looked it seemed some inventor in a backyard or a barn or a pasture was putting together some kind of bizarre flying machine. Most, as might be expected, remained in the turkey class and fell instantly into oblivion. Moore-Brabazon, who held Pilot Certificate No. 1 of England, decided to place his name in the history books in yet another manner. There was that old expression, "I'll believe it when a pig can fly." Moore-Brabazon brought the whole world up short when he made the old saw come true; he took along a pig as a passenger, and whatever was impossible before, it would now seem had come to pass!

Kings and dictators and queens and princes and all manner of royalty took to the skies as fascinated and delighted passengers. It was still too early in the game for air transport, as such, because machinery was so unreliable, ground facilities were scarce, and the weather ruled everything. But the military was moving closer and closer to accepting the airplane as part of its arsenal, and a glimpse of the future came when Eugene Ely made a daring test flight. He took off from the deck of a cruiser in a Curtiss biplane at Hampton Roads, Virginia, in 1910. Two months later he astounded the navy by alighting on a wooden deck hammered across the afterdeck of the U.S.S. *Pennsylvania*. The seed for a future aircraft carrier had just been planted.

As fast as new and stronger and more powerful aircraft appeared, so did their pilots. There was hardly any difference between a pilot as such and a test pilot. With rare exceptions, every pilot was a test pilot, since so many flights were made in machines that had never before flown or were modified between each flight. Then, gradually, those who had been flying for a while and had come to know their machines well, graduated to a new status of *experienced* pilot, and with millions of people enthralled by flight, these pilots and their ragged machines rushed to county fairs and racetracks to put on exhibitions.

Barnstorming exploded on the aviation scene. The daredevil pilot, the stuntmen and stuntwomen were with us, flying, whirling like dervishes in the air, doing the impossible. And many in the crowds came to see these aerial maniacs overdo their maneuvers, fly their machines beyond their limits.

Doom thumpers waited to see a plane tear off its wings and rip away the tail. The falling wreckage and hapless pilot would then plunge to the ground in an all-too-often fatal crash. Perhaps the miraculous unreality of what was happening in the air made even the failures seem unreal. But never for the pilots.

Among the stunt pilots none matched the daredevil, skilled antics of Lincoln Beachey. He not only flew beautifully, but was described by Orville Wright as "the greatest aviator of all." Crashing airplanes was part of the game. It happened to almost *all* pilots in those days, and Beachey had his own share of crumpling fine machines into sawdust and torn fabric. He raced across fairgrounds before stunned crowds and snapped up handkerchiefs with his wing tip. He would find a row of hangars or sheds, and he would fly down the row, snapping his wing down as he passed each hangar so that the wing extended *into* the hangar, and had to be withdrawn instantly before it struck the wall rushing at it. In 1911 he rose to an altitude of 11,600 feet, climbing until he ran out of fuel. Simple enough. On the way down he performed unpowered wild maneuvers for the fun of it. Beachey was angered when he learned that Pégoud in France had made the first inside loop—i.e., his plane went up and over on its back and continued around to fly, level with the ground. No one was going to outfly Beachey! He began flying loops with incredible abandon, faster and faster and too close to the ground, leaving himself no way out of a bad moment or a changing wind. One day he might have to pull out with a tremendous load on his airplane to keep from striking the ground. That moment came finally in 1915 where fifty thousand people at the San Francisco Exhibition thrilled to Beachey's madcap barnstorming antics and then cried out in horror as he tore back the wings of his aircraft and plummeted into San Francisco Bay. Ever the showman in his brief life span, he went out in a death-embracing performance.

Airplanes went from one engine to two, then three, and by 1913, Igor Sikorsky in Russia was flying his *Le Grand* monster with four one-hundred-horsepower engines and with enough internal capacity and power to carry up to fifteen people.

By the time the first decade of flight ended there were well over 350 government-certified pilots in France. Right behind the French came Great Britain with sixty, and official pilot license certificates were being handed out in Germany, Italy, Belgium, and the United States. But the slips of paper meant little, for hundreds of men were already stumbling into the air on their own.

The price continued high, and became ever dearer, as more powerful engines appeared and new challenges beckoned. Little real attention had been given to safety (and would not until testing became a permanent part of aviation growth, and the experienced, skilled test pilot was singled out for his particular role). In the very beginnings of flight, Lady Luck walked among and flew with most of the men who challenged the skies. But even in the years after the first flights, safety devices such as seat belts—about as common, ordinary, and sensible as might be imagined, even in the form of a *rope* securing the man to his machine—were absent from aircraft.

The names began to mount for what might one day be an honor role. Lefebvre, Ferber, Delagrange, and many more, some known and the majority unknown. Of those whose names were recorded in 1919, the deaths of thirty-two men were confirmed.

Two events will bring us to the close of this period. Within less than ten years since the miracle at Kill Devil

Hill, Roland Garros, a French musician, who put aside his instruments to become a pilot, flew the incredible distance of 435 miles, nonstop, in less than eight hours to cross the Mediterranean Sea. Again the feat was marvelous, the promise almost blinding.

One more event went unnoticed by the world press, and even today it can hardly be found in even the most thorough histories of flight from its earliest beginnings. Most of our history books will record that jet flight began in the mid and late 1930s with developments in England and in Germany. But the books are wrong. Almost no one—*almost*—is aware that the first *unplanned* jet flight was attempted in a machine designed by and cobuilt by the brilliant French mathematician, scientist, and aircraft designer Henri Coanda. For some years, long ago, I spent many long hours with this frail and marvelous gentleman, whose "Coanda effect" is as valid and important to flight today as it was when he first brought it to the drawing board many decades in our past.

Coanda had that knack of peering far into the future, beyond the turmoil of the present. So in 1910, a revolutionary machine he had designed and brought to being was ready for tests. It was as sleek as an aircraft off a production line today, a biplane with two long, thin (high-aspect ratio) wings, a long fuselage, and finned tail for stability and control. It was built for strength without the flailing stays and wire braces of so many other planes of that time.

And it lacked a propeller *because it was the world's first jet aircraft.*

Coanda had taken a fifty-horsepower piston engine and severely modified that powerplant so that it drove a compact and extraordinarily efficient centrifugal air compressor. Air was drawn in from the front, compressed and mixed with fuel, and ignited in the enclosed chamber, hurling back from the rounded orifice of the engine not only heated air under tremendous speed and pressure but also visible flame.

His intent was to do away with the vibration of the propeller, to get rid of its drag, and to make power smoothly effective. And to everyone's surprise, except Coanda's, it was designed so perfectly that it would have flown on its first test flight.

And that is exactly what it did—unbidden by its builder,

Henri Coanda. He was not a pilot, but well before he planned for his biplane jet to take to the skies with an experienced (i.e., test) pilot, he would make ground-taxiing tests himself. His problem was that his machine was far more effective in power and lift than he had anticipated and, in his own words, "I had no intention of flying that day. . . . I was concentrating on adjusting the gasoline flow and did not realize the aircraft was gaining speed. Then I looked up." *The jet biplane was already in the air.* "I saw the walls of Paris approaching rapidly. There was no time to turn around—I decided to try to fly. Unfortunately, I had no experience in flying."

He sat, stunned, as the jet biplane raced from the ground and plowed into a stand of trees, knocking the inventor about and destroying the incredible machine. The date was December 10, 1910—just seven years from the first successful powered flight of the Wright Brothers!

And a second Coanda jet biplane still hangs in a museum outside Paris, a silent testimonial to what might have been, to a world that would have been changed vastly, if only its pilot, thrust so abruptly into flight, had known how to fly.

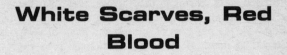

White Scarves, Red Blood

There is an irresistible urge to paint the canvas of flight in the fighting glory of the period from August 1914 through November 1918, for this was a time of aerial combat on a scale that only a few years before would have been considered absolutely impossible.

It was a huge arena, with swirling dogfights, early bombers droning through the night, and giant zeppelins raining bombs on the frightened cities below. There were brave and gallant men, and there were frightened men who also endured. Brave or frightened, or both, they flew in skittish observation planes, they hurtled earthward in fighters, heaving incendiary bullets into observation balloons, photographing the carnage and blood in the muddy trenches far below. World War I was a miserable, stinking, horrible war, masses of men ground up liked chopped meat, women and children torn apart by bombs from planes high and unseen. It was hunger and disease run rampant, terrifying and brutal attacks with gas that choked, or gas that blistered and burned, men coughing their lungs out, men gone blind and hideous with their skin burned from their bodies and their eyes reduced to watery pulp. It was day-in-and-day-out, ceaseless artillery barrages, millions of men manipulated by desk-borne "leaders" in different lands with different languages and customs, but each squandering the lives of countless men and inflicting horror and misery from far behind the combat lines.

That was World War I, killing fields unlike any other ever known at any time in history before, or since.

But above all, for us in these pages, there was that war in the air. It is not simply a broad swath across the pages of history, for the numbers of aircraft and men, of weapons and systems, of missions and deeds, surpassed both expectation as well as providing innovations never before even conceived. The air war broke down into classes and categories, into small and large, into varieties of assignment, into missions for both day and night, into different purposes of scouting, filming, photographing, observing, recording, shooting, bombing. On and on, with every day seemingly a new dawn of discovery for some new means of utilizing flight to bomb and kill and maim.

We have, most of us, clung tenaciously, above all else, to the glorious memory of one-on-one aerial combat, the fighters (or scouts, as they were then known) swirling madly about in whiplike maneuvers, man-to-man battling to the death, diving and spiraling, looping and twisting, always aiming their chattering machine guns at their opponents. In a war of utter misery, both sides sought madly to find heroes they could place on high pedestals and shower with honors and medals, for the greater the adulation for these warriors of the high blue, the easier it was to forget the stinking horror that was true for more than 99 percent of the rest of the men in battle.

Somehow we sought out that special niche of the war, and we, *all* of us, Germans and French and British, Italians and Americans and Russians, and many more, wallowed in the honor among and between airmen—ah, that fair duel with rules, with the game to be played as gentlemen.

Never mind that well before the war began in August of 1914 the first machines had already been in battle. Not in what officially was World War I, but in smaller but equally nasty engagements from the African deserts to the mysterious ports of Asia. Give man a new device, no matter if it is weapon or kitchen utensil designed for a housewife, if it can be applied to kill other men, it will receive enormous sums of money and, eventually, powerful political support.

The balloons, those swollen and clumsy oversized onion bags of hydrogen and heated air and other gases, first lofted into the skies with animals, and then men. Initially it was because there was adventure and fun and challenge, and the prospect of fame. All too quickly the military assembled special units to bring together the balloons, their support systems on the ground, armed men to defend these units in the field, and as fast as they could be gathered, they rushed explosives in every imaginable form to where the balloons could carry them aloft and then shower them down upon an enemy, and with one purpose and one purpose only—to kill the other souls trapped beneath them.

Air warfare came into being with the balloons of Napoleon at the raging conflicts of Maubeuge and Fleurus in 1794, when the balloon was still a fledgling vehicle, but already bearing its fangs. Then onward in 1796 to soar with Jourdan's army before Andernach and Ehrenbreitstein, and to be captured by the Austrian army of Duke Karl at Würzburg, and so spread the use of this new infernal device.

Three years later, in 1799, the military balloon forces rushed off with their French aerostiers to Egypt to support the Battle of the Nile. Then there was a pause in the slaughter and the rushing about of armies with their air weaponry, and not until 1849 was the balloon (much improved, of course, with the ability to lift much heavier loads of explosives, chemicals, jagged metal, and other fun implements of warriors) back in style, with now the Austrians bombarding Venice with what they fondly called their "aerial torpedoes." French balloons drifted across the Battle of Solferino in 1859.

Two years later the Yanks and the Rebs were having at one another with everything that could kill and destroy, including balloons on both sides, mostly for the purpose, from 1861 through 1864, not of bombardment, but of directing massive artillery fire at the "enemy" that killed tens of thousands of Union and Confederates alike.

Aerial survey and accuracy of ground weapons fell behind the balloonists of Asia, when in 1869 high explosives rained down on the imperial troops of the Japanese army during the siege of Duke vs. Aidzu's bastion at Wakamatzu. Balloons soared and landed with amazing regularity through the siege of Paris in the Franco-Prussian War of 1870. They flew with the French army in 1884 at the battles of Hong-Hoain Tonkin (those people knew aerial warfare from Western nations a *very* long time ago!). The aerostats moved through the skies after launch from the British army in the 1885 campaigns of the Sudan and Bechuanaland. They flew with the Italian military in their fierce combats in Abyssinia in 1887, and they floated through the skies over Santiago in the Spanish-American War. Two years later in 1900 they were again in battle with Lord Robert's forces in the brutal Boer War. That same year balloons were again battle-proven by both French and English combat forces engaged in fierce fighting in China.

Four years later they played crucial roles in the Russian-Japanese War in the slaughterhouses of Port Arthur, Liaoyan, and Mukden—from which Japan emerged as a new world power. They were again in battle with the Spanish army in 1909 operations against the Moors.

Then came the first mixed operations. Balloons, airships, *and* airplanes proliferated on battlefields. Even in the isolated, dust-choked, and mountain-strewn stretches of the border between the United States and Mexico, airplanes joined the forces of General John J. Pershing in pursuit of Pancho Villa. The Mexican bandit had stormed into Columbus, New Mexico, and left seventeen American corpses behind him when he began his return to Mexico. The American government sent Pershing after Villa with orders to bring him back either alive or with his body punched full of holes from rifle bullets.

The fledgling military was barely ready for operations in rough country. Tests of rifles, machine guns, radio communications, and bomb dropping were already behind this first meaningful operation, but the Aeronautical Division of the army had scrimped along on meager funds for years. They had sent one of their new Burgess-Wright biplanes on reconnaissance flights over Mexico in 1913, hardly a stirring engagement, but nonetheless a beginning. More flights followed. The army soon had aircraft as far afield as the Philippines, flew new scouts from floats, and watched with amazement as the U.S. Navy, under the helm of Bradley Allen Fiske, successfully tested the dropping of aerial torpedoes against shipping.

The rule to follow would never be elucidated better than by General George S. Patton in World War II, when he surveyed his assembled troops and offered them a battle-proven homily. "I don't want you sons of bitches to die for your country!" he thundered, and then pointed his hand in the general direction of the German army. "I want you to make *those* sons of bitches die for *their* country!" Such is the motto of battle, and lifting upward from the earth—no matter how harmless and friendly and exciting those early flights—simply widened the canvas across which men would slaughter one another with greater and greater zeal.

As fast as men joined flying ranks, they paid the ultimate price. P. O. Parmelee, loaned to the army by the Wright Company, was killed in 1912. Lieutenant John C. Walker was so terrified by a crash in Texas he never again flew. Lieutenant G.E.M. Kelley died of a fractured skull in another crash. By 1913, however, the army's signal corps had enough new planes and pilots in its First Aero Squadron to be flying regular patrols with nine airplanes along the Mexican border. Yet the planes crashed regularly, men were hurt or killed, and our military struggled to stay in the business of flying. When war erupted in Europe, new favor attended the purchase of airplanes and the training of pilots.

The army had enjoyed its first ten years of military aviation, and it received its summation from a veteran infantry officer who cracked that "airplanes could go higher and faster than horses."

But the muddling, underfunded, and miserable performance that so characterized military aviation in the United States truly masked the future. It was all too easy, and in many respects fully justified, for even the highest-ranking officials of different nations to sneer at the very idea of airplanes having any effect on the battlefield. Far more dangerous to these leaders were the enormous dirigibles rushed into production, and performing in magnificent fashion, under the leadership of Count Zeppelin of Germany (who had been trained by Lincoln's balloon brigades in the American Civil War!). Those who understood the size and might of the zeppelins, despite their horrifying lift from dangerous hydrogen gas, foresaw French and British cities being bombarded from the air and helpless to do much about it.

But few really understood the incredible advances of all

manner of airships and aircraft. When war broke out in 1914, planes were flying better than 125 miles per hour. Several had climbed to more than twenty-five thousand feet above the earth. Others were crossing the Alps and the Pyrenees. The first nonstop flight of more than one thousand miles was an accomplished fact. The ability to lift heavier and heavier loads became glaringly obvious, because the carriage of up to fifteen people could easily be replaced with an equivalent weight in high explosives.

The Wrights were stunned by the development of aggressive military aircraft. Orville revealed their crushed hopes when he wrote, "When my brother and I built and flew the first man-carrying machine we thought we were introducing into the world an invention which would make further wars practically impossible." And in 1910 the British war secretary made a sour face to the press and announced: "We do not consider that aeroplanes will be of any possible use for war purposes."

Despite the negative attitudes of military and political leaders, governments had started full-scale aviation on its way. Consider all that had preceded the growth of aviation where every man had to be inventor and test pilot in order to ascend into the skies. The growth was seeded at first by just a few individuals, then a few more, and finally small clubs gathering to form groups of pilots and planes, and from the first blazing feats (in clattering flimsy machines, to be sure) there came the first production orders for airplanes, such as the one hundred machines ordered from Bleriot after his Channel crossing.

Now it is August 1914, and the opening shots of World War I have been fired. In America, the potential of airpower continued to founder on the shoals of official opposition to the military use of aircraft. But that was in America, far from where military forces mimicked the glowering looks and fist-shaking gestures of their governments.

And if military aviation groped forward in England and in France, nevertheless it made strides that would have been considered so fantastic as to be entirely unbelievable by the government leaders of the United States. While many of the aircraft still were unwieldy, fragile, tricky to fly, and contributing more than their share of broken bones and burned bodies, there was no question to field commanders that these planes would become the new high eyes of ground forces. And so as war erupted, the British and French had between them no less than a thousand planes of all types.

The Germans faced them with an array of twelve hundred aircraft ready to do battle.

But at first there was little battle, indeed. Few people really understood the needs, forces, and aerodynamic loads of aerial battle. And at first there was a marvelous situation of "no contest" in the air. Cumbersome two-seaters droned like great dragonflies over enemy lines, looking down, marking maps, and taking photographs. They carried no weapons. More and more often they would see an enemy aircraft on its way to or returning from the same mission.

The slaughter that was taking place was far below. Up here the air was fresh and clean, there existed an élan to be shared by all aviators, and the enemy pilots and crews would wave merrily at one another. *This* was the way to fight a war!

But that feeling met with sodden anger by German commanders taking the brunt of accurate artillery fire because of the high-flying observers who gave exact positions of German forces to British and French batteries. They called for Berlin to bring on faster airplanes, and the men were to carry guns or whatever was needed to get rid of those *verdamnte* observation bugs in the air. Demands notwithstanding, the air "war" continued for a while in its laconic way, the planes droning back and forth like stingless wasps visiting fields of flowers. Berlin also ignored the outcry of its field commanders. Faster airplanes? How stupid! If they flew too fast, there would not be enough time for the observers to mark their maps. The photographers would barely have time to steady their cameras before their targets would whiz beneath and by them. Slow, stable, steady; *that's* what the high command wanted and that's what it got.

Of course, there are always *some* pilots who stand out from the crowd, and this applies to the military just as it did to Lincoln Beachey who made women shriek and men gasp with his sensational flying antics as a crowd-pleasing barnstormer.

Many weeks after war began a German officer flew above the suburbs of Paris, and manually heaved two four-pound bombs over the side of his airplane. Those eight pounds of metal and high explosives marked the official beginning of aerial bombardment in what went into the history books as the Great War. There had been an earlier attempt to do battle in the skies when the first British aerial units arrived in France. Lieutenant L. A. Strange hauled a Lewis machine gun to a French Farman, rickety and blundering, and took off for enemy lines. There he found a German plane and began immediate pursuit.

But here is where not knowing what your airplane can do voided the conflict. The German plane simply climbed away from the Farman, staggering with the additional weight of that machine gun, which no one had computed, or even roughly estimated. The Farman hauled desperately to a height of 3,500 feet and then simply wallowed in the air while the lieutenant watched helplessly. There was a lesson implicit in this, and if you conclude that better planning was in the offing, you are wrong. Returning to his home field, Lieutenant Strange was chewed out by his commanding officer, who figured out (certainly correctly for the Farman) that the reason the German was able to thumb his nose at Strange and fly blithely off was the weight of the machine gun. "Next time," he admonished the lieutenant, "leave the bloody thing on the ground with the infantry, where it belongs."

It was a tiny beginning, but it was critical. Figure out what your machine can do with what it carries before you go off to do what might be fatal contest with the enemy.

Test your aircraft.

Fly it under all kinds of conditions. Fly it light, fly it heavy. Climb to its maximum height. Dive it until the wings threaten to break off (and so many did in training and in combat!). Do the wings need a change in the angle of incidence so that a minor shift in location improves lift? What about a different engine? And can the propeller be modified to give more thrust? The questions run into the hundreds and each and every one of them was not only valid but critical. And had to be tested.

Credit for the initially audacious and irreverent goes not to the French, who accepted such evaluations as awe-inspiring and deserved, but to the stoic Germans. None other than Lieutenant Max Immelmann, who would become one of the most famous fighter pilots in history. Early in September, with the German army only twenty-five miles away from and battering at the gates of Paris, Immelmann flew over the city. Moments later an old cavalry boot with a note attached, demanding the surrender of Paris, tumbled through the air and thumped to the ground before startled citizens.

Perhaps there was a shortage of boots or Immelmann realized quickly this was pretty ineffective stuff. The next day he flew over Paris at five o'clock in the afternoon, hurling packs of leaflets to flutter across large areas of the city. "People of Paris! Surrender! The Germans are at your gates! Tomorrow you will be ours!"

Many Frenchmen and women read the leaflets. But just as many did not, or simply threw away the surrender notes. Paris was fighting for its life, and in a military move that is singularly and splendidly French, General Gallieni gathered every available taxicab in Paris, jammed soldiers and weapons into them, and the French army sallied forth to battle, and threw back from the outskirts of the French capital the almost-victorious German army.

There'll never be another war like *that* one. . . .

The fighting inevitably widened, and the equipment and performance of the aircraft on both sides was dictated by needs in the high arena. It became evident all too quickly that the observation planes were dangerous far beyond their sputtering and ungainly size. On each side of the battlefront the word went out: knock those things out of the air.

That meant *faster* airplanes. Faster airplanes were dictated largely by high power and low weight, and the rush was on to convert what was officially a scout to a pursuit or a fighter plane. While both sides began mass production (another startling innovation that would forever change the world) of aircraft, those already in the air took matters into their own hands. Or, *from* their own hands. The crew of an observation plane would fly over an enemy of the same type. They'd wave to one another as they had done, and then the fellows on top would drop bricks, rocks, and hand grenades onto the trusting souls below. A brick may not seem like much, but after hurtling downward through the sky, it will kill a man, or tear up a wing, or splinter a propeller. Accuracy was not the sort of thing you'd give medals for, but it sure was a start. Soon people were banging away at one another with pistols, shotguns, and rifles, and the machine guns, now that engines were more powerful and performance had improved, were back on the scene.

The air war was in full tilt. Yet innovation was still the name of the game. With machine guns blazing away, it was obvious that pilots would like to do *something* to protect their hides. The single worst way to be attacked was from below by an enemy climbing unseen against the vulnerable belly of the higher plane. The first a pilot might know of the attack was machine-gun bullets smashing into his own soft body as well as his aircraft. The designers and suppliers of these aircraft had made no provision to protect pilots from such lethal attacks.

On both sides of the battle lines, stove lids began to vanish from kitchens, barracks, and ready rooms. It was an epidemic, and the authorities at first went mad trying to understand what possibly was so great about stove lids that they would be stolen in such numbers.

Easy enough. What the designers and builders would not do the pilots did for themselves. They sat on those lids because they were most effective armor plating against bullets!

Let us now return to the memories of aerial duels, the one-on-one swirling dogfights we have emblazoned in our histories as "the aerial jousting between knights of the sky." Well, in some ways it *was* like that. In some ways men fought one another with valor and honor, and there were pilots, from newcomers to great aces, who would not fire on a crippled plane, or who, when seeing their opponent was out of ammunition, would fly alongside his enemy, salute him, and peel off for home.

Just as knights painted their colors and markings on their shields, so did pilots paint their pursuits with crossed swords and griffons and battle-axes and other carryovers from medieval times. Men went into battle with long silken scarves fluttering in the wind from where they were tied to struts or wings. Pilots in leather helmets were recognized by the colors of their scarves, whipping behind them from the air blast as they hurtled into battle. Whole squadrons adopted the same insignia, but with space left for individual identification so that the top contestants on each side could search for their chosen enemy with whom to do individual battle.

Pursuits would fly over an enemy airfield at night or in a swift daylight dive and drop a challenge to a particular fighter pilot. And they jousted, all right. Honor to these exalted few was everything. Two huge formations would meet at a certain height, each circling above its own lines, while the two aerial knights would leave their formations and set up their approach just as would knights on horseback preparing to battle with lances. The two planes, at a given signal, would rush at one another head-on, and then break sharply right, and the battle was on.

Bizarre life-styles gave rise to bizarre romanticism, and much of it was either true, or at least based on truth. Pilots flew with leather helmets, with spiked helmets, with headgear of their own choosing, or like France's Jean Navarre, a sensational fighter pilot, who rushed into battle wearing a woman's silk stocking for his helmet. Fiercely impulsive, reckless, he once charged off from his airfield in his pursuit, wielding a large butcher knife which he said he would use to "disembowel the monster," referring to a German zeppelin on a bombing raid. If one presumes Navarre at the time was either whacko, or simply lusting for some kind of fight, it would be difficult to fault such a conclusion.

The romantic inclinations of a war that at its best was brutal and murderous in the air even carried to the acceptance of death. If a skilled pilot were killed and fell within the enemy's lines, he was often given a burial with full military honors. Each side dropped wreaths and "letters of regret for a fallen comrade" over their enemy's airfields. And the fighter pilots who returned to their own cities for rest and recreation were lauded and feted. Small wonder they felt like, and were to their adoring crowds, true heroes.

But there's the other, dark side of men: pilots who enjoyed killing and were as savage in the air as any wild animal in the jungle. The superior pilots were men of excellent vision, of natural flying skills, and of that hard and relentless urge to kill and the ability to bring their desires to reality. This did not take great physical strength. Georges Guynemer, one of the all-time great aces of history and almost a saint to the

French, suffered from tuberculosis and at times could barely walk to his airplane. Some men were deeply religious. Others were patriotic to the point of accepting death; these were the battle-seeking "madmen," who, despite terrible wounds that would have left most men bedridden, crawled into their planes to climb away to fight. Two of the best known of these men were France's Charles Nungesser and Germany's Rudolf Berthold.

Some pilots were perfectionists, cold-blooded, wily, superbly careful, chess masters of the air who planned every move. Others were wild-eyed berserkers whose very skill and ferocity carried them through fights they should never have survived. Others prayed for forgiveness for the lives they had taken.

Still others acted as if they *were* knights. None other than the leading ace of the war, Baron Manfred von Richthofen, with eighty confirmed kills (he had many more, but a kill was considered confirmed only if the pilot had three eyewitnesses), who after each victory awarded himself a beautiful silver cup. He had a hell of a lot of silver on his mantel before a relative newcomer "from the other side" pumped bullets into his body to end the reign of the Red Baron.

Yet in so many ways the air battles were a slaughterhouse for the many, and romanticism for a very, *very* few. In the long run, we have emblazoned the very few into our historical memory, and given the vast majority of pilots very short shrift, indeed.

Even the best of the airplanes were incendiary bombs waiting to be ignited. Fuel tanks could be set ablaze by a single bullet, and the introduction of incendiary bullets into battle only worsened what was already the most terrifying fear of pilots—burning to death in the air. Airplanes of wood and fabric, of dope and oil and gasoline, are winged tinderboxes, and they burned with furious speed and horrifying results to their pilots and crews.

And there was little or no escape! Pilots in flaming airplanes close to the ground had a ghost of a chance to sideslip their machine and crash as quickly as possible and get away from their blazing coffin. But too high in the air, and the pilot had three choices: burn to death, writhing in torment until the brain finally fled the torture of its body; shoot himself in the head to get it over with as quickly and painlessly as possible; or, and many pilots took this option, throw himself out of the airplane.

But what about parachutes? They were there, they were ready and available, they had been tested and proven! Parachutes were provided for the observers in observation balloons, which when hit ignited with a furious speed difficult to comprehend. The parachute was attached to the man's body, and hanging from the basket suspended beneath the balloon. Comes the fusillade of incendiary bullets, a single spark before the mushrooming blaze, and that observer was gone, flinging himself wildly away from the balloon, the parachute filling almost immediately.

Why not, then, parachutes for pilots, especially in raging air combat where fire was the most feared of all adversaries? Here, once again, we must leave the arena of battle and visit the headquarters of military commanders and the political leaders of the combatants. Were parachutes available? Absolutely, because well before the first shot of the war was fired, an American barnstormer, a wild and fearless exhibitionist, had perfected the pack parachute so that it would harness closely to a man's body and be quickly and easily opened in flight, and he proved this repeatedly with his exhibition jumps. They could quickly have been produced by the tens of thousands.

Not a single American, British, Canadian, French, or other pilot fighting with the Allies ever saved his life from a burning airplane with a parachute. The high officials of each nation refused their delivery to the front. If pilots had parachutes, they claimed, they "might be tempted" to leap from their craft at the first signs of trouble.

By war's end, only a handful of German pilots were given parachutes, and one of the kaiser's greatest aces, Ernst Udet, demanded one be placed in *his* fighter. One of the reasons Udet became one of Germany's greatest aces is that twice he saved his life by parachuting from his plane, either broken or burning, in the air.

Most airplanes were produced in that war not by engineering and testing, and not even by factories, but in giant workshops where the sheer numbers of workers rolled planes out the doors by the hundreds. Many never saw combat. The training airfields were littered with the wreckage of the planes. Men would be given perhaps four or five hours of training and sent off to the front into combat. They could barely fly and certainly they did not fly with skill or the knowledge born of experience, and they were slaughtered by the veterans. Quality control in production was a grisly joke. The single greatest danger to any pilot was letting the speed of his airplane get away from him, for fabric tore all too easily from wings and fuselage, and even the wings would finally break in their supports and turn to instant wreckage.

Engines were as prone to fire as they were to clattering away steadily. Worst of all were the rotary engines; strangely reliable in that they ran for long periods of time, they were devilish to their pilots when used as "tractor" engines mounted in the nose of an airplane. Certainly the men who churned out thousands of these engines in factories never sat behind them. The rotary, in which the propeller is fastened securely to and then locked to the engine, is that unusual design where the entire engine spins all the time. You fire it up, it runs at full speed, and that is *that*. But such a device demands a waterfall of lubrication.

It sprays oil like the bottom of a bucket shot full of holes and then blasted with a fire hose. To lubricate the rotary engine you don't use just oil; you use *castor* oil. This mixes with fuel dumped down a hollow crankshaft into the engine, and it's off and running full bore. But not all the castor oil is burned. And what is not burned is bestowed upon the pilot and much of his airplane in a ghastly, foul-smelling spray that would gag Bigfoot and bring him to his knees. Everything else becomes coated, smeared, and awash with this spray, including windscreen, cockpit, goggles, and the pilot. It's terrific fun.

It's difficult to believe, in our times of understanding the air ocean and the rapidity with which it thins with ascent, that so few pilots really knew what they were getting into when they went for altitude to "get a jump from above on the enemy." In their fabric machines, with massive wooden propellers and dangerous engines, and flight characteristics often just short of terrible, the pilots would climb and climb. They would climb to fifteen thousand and seventeen thousand

and often over twenty thousand feet. These are heights that today are considered virtually fatal. At such heights the pressure is so low and oxygen so thin that the pilots suffer from double vision, dizziness, loss of peripheral vision, and clumsy coordination of mind and body—and not know why. If they could have taken off their gloves, they would have seen their fingernails turned blue, a sure sign of hypoxia (oxygen deprivation). Well, why not do that? Why not check for a visible sign of hypoxia?

For one reason, at those heights—no matter how high the temperature on the ground—it is colder than at the north pole, and to remove gloves was to watch your hand freeze right before your blurry eyes. Another reason is that a man can barely think straight at such heights; he's like a drunk who *thinks* he's doing great, but is actually a groggy and near-helpless victim of an oxygen-starved brain.

All too often the pilot would simply pass out. That wasn't the best way to go, because when he went into the black, his engine was still pounding with all the power it could produce, and that meant the airplane falling off into a power dive. By the time the man emerged from foggy bottom it was usually just in time to hear the wind shrieking through his struts and wires. This got his attention, but not before the fabric tore loose from the wings, the struts failed, and the wings crumpled, and he knew his power dive had become a death plunge.

Yet, for all these reasons and more, this was the very edge of the dawning of the age of the test pilot, who would become vital to future aeronautics. The sheer numbers of that war established beyond any turning back that testing and retesting was the only way to advance into the new performance envelopes that superior engines and construction would bring.

The performance of new engines and structures meant that the airplane was no longer the exciting premonition of the future; it *was* the future at our doorstep and in our grasp. And there was yet another impelling and compelling factor that overrode all else, that not only would not be denied, but beckoned with glittering shine like the pot of gold at the end of the aeronautical rainbow.

Because it was the pot of gold.

Passenger and cargo flight was upon us. That meant designing, testing, manufacturing, and carrying people and cargo for money. Scads of money. It meant hiring thousands of peope as mechanics, service personnel, administrative work, ticket sellers, baggage handlers. It meant building airports, massive runways, connecting systems. It called for massive investments in radio and other communications, for navigational aids, for a vastly increased understanding of weather so that the skies would be less filled with unknown rocks and lethal weapons of nature.

And when you have *billions* of dollars in the offing, you do not hold back on *anything*.

Before we enter this golden age of aviation, when barriers fell as quickly and in bunches like tenpins at the end of a bowling alley, pause for a moment and consider the sheer numbers of this war from 1914 through most of 1918.

In those four years armies numbering more than sixty-five million men were mobilized. Now consider, if you will, simply on the scale of logistics and finance, the cost of supplying, feeding, housing, equipping, transporting, and caring for these same men who would be expending gigantic quantities of death-dealing explosives and other armaments against one another.

Before that war ended, Europe was able to count a confirmed casualty list of 37,499,386 men, women, and children. Of that number, 8,543,515 human beings were killed, starved, died in accidents or from disease. Another 21,219,452 were wounded, taxing the medical facilities of most of the world. Add to that, 7,750,919 listed as prisoners and missing, so that the numbers of dead and wounded soared even higher.

That's flesh and bone and blood and lives for all combatants on all accounts. Now we can narrow down our sights to things aeronautical. But before these numbers for these four years parade before you, recall the slow, agonizing pace of how aviation came to be, and that this war began only eleven years after Orville and Wilbur Wright flew at Kill Devil Hill.

The official records show that more than twenty thousand air battles, small and large, in daylight and in darkness, raged between enemies, the vast majority across the European continent.

By the time the armistice was declared, more than 150,000

men and women (including nurses and administrative personnel) were involved directly in the various aeronautics branches of these nations committed to battling one another. There had been more than twenty thousand officially recorded combats, but this is far less than the additional number in excess of a hundred thousand missions by scouts and pursuits, by bombing raids from aircraft and zeppelins, and the observation flights that went on through the war.

From the handful of aircraft available—aircraft truly fit for battle—at war's beginning, the fighting stopped with 10,316 combat machines poised in forward combat areas to continue and then to expand the air war. Had that war continued but one more year, the new sprawling workshops would have sent another fifty thousand planes to the various fronts.

That's hard money.
And that's what makes airplanes fly best of all.

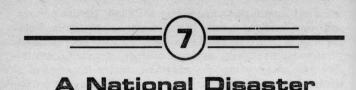

A National Disaster

The understanding of great events in history rarely comes with a rush. It requires time, lots of time. It demands laborious investigation. Men of science and technology *always* stand on the shoulders of all who have gone before them. Most of this effort takes place far from the public eye, because it is innovative and it shakes the trees of accepted science. A breakthrough is always rejected when first proposed, it is then accepted on conditions of great distrust, and finally, when it has come of age and fits neatly within the framework of our daily lives, it is already obsolete and on its way to being discarded.

But there are those wonderful times in between, when a new methodology is the key to the future. In this new world of aviation that spread swiftly across the globe, once the military impetus of a world war fell behind men, the driving force was a combination of many factors. We have touched lightly on them. To build an aviation industry you need more than airplanes; we have reviewed the need for airports, maintenance facilities, huge supplies of fuel and oil, pilot-training programs, navigational systems—a list that simply added one to the other that would fill this entire book.

At the end of a war, with the promise of the age of aviation in which aircraft would become practical and potentially profitable, the new breed of pilot emerged. This was the pilot experienced in flight, but also versed in the mushrooming technology and science of flight.

This was then, and is today, the test pilot.

Flying, even superb piloting, was but the beginning. The test pilot needed to match daring with skill, courage with know-how, willingness with engineering savvy, the pleasure of flight with a discerning eye for what was being sought in his flights. He needed an engineering background, a thorough understanding of meteorology, an intimate relationship with electrical systems, with radio and other forms of communication. His life would depend on his knowledge of stress on wings and fuselage. New challenges would greet him on almost every flight, for he would penetrate areas never before touched by man. He would come to know vibration of unparalleled ferocity, fluttering of surfaces that could tear apart the strongest airplanes ever built. Engine overspeeding, heating, choking; all these would become his heart and soul.

He must be the best.

Great fortunes rode with these test pilots. As aircraft became more powerful, larger, longer ranging, higher flying, and faster, they called for huge industrial investment. Where men had individually designed their first machines and built them in worksheds or backyards or a convenient garage, now engineers would study every possible aspect of a new design so that it would conform to the needs of its manufacturers and, subsequently, of airlines and governments that would pay hundreds of millions of dollars.

If the products failed, so did the company. If the new machines faltered, or broke apart, or failed successively to meet the specifications laid down for them, huge companies would collapse as their funds vanished.

Many test pilots worked for themselves, or for small companies assembled by their friends about a man who was both designer *and* test pilot. Others flew for the military. Now weapons would be tested with the aircraft, and some machines, beautiful to the eye and superb in performance, were disastrous failures when placed under the strain of simulated combat. Now they had to carry ever greater weight in the form of machine guns or cannon, to haul bombs aloft, and to perform crushing maneuvers under which their structure *must* remain sound. So the aircraft were designed at great cost, built at greater cost, and then tested while investors hoped that the end result would be that holy grail of all industry—the fat contract.

All the test pilot had to do was know the engineering and science of a hundred men, fly with the smoothness and skill of an angel, accept challenges that had never before been known, and be willing to hurl himself into situations that could snap metal like a toothpick, or roast the man alive, or crush the breath from his body.

Now, let us better understand the intrinsic nature of this business. Some pilots of great skill and experience flew, above all else, for the money. Others flew for the thrill. Simply to fly faster, higher, farther, was *everything* to them. Many pilots flew for these reasons and perhaps also for fame. After all, a hero is a hero in any language and in any land, and these men were not in the business of killing people, but of risking their own lives.

The more sensational flights in testing have almost always grabbed the headlines. Men ascended to heights long considered impossible, dove their machines at speeds everyone *knew* were impossible, crossed oceans and continents in single nonstop journeys.

In the future, there were ever new barriers. Soon they would be flying so swiftly that air massing about their airplanes would prevent their machines from going any faster, and the enormous shock waves they were creating would in an explosive instant tear the aircraft to jagged metal. Broken airplanes and dead pilots; that was the price. They flew so high that they finally had to consider that our atmosphere had its limits and these limits sorely restrained what man and machine could do. The dream of flight without propellers emerged from proposals and tests, and new words leaped into the language: rockets and jets, supersonic and transsonic and hypersonic, exoatmospheric flight, afterburners and swept-wings, Mach numbers and compressibility.

The history of test piloting is one of always being told that what the engineers wanted and the test pilot would do was, flatly and absolutely, impossible. Even the sound barrier became a household word, for it was a daring and dashing thing to contemplate, that men could fly faster than the speed of sound.

Realists said, no way. Other realists, who knew their machines were already flying faster than a bullet, said, why not?

There was always, then, as it is now, only one way to find out.

Test the machine.

Even today, with computers and supercomputers, with all the science and technology and vast experience of close to a century of flight, there is always that acid test.

Fly the machine. Take it up into the bared teeth of the unknown and wring it out.

And, as it was in the early days, so it remained: men risked their lives, and men died.

World War I opened with the United States in possession of the most miserable, underpowered, outdated, clumsy, unreliable handful of airplanes—they could not be called warplanes—of any major power in the world. By the close of 1913, only one year before war broke out in Europe, the United States Army had purchased the grand total of twenty-eight airplanes. Nine had already crashed and were either destroyed or burned. The signal corps of the army had trained forty of its officers as pilots, and eleven of those were dead. The twenty-nine remaining were just about the sorriest bunch of military pilots to be found anywhere on the planet. Few high officers had any real interest in developing aviation, and as complaints from the army's Aviation Section reached Washington, a top officer castigated these surviving pilots as "deficient in discipline and the proper knowledge of the customs of the service and the duties of an officer."

If you searched for high morale among dedicated young officers, you would have to look elsewhere than the Aviation Section of the U.S. Army. It was a cruel joke against the progress of aviation in other lands. By comparison we were still in the age of the dugout canoe. Almost three years later, in April of 1916, the U.S. Army had a total of *two* airplanes left in its arsenal, and both were fit only for the trash heap.

While complaints went over in headquarters with all the flotation of a lead balloon, they couldn't be disputed. And enough officers had managed to reach the ears of congressmen and senators. After all, it didn't require earthquakes to reveal the abysmal state of aviation in the American military, or that had it not been for enthusiastic inventors and builders and pilots risking their lives in untested machines, the entire country would have remained in the dark ages of flight while Europe thundered ahead with enormous production of aircraft.

To go back in time a bit, the conduct of the army with the Wright Brothers had caused scandal enough, tempered only a little by the actions of a private group. This was, in 1907, the world's first organization intended specifically to design, build, and then test-fly the new airplanes. The members would keep meticulous records of everything they did, details of every flight, so that each new test flight would have for its pilot the full support of whatever experience had been gained by others. This was the Aerial Experiment Association, to which great amounts of money, and official sponsorship, were provided by none other than the eminent scientist Alexander Graham Bell. Fortunately for members of this new association, they were in full agreement with Mr. Bell that airplanes should not be designed by-gosh-and-by-guess but by the latest scientific and engineering methods. They set rigid construction goals that would permit an airplane to make repeated flights rather than single hops to crumbling wreckage every time it flew. They wanted the maximum performance consistent with structural integrity. They wanted to be able to construct several aircraft of each type so that as many pilots as possible could be taught to fly. And into each of these activities they would hold as paramount the element of safety.

Enjoying the cloak of respect and integrity provided by Bell, they constructed their first aircraft, and with perhaps an eye cocked back into some Indian history, named the machine *Red Wing*. Their flair for what could have been great advertising copy was far superior to their craftsmanship. Despite intensive effort, they were woefully ignorant of the new science of aeronautics. *Red Wing* lurched drunkenly into the air for its first flight, wobbled precariously, and then decided to abandon the air for the ground. The airplane could fly no better than its pilot, and this first return to earth did a really neat job of crumpling the machine into splintered mush.

Immediately the gang started on their second model and soon rolled out *White Wing* (somehow an airplane *not* the color of blood seemed appropriate for the second try). At this moment fate intervenes. Watching *White Wing* under construction, army Lieutenant Thomas A. Selfridge approached Bell and his group. "I urge you to do whatever you can to train your members as pilots," Selfridge told them. With the painful reality of the army's own situation, he was desperate that pilots be trained by anyone, for if there *were* pilots about, the army would have some recourse should it ever decide to buy more than a few rickety machines.

Selfridge, meeting with the association members, told them that they needed more than simply flying experience. They had to know the theories and practice of flight. They must know what was happening to their machines in the air *and why*. "Build your aeroplanes so they will carry two people rather than one," he recommended. "Make your flights training flights as well as testing flights."

Perhaps Selfridge provided that final impetus, for *White Wing* turned out to be a smashing success. On May 22, 1908, Glenn H. Curtiss test-flew the only-one-of-its-kind *White Wing* along a measured distance of 1,017 feet in nineteen seconds. Much more important, the airplane was stable and responded extremely well to its controls.

The association members never had much of a chance to meet again with Lieutenant Selfridge. On September 17, 1908, he was killed in the test flights of the two-seat Wright biplane at Fort Meyer. But Selfridge had started something that would slowly develop American aviation.

Alexander Graham Bell certainly had great influence in the highest political centers. He had listened carefully to Selfridge, he had watched his own small group prosper in knowledge and experience, he was shocked and dismayed at the tremendous advances in aviation in Europe, and he was demoralized by the state of American aviation. One of the events that rattled the great scientist had to do with the man who would later become known as the "Father of Marine Corps Aviation," Lieutenant Alfred A. Cunningham.

Cunningham was a man totally dedicated to the U.S. Marines, just as he was dedicated to the concept that the marines *must* have aviation to support their operations in the future, and the beginning of that force, desperately small as it might be, needed to be butt-kicked into life *now*. With so few pilots surviving their first flights, and just as many willing never to take a second chance at what they had barely survived,

Cunningham determined that *he* would not only have to promote the cause of marine aviation, but that he must lead the way.

Easier said than done. Determination and grit makes up for many things missing from the human experience, but they do not permit a man to fly just because he wants to. And Cunningham did *not* know how to fly. Jaw set in granite, he pushed through all obstacles and obtained permission to fly a decrepit, wing-sagging, belly-laden critter known as *Noisy Nan*, so named because of the uproarious clatter exploding forth from its engine. Casting sanity and caution to the winds, which was farther than *Noisy* promised to go, Cunningham took his seat in the winged garbage heap. The men who watched were aware that not only had Cunningham never flown, but neither had his sorry steed.

The engine clattered, birds fled in panic, men moved back by reflex, and Cunningham pushed *Noisy Nan* as fast as it would roll across a grassy field. History was about to begin for marine aviation as he sped down the field toward takeoff.

Nope. Cunningham and *Noisy Nan* both ran out of open field before the machine would deign even to lift its bottom from the ground. Cunningham turned about and tried again. And again, and again. "I called her everything in God's name to go up," he later confessed. "I pleaded with her. I caressed her. I prayed to her, and I cursed that brick of an old maid to lift up her skirts and hike, but she never would." To the hilarity of watching friends, the would-be marine aviator climbed from the "old maid," violently kicked the airplane, and ordered her taken to a junkyard. He would later go on to other airplanes to win his wings and become one of the great forces in American military aviation.

But that was far in the future, and this sorry episode prompted Alexander Graham Bell and other powerful figures to *do* something about the grimly unacceptable state of affairs. War broke out in Europe, the opposing forces had over 2,200 planes already soaring into combat. Bell and others castigated official Washington for their failure to act. The first Aero Squadron sent to Mexico in 1913-14 had barely managed to keep its pilots alive, which was the best the army had to offer, as the men ran short of water and food, ate dust, and suffered from insects, blistering heat, snakes, scorpions and vermin.

In the Philippines, the tiny detachment found flying in the open biplanes almost more than they could bear. They had no decent clothes for flying, the weather was brutal, the rains torrential, and the two planes that finally arrived in that island nation were often seen diving frantically for the ground as dense swarms of locusts smashed into the faces of the pilots.

It was hardly better in the States. Some men had learned to fly at a Maryland field under the direction of the Wrights. Glenn Curtiss had taught others. Finally, in the early winter of 1911, the Aeronautical Division of the army's signal corps made its big move to churn out pilots by moving its few airplanes, horses, mules, all equipment, mechanics, and a small group of weary pilots to the Barnes Farm in Augusta, Georgia, to open a new flying school. Hopes ran high; the army was doing *something* on a decent scale!

The gods *do* have a sense of humor. No sooner had the army settled into the Barnes Farm to prepare for the first training flights when a devastating snowstorm roared down from the north, blanketing the farm in a thick white mantle.

Ah, but the storm passed quickly, the sun once again appeared in the heavens, and . . . came the rains. Day after day and night after night it rained. The streams and rivers swelled, overran their banks, and floods raced through the countryside. The pilots and crews lifted their airplanes to the highest scaffolds they could build, tied them down as best they could, and then hitched up horses and mules to execute that famous military maneuver of "Let's get the hell out of here."

The men who wielded clout in Washington shook their heads at the continuing debacle of aviation in the United States. They noted that during the comparatively brief period of three years before the outbreak of war in Europe, the Congress of the United States appropriated a total of $350,000 for military research, construction, aircraft purchase, and training of pilots.

Flying officers choked back their rage at this dribbling of funds. In the same period they noted that Germany, for its air forces, had expended no less than twenty-eight million dollars!

Finally, enough hell was raised in Washington for the Congress in 1916 to appropriate no less than thirteen million dollars for military aviation in the nation. As noted, in April of 1916, two grounded (nonairworthy) airplanes constituted the entire flying force of the U.S. Army. The Congress ordered 366 new airplanes to be delivered immediately.

Easier said than done. Of that number, only sixty-six were actually brought to the few military fields available. What of the others? Well, there's no magic in building airplanes. You can't wave dollars and convert the money overnight into flying machines. For years the army had rejected production; now it wanted everything overnight. To its everlasting consternation, the army found itself loaded down with cancellations from most of the companies to which it had given enormous contracts. When World War I ended in November of 1918, not a single airplane designed in America had seen combat. Every machine American pilots used in battle was of either European design or manufacture.

But there was *that* moment in 1915, when pressure came to bear in a way that would reap incredible rewards in the future. It was the sort of moment that rarely if ever makes headlines. No one broke any speed records, no one soared to formerly unattainable heights, and no one crossed a continent or an ocean. To the contrary, one of the most epochal moves that would one day lead America into a position of world dominance in the air passed quietly. Acting with extraordinary common sense, goaded on by the rage and outcries of those who saw America floundering about helplessly as a stepchild of aviation, the Congress assembled the most knowledgeable military and civilian authorities, engineers, and pilots it could find and, by an Act of Congress, formed the National Advisory Committee for Aeronautics (NACA), with specific mandate "to supervise and direct the scientific study of the problems of flight, with a view of their practical solution."

As quickly as possible the NACA established the Langley Memorial Aeronautical Laboratory in Virginia, and with virtually a free hand from the Congress, began not only its own research program, but became a clearing house for *all* aeronautics in the country. Individual designers, companies, groups of engineers, and pilots, reported their efforts to

Jenny

NACA, and NACA in its turn made this data available to others. In this system, if a company wished to design a new airplane, they could go to NACA, review the designs and the records of virtually every wing (airfoil) ever built and tested, and know they could build that same wing for their new designs, and know the design would work.

NACA could not undo all the harm and chaos infesting aeronautics in the country overnight. During the years immediately after its formation, military aviation dominated virtually all research and development in the land, an obvious necessity with the nation approaching its own involvement in war.

Once again, money alone proved dismally inadequate to overcome the long and miserable hiatus of applied research in the United States. On July 24, 1917, the Congress threw away all fiscal restraint by appropriating $640 million to build up the air strength of the country.

Money flooding into aviation produced results. Thousands of young applicants stormed flying schools. The Curtiss Company, the only true production facility in the country, rushed hundreds of Jenny trainers from its shops and factories. But these were slow and ungainly machines totally unfit for combat, a point many people missed completely. But it brought forth a great carnival atmosphere and flying circus that spat forth a torrent of young new pilots. What few people really understood was that while these men had learned to fly in their cumbersome biplanes, they had only the haziest notion of how to *fight* with an airplane, and very few had ever so much as fired any kind of weapon from the air.

By December of 1917, the army had graduated 1,800 men from its ground schools, and shipped them off through submarine-infested waters to receive their flight training and instruction in combat tactics from the French. A spirited concept, certainly, but one that followed in the path of earlier hasty programs, and the great training effort disintegrated as quickly as the new men departed their ships and set foot on French soil. Rather than rushed into flying, they were herded like cattle into mobilization camps where they were sorely mistreated by officers who regarded them as draft dodgers and worthless scum deserving only the strictest discipline.

Colonel Hiram Bingham reported that these hapless men were the undeserving victims of "serious and exasperating delays, disappointments, and 'raw deals.'" He concluded, sadly but honestly, that this had become "the worst page in the history of the Air Service."

By May of 1918 a miserable situation had degenerated into total chaos. Many of the thirty thousand Americans finally assembled in France, England, and Italy despaired of ever receiving their promised airplanes. The air historian Lieutenant Colonel H. A. Toumlin, Jr., reported that the air-service program "was a practical failure; was facing the possibilities of disaster . . . and was faced with moral and mental disintegration and disarrangement, which was insidiously wrecking the very integrity and the morale of the entire service."

Well aware that American production of airworthy combat machines promised to be a grisly joke, General Pershing in desperation contracted with the French and Italian governments for the delivery of six thousand new planes and twelve thousand engines before June of 1918. But even this measure of desperation came to naught, for the Aircraft Production Board in the United States failed to meet its obligation

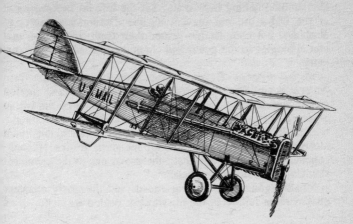

De Havilland DH 4

to France and Italy in sending promised tools and other materials, and both those countries in disgust canceled their contracts!

It was this failure that forced the United States to purchase, as Pershing noted bitterly, "inferior types of planes from the French." Our pilots flew old Nieuports discarded by French pilots; many an American pilot discovered to his horror that his Nieuport had shed the fabric from its wings, causing the airplane to disintegrate in midair. Before the war ended, every single American squadron at the front saw men die because of these defective aircraft.

A desperate attempt was made to overcome the staggering faults by producing the British-designed de Havilland DH-4 in huge numbers and rushing them to the battle front to overwhelm the enemy. These planes were so inferior in workmanship and in equipment that most had to be rebuilt at the American aircraft center at Romorantin. The heavy and clumsy DH-4 flew with all the grace of an overloaded garbage truck. Pilots were distressed to find a large and fragile fuel tank, which could be exploded with a single incendiary bullet, jammed behind their seats. Yet the inferior performance of the DH-4 did not prevent its use. Desperately short of airplanes, our commanders gritted their teeth, made their silent apologies to the gods, and committed the pilot killers to battle.

Justice Charles Evans Hughes, upon investigating the American air industry, noted the rampant waste and inefficiency and deplored the "defective organization of the work of aircraft production and the serious lack of competent direction of that work." In the most damning indictment ever received by the American aircraft industry, Justice Hughes concluded with the regret that "the provisions of the criminal statutes do not reach inefficiency."

Finally, gratefully, the war ended, and the grisly chapter of American failure in the air was put behind us.

PART II

PART II

The Test Pilot Comes
of Age

There were a great many comments attending the formation of the first full-scale engineering and flight test organization in the United States. The advent of any new system is always a rich field for speeches and pronouncements, even if only a few of the people involved really understand what is already happening, and fewer still can see well enough into the future to comprehend long-term consequences. As created by Congress in 1915, the NACA was largely a paper organization. It's all well and good to hang a big sign at the entrance of Langley Field in Virginia saying it is now a great aeronautical research center, but you've also got to get down to the nitty-gritty and put up your buildings, gather your measuring devices, and even figure out just how you're going to do what you've been mandated to do when the field is still less organized than a sixth-grade classroom in a spitball fight.

The army and navy envisioned the military research centers as part of the overall research plan and program. NACA and the military services, as well as private and commercial undertakings, were in the long run configured to be a *national* asset. One reason for creating these various organizations was to permit the different groups to march to the beat of their own drummers. Regimentation stifles the mavericks, chokes imagination, and sends some of the best pilots elsewhere. Thus the creation of NACA was also the beginning of a far-flung, individualistic yet generally cooperative national "fund" of aeronautical knowledge.

To those who'd been fighting to apply sense and direction to American aeronautical engineering, the shabby performance of the nation in the air war over Europe, and the production mess in the States, would be a blessing in disguise. Leaders in Washington are not always myopic. The word, in effect, went out through both official channels and in private meetings: *Get this project off the ground. Get the hell back to your base and kick butt and let's see some results.*

That was the word and the word was good. By late 1917, the production and combat disasters were already becoming distinct through the war clouds over Europe. Public indignation was rising as letters sent home to families by pilots wasting away months in mobilization camps, were made known to newspapers. The idea of some men being so frustrated that they quit the aviation sections to which they belonged and volunteered for infantry duty was enough to splash the front pages. And even those men who reached air combat duty were flying the hand-me-downs of our allies. (There are always those inevitable few who rise above the quagmire, such as Eddie Rickenbacker, who shot down a total of twenty-six aircraft and balloons. But those in the know understood that Rickenbacker, after shooting down five German planes, came within a hairsbreadth of being killed by his own airplane—a Nieuport fighter that shed the fabric from its wings and was coming apart in the air. Brilliant piloting, and the good fortune to be at low altitude, enabled Rickenbacker to land the disintegrating airplane safely. Not long after, he and his squadron mates managed to acquire French Spad fighters, heavy and even trucklike compared to the flyweight Nieuports, but many times stronger and capable of high-speed dives while staying in one piece. Flying these machines, Rickenbacker went on to become the leading American ace of the war.)

Guilt and frustration work wonders, and foresight adds to accomplishment. By the final months of 1918, as the war in Europe ground to its bloody halt, the War Department in the United States had already laid down the foundation for immediate and longterm future flight engineering programs. The Air Service Engineering Division was now a reality, and began to tie together in a cooperative venture the results of both testing and operational experience. More to the point, the new Air Service Engineering Division had established the Flying Section, the first flight-test organization worthy of the name. The flight test group, gathering the most experienced engineers and pilots to be found in the country, set up its headquarters and facilities at McCook Field in (appropriately) Dayton, Ohio.

(In the future another organization, immense in facilities and manpower, would become the world's leading flight test center—only ten miles distant from McCook. This would be known the world over as Wright-Patterson Air Force Base, and it would owe its existence to the accomplishments that came swiftly and steadily from McCook. This first field, McCook, would remain for the next ten years where it was established and then become part of the huge flight test center at Wright-Patterson.)

So the impetus of war and the gross failure of American aviation helped create McCook Field and its growing engineering and test divisions. But as quickly as the war ended— and it is necessary to recognize that this four-year holocaust was known worldwide as "the war to end all wars"—government aircraft research slackened.

And this is where and when individual drive, perseverance, and determination finally overcame economic barriers. At McCook, the objective was not to gain more and more money, but to work on new concepts and experiments. Results were what counted, and the Flying Section lost no time in doing what was paramount to its success—getting into the air to test, to learn, and to succeed.

The engineers at McCook set their sights on high-altitude tests, and they leaned heavily on the skills of one Captain Rudolph W. Schroeder. He was known as "Shorty" Schroeder, because of his six-foot-two-inch frame. Naturally. However, height wasn't Schroeder's most striking feature. His eyes seemed to burn with a deep fire, and his intensity struck people meeting him for the first time. Physically he was superior to every other pilot, heavily muscled but flexible in his movements, and he was equally recognized for his flying skills and swift reflexes.

Several years before McCook Field gained its primary position for aeronautics, Shorty Schroeder was already recognized as "the man to watch." Competing in air races in 1914, he had won repeatedly. All that was well behind Schroeder by 1918 when he was chosen for the new high-altitude program.

Before the "war to end all wars" had ended, the army managed to build a promising new biplane, the LePere Type C-11. It was rushed into production for use in Europe. The war outsped the production lines, and the LePere became the first new aircraft in the United States to enter the postwar era. Powering the LePere was probably the single greatest contribution from American industry to the war effort—the four-hundred-horsepower Liberty engine. Designed finally as a twelve-cylinder V-type engine, it proved remarkably dependable in flight and quickly went into many different types of new aircraft.

McCook designated their LePere as the first aircraft designed specifically for flight research. (This looked much better on paper than merely listing the airplane as a convenient leftover from a war it did not arrive in time to enter.)

Still, going after scientific data for high-altitude flight was a search for answers to problems pilots were encountering in combat. Getting the "high ground" is critical to fighter combat, and pilots on both sides often climbed as high as their fighters would take them. As mentioned earlier, this placed tremendous physical strains on these men. Reaching heights of seventeen to twenty-two thousand feet, above which their laboring engines could not take them, both men and planes suffered severely from oxygen shortage and the frigid cold. Many pilots collapsed, unconscious, from lack of oxygen.

Shorty Schroeder was bundled up in a heavy flying suit. Any winter suit with a new name tag was called a flying suit at the time. He wore a leather helmet, flying goggles, fur-lined boots, and thick gloves. On his first flight, the solid LePere climbed steadily until Schroeder was shivering and dizzy from oxygen starvation. He wanted to go to sleep; the desire was overpowering. Still the LePere climbed, the engine roar drummed against his senses. Then hunger pangs assailed him, none of which Schroeder understood. The different moods coursing through him then became the exact opposite of what most men experienced with hypoxia—rather than warm feelings of well-being (which sent many men into sleep), Schroeder instead became angry with his airplane, himself, the whole bloody experiment.

He forced himself to *think,* angry at his sudden weaknesses. *The oxygen bottle!* Snug against his face was an oxygen mask with what was then known as a "very positive regulator," which drew oxygen from a small cylindrical tank and fed it through the mask to the pilot's mouth and nose. Schroeder hated the mask and it had become his single greatest source of irritation on the flight. With good reason, he would recall later; the men fitting the mask to his face concentrated on a tight seal from mask to skin so that Schroeder wouldn't lose the oxygen he would need so urgently at altitude. They did their job too well; the tightness of the mask numbed his face and the severe cold aggravated the pain that grew steadily.

He fought off his emotions to concentrate on flying and following his test program. Was he getting oxygen? It didn't seem so. The oxygen that ran to his mask was manually controlled by Schroeder turning a valve. The oxygen was then forced upward through a rubber hose and pipe stem into the mask. But Schroeder didn't have a regulator and there was no visual means to determine whether he was or wasn't getting oxygen.

Immediately he thought of a test that would work. He placed his tongue over the pipe-stem opening. Sure enough, he could feel the pressure of the oxygen, and he felt secure in continuing his climb. He also noticed that at the twenty-thousand-foot-mark his oxygen flask and hose were no longer recognizable; they were already covered with a quarter-inch-thick layer of ice. (So was much of Schroeder's clothing; he was already coated with frost that grew thicker with every passing minute.)

Schroeder fought his way to twenty-four thousand feet, but there the airplane would climb no more. The Liberty engine, hammering away under full throttle, barely managed to keep the LePere "hanging in the sky." Schroeder sucked deeply on oxygen, his head clearing sufficiently for him to realize it was time to "get down and out." He was also aware he might run out of oxygen before he could descend to the lower levels of thicker air.

Gratefully, he eased the stick forward, the heavy biplane wallowing in the high thin air, and down he went, the LePere showing a tendency to dive faster and faster. But as quickly as he was descending, Schroeder's head was clearing and his senses were quickly back to normal. He eased his descent and landed back at McCook Field.

Grinning faces told him what he wanted to know. Shorty had flown to twenty-four thousand feet to set an American altitude record.

More important, he was now experienced with flight at extreme altitude. Medical researchers wanted more information on physiological reactions to altitude, and the aircraft engineers climbed over the airplane, instrumenting it for data on pressure, temperature, and other effects. Schroeder went up again, and with his first high-altitude launch behind him, he was able to handle the airplane with greater precision. He maintained a better rate of climb, holding a specific airspeed, and soon he was back in that rarefied world miles above our heads. This time Schroeder passed his former record by three thousand feet.

The war was still raging in Europe, and thousands of planes were in combat daily. By September of 1918 it was also clear that the best fighter plane of the war was Germany's Fokker D-VII; fast, maneuverable, fast climbing, and capable of reaching unprecedented heights. The need for more data on high-altitude exposure to both plane and pilot was greater than before.

The army scheduled Schroeder for another stab at even higher altitudes, set for September 18, 1918. The tests continued with combat-type equipment, for the LePere was intended as the first American-built fighter (two-seat) to go into combat in Europe. (Officially the airplane was the Packard-LePere LUSAC-11.)

Schroeder's equipment was the best available. Mechanics fine-tuned the Liberty engine. Everything on the LePere was checked and with the weather perfect for the high-altitude test, tanks filled, Schroeder took off and began his steady, circling climb.

This is the flight that would earn him the title of the Icicle King.

More experienced now with his body's needs and his oxygen equipment, he climbed steadily, passing his first record. At twenty-five thousand feet he recognized the danger signs of hypoxia. His thinking was muddled, he alternated between an overwhelming desire to sleep and bursts of anger. Only one thing to do. Limbs moving stiffly in bitter cold, he increased his oxygen flow, risking that he might run out of oxygen before he could return to denser, lower air. The gamble was worth it; he knew he couldn't continue his climb in his mental state and deteriorating physical condition.

Up, up; higher and higher. The LePere thundered hollowly in his ears and the dazzling clear sky of extreme altitude seemed to burn his eyes. He wrote, laboriously, in his flight log attached to one knee that the temperature was sixty degrees below zero Celsius.

The LePere drove steadily through thinning air. Twenty-seven thousand feet . . . matching the highest he'd ever flown. Frost seemed to cover the entire cockpit and everything about him. In that open cockpit he might as well have been standing on an Antarctic mountain in the dead of winter with a screaming gale of a hundred miles an hour.

He could no longer see. Solid frost covered his goggles. Calling on reserves of strength and will, he managed to lift the goggles from his face so he could check his height on the aneroid altimeter. Immediately the screaming wind and terrible cold forced tears from his eyes; just as quickly as they appeared they froze solid. But he was able to keep the goggles away from his face long enough to read his new record: twenty-nine thousand feet. For a long moment he wondered if he could continue his climb. He couldn't see through his goggles, and if he left his eyes unprotected, they teared so badly that he would quickly lose his vision.

The LePere answered his questions. The thunder from the Liberty engine ended with that crash of silence so well known to pilots who in an instant change from flying an airplane to holding the controls of a lead brick. Immediately the biplane fell rapidly. Schroeder knew he must not let the airplane dive; strong as it was in this thin air, and for so long a descent, it could quickly achieve a speed that might overload the structure. Freezing cold, eyes watering, without power, he swung into a wide descending spiral so that he would have enough altitude to make his deadstick approach and landing at McCook.

At twenty thousand feet his head was clearing and he could judge his situation. And apparently just in time, for a weather front had moved in during his climb and the powerless airplane dropped through thick clouds and snow—without blind-flying instruments in the airplane. Now his very existence hung on his flying skill and his ability to retain control, unable to see anything but blinding white. He kept the controls set for that continuing downward spiral and suddenly broke through the clouds. No landing at McCook Field. He was over Canton, Ohio—more than two hundred miles away, blown far off his original position by powerful high-altitude winds.

The field below him was rough-hewn, but Schroeder had no time to consider anything but his approach and landing. He came down hard, bouncing, fighting for control. The tail came up, a propeller blade slammed into the ground. As fast as the prop tip snapped off he had the stick back to save the landing.

All in all, it was a sensational, wonderful, marvelous landing—considering that the Icicle King's face was a block of ice, both hands were frozen numb, and four of his fingers, and his lips, were so badly frozen he was rushed from the airplane to a hospital.

Captain Schroeder quickly became Major Rudolph Schroeder and was officially assigned to the position of chief test pilot of the Air Service Engineering Division.

The year following his record altitude flights and close brush with death, Major Schroeder had a rare opportunity to demonstrate his skills in a flight that hearkened back to his early flying days. Schroeder had learned to fly in 1910 at a Chicago field and held Commercial Pilot License No. 7 as issued by the U.S. government. Aside from his flight records, he was the first army officer to wear a parachute in the line of duty, the first chief test pilot of the army, and would soon become the first man to flight-test a highly supercharged aircraft engine.

But in between his last record altitude flight and a new test scheduled for 1920, Schroeder's commanding officer heard of a great air race from New York to Toronto. Well, hadn't Schroeder already proved himself in low-altitude air racing as well as his world-record altitude flights? He gave Schroeder the nod to "have at it."

The first problem was to get an airplane they could use in a *civilian* race. The LePere was out of the question. The McCook engineers and mechanics searched the hangars and shops, and lo and behold, they discovered an abandoned Vought VE-7. The crews went to work day and night. Knowing that the Icicle King would be flying, they performed their own sort of miracle. What had been close to a dead buzzard now sported a new engine that ran sweetly. Shorty had told them: "You fix it, I'll fly it."

An engineer grinned. "And *win* the race in it," he added.

That's just what the Icicle King did!

On February 20, 1920, Major Rudolph Schroeder prepared to take off from McCook Field in his now-familiar LePere, but the plane he had flown before lacked the new modifications and additions on this one. The big biplane had been fitted out with a new Moss turbosupercharger built by General Electric. The company was risking a fortune and its reputation on the turbosupercharger that in the thin air of high altitude would ram air into the engine so that it mixed fuel and air as if it were operating at lower altitudes. If the flight went as planned, Shroeder would be airborne for about two hours.

He climbed out as before, but as he soared upward he felt the airplane surging with power he'd never known at high altitude. The LePere climbed steadily, but Schroeder was close to making the last flight of his life. The airplane and its Moss turbosupercharger functioned beautifully, but Schroeder fell prey to equipment failure—not with his airplane, but with the oxygen system he carried along to keep him conscious in rarefied air.

Near peak ascent, Schroeder felt the sudden onset of hypoxia. Had he used up all his oxygen? He didn't know what the problem was. His peripheral vision began to fade, a sure sign that his brain was lacking oxygen. He knew that he was close to disaster. What he could not tell, as best the engineers could determine later, was that his oxygen system had what went in the official reports as a "valve problem." He struggled to maintain control of the airplane, wobbly in air thinner than any he had ever flown through before. Desperate to remain conscious, he pulled his goggles from his eyes so that he might *see* what could have failed him.

Instantly Schroeder was struck blind. The airstream blasting into the cockpit with temperatures estimated at eighty degrees F below zero hit his eyes and froze them as hard as ice. All vision was gone.

He reacted instantly, swinging down the nose and maneuvering into a steep spiral. He pulled back on his throttle to kill power that would only accelerate his descent. Blinded, Schroeder couldn't tell that the airplane was already plunging into a steep dive.

The blinded pilot could only struggle to clear ice from his eyes as the LePere screamed earthward. The speed continued to build up, and in the World War I–era fabric-covered biplane, breakup was only seconds away as the LePere raced past three hundred miles per hour. For six miles the biplane dove madly as Schroeder fought for vision. Finally, in the heavy warmer air at two thousand feet, he regained partial vision. Still half-blind, his body crying out in pain from the plunge into high pressure from the thin air at the top of his climb, he fought his own physical problems *and* the LePere, finally curving into a landing approach at McCook Field. Many of the men on the ground, watching the airplane shrieking downward, were convinced it would either come apart from the tremendous forces of the dive or it would hurtle straight down into the ground.

Schroeder landed safely—with his eyelids frozen solid.

He had also set a new world's record for altitude—33,114 feet.

The high-altitude flights were already bringing major changes and improvements in oxygen systems and cold-weather gear. There was no longer any question but that the old Liberty engine was a marvel for reliability or that turbosupercharging worked beautifully. But there were problems up so high. Schroeder flew through air that should have been as calm as the surface of a still lake. Instead, every now and then invisible currents rattled and shook the airplane, threatening to throw it into a steep bank, which, at that height, would have caused it to a stall. It was also obvious that much more reliable oxygen equipment was needed. The open cockpit was a disaster that blasted the pilot with all the fury of Antarctic gales. Getting heat to the pilot was now as vital as getting power to the engine. More high flights went on the schedule.

It was time to pass the baton to another test pilot. Engineers modified the LePere again with a revolutionary new propeller. This was supposed to operate at slower speed at low altitude so that it would not exceed its "load limits" in dense air, but once the machine climbed into rarefied heights, the propeller could be brought to full thrust with full power from the engine. The engineers tested a four-bladed propeller, discarded it, and produced a huge two-bladed experimental prop that had already gone through some wild moments.

For climb at low heights the propeller was to turn at 1,100 rpm. As the plane climbed into thinner air it would speed up to an expected 1,400 to 1,600 rpm. The pilot selected for the new record altitude, Lieutenant John A. Mcready, had been working his way slowly toward the record attempt. In test flights Macready had more than his share of harrowing moments. Once the propeller flew completely off the airplane, and Macready returned to McCook in a pure glider. On another flight at thirty-one thousand feet the propeller "ran away," overspeeding wildly to 2,400 rpm and threatening again to rip free of the LePere. Macready had flown his proving flights for more than a year, and every time he went up, something else went wrong, and he came back in "emergency" descents. Bearings and oil pipes in the engine cracked and broke loose. Parts of the supercharger would suddenly fail, hurling pieces in all directions and reducing the engine to gasping stuttering. Most of these failures took place at the heady altitude of twenty-five thousand feet, and it's a long time and a far ways down to fly a crippled machine.

Finally, on September 28, 1921, Macready was ready. He had put on heavy woolen underwear from ankles to neck, then donned a heavy leather flight suit with a huge fur collar about his neck and head; the leather suit was packed with feathers and down. So were his boots. His usual flying helmet had been modified into a "leather mask" lined thickly with fur. His gloves also were filled with fur. On this flight Macready would use a mask that sent oxygen through a manually operated valve and regulator, leading to a pipe stem he held in his teeth. He also had an emergency flask in the event the system failed. The problems of the Icicle King had brought about new goggles. Each eyepiece was inserted separately into the goggle straps and the insides of the lenses were then coated with a gelatinlike material that, it was hoped, would stave off freezing.

It was a perfect day, warm and clear. Macready climbed out steadily, the LePere functioning perfectly. At ten thousand feet he pushed up through a layer of clouds. Again at twenty thousand he encountered a cloud layer. At this height he opened the valve to start his flow of oxygen. He was getting sufficient oxygen and his new clothing kept him comfortably warm. Then the LePere climbed above thirty thousand feet.

His first indication of trouble was with his oxygen flow. Any exertion he made brought on a feeling of dizziness. As he looked earthward, the world was blurred and the cockpit instruments appeared "dim and shaky." He kept increasing his oxygen flow. "I was worried at no time until approximately 39,000 feet was reached," he described in his official report. Then, trouble moved into the cockpit with him as his breath froze in the tube of his oxygen mask. He tried to blow his oxygen tube clear "and did succeed in getting a taste of the ice." But the flow was still severely restricted. Immediately, Macready grabbed for the emergency flask and "tore a small plaster from the side of my mask, placing the tube through this aperture directly into my mouth within the mask and in an instant was feeling comparatively normal."

He could hardly believe the effects of the turbosupercharger and the new propeller. At 40,800 feet indicated altitude, "I was supercharging to sea level conditions," he later reported, adding he was astonished with the performance of the airplane. But that was just about all the airplane and its systems could deliver, and abruptly engine power diminished sharply. Macready fought the airplane up barely another hundred feet and realized he had reached the absolute maximum ceiling of this flight.

By now, with the steady loss of power, he could barely

control the LePere. It needed the huge blast of air from the propeller, which had slowed drastically in its turns. From a solid platform the LePere became a wobbly drunk of an airplane, and its slow speed rendered its controls almost useless. Macready was, in his own words, "hanging suspended at an indicated altitude on the dial of 41,200 feet," and the biplane "swung and rolled. . . . The controls were almost useless."

He staggered along for another five minutes, the LePere refusing to climb another foot. He knew when to call it quits. With extreme care he eased back on the throttle to begin his long controlled descent.

The LePere simply didn't have it. Suddenly it gave up its lift, "the bottom seemed to drop out," and the airplane began to descend much faster than Macready wished to go. That sudden plunge was nearly fatal. The engine and its systems went through shock cooling, losing their ability to continue sending heat through pipes for warming the man in the cockpit. From being "comfortably warm" Macready might have been plunged into ice water that was freezing faster than the airplane was diving. Whatever had been smeared on the inside of his goggles proved useless. The goggles froze solid and Macready in the next instant was blinded. For an undetermined time he found himself unable to control the diving airplane. His limbs felt useless and he hovered on the edge of unconsciousness. He feared he would collapse. Groping through the fog in his mind—"I could not think fast and correctly"—he knew he must hang on long enough to regain control of the airplane.

For eleven thousand feet the LePere plunged like a bomb falling from the sky. Instead of exerting himself, Macready decided to let his ship fall until he descended into thicker and warmer air where oxygen would be easier to mix with ambient air and his wings could grasp the atmosphere for flight.

At thirty thousand feet he felt his head clearing and he was regaining full use of his limbs. The engine systems were again functioning properly, and Macready brought the plunging ship under control, maintaining a steady glide. He pulled away his useless goggles and slipped another pair before his eyes. Then at twenty thousand feet, he circled for twenty minutes to check out all airplane systems. Once again, unexpected high-altitude winds had blown the airplane far from Dayton, but now with everything working normally and the pilot feeling as strong as he was before takeoff, he headed for Dayton and landed at McCook Field.

The altitude flights of Schroeder and Macready ended all questions about the need for experienced test pilots to break new high ground in flight. From these tests there came the turbosupercharger, special propellers, new and reliable oxygen systems, and heating systems for the pilot. Flying in an open cockpit at such heights was both foolhardy and unnecessary, and plans were already being laid down to design ships with closed cockpits or cabins. The LePere had never been designed for high-altitude experiments. Another point made painfully clear was that were the landing gear retractable, the airplane could have climbed faster and reached greater altitude. Even the wings were antiquated, for the LePere was designed to fight at low and medium altitudes in European combat, not produce maximum lift at the highest altitude possible.

From these tests flown by these two men, and one other in which Lieutenant James H. Doolittle (who would become one of the most famous test, racing, and combat pilots in the world) pushed an army XCO-5 above thirty-seven thousand feet and lost consciousness, racing earthward out of control and recovering barely in time to swing into his landing approach, a vast new experimental *series* began.

There was one more item to be added to the list. From these days on, experimental test pilots would all have another piece of equipment—a parachute. A great many men lived longer than they ever expected when their machines broke apart in the air, or burned, or tumbled violently out of control.

The new age had arrived.

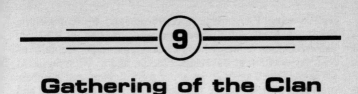

Gathering of the Clan

"What everybody wanted in those days after the war ended," reminisced a gray-haired pilot at a meeting of the Silver Wings flying fraternity (of which this writer is a life member), "was power. I don't care what they did in the way of design, you know, by cleaning up the ships. They reduced the struts and the cross-bracing wires, and they put little streamlined covers on the wheels, and lots of stuff like that. So you'd get a little more performance from your ship. But it wasn't enough. Then, sometimes, especially for the boys who wanted to get into racing, you know, flying against one another in wild racing competitions, and there got to be a lot of money in that, well, they'd design their own ships. Little killers, we called them, because they were so damned small and sleek it was like trying to fly a *fish*. That doesn't sound like it could be real, but believe me, it was. They were really tiny little things, with short wings and the biggest engines they could stuff into the nose, and crazy propeller designs. They were so damn small you felt like your behind was going to scrape ground when you taxied. And, my God, on the ground, especially over those rough grass fields, running along the ground, they'd try to shake you to pieces. You saw everything through a blur until you got into the air, and then you were flying for your life—just trying to stay alive, let alone get into a full-throttle fracas with everybody bunching together to get an edge as we all went around the pylons."

The old pilot—ninety-two years old and still flying—still

with a valid FAA medical certificate and his commercial ticket—went silent for several moments. He had to. We were gathered at the annual whoop-de-do of the Experimental Aircraft Association at Lakeland, Florida, and as we reminisced we were forced on hold as about forty fighters and bombers of World War II vintage thundered overhead with a roar and vibration that shook our wooden building. It was a meeting this writer would never forget; Silver Wings had just nailed me with absolute surprise when I was awarded a plaque as a Master Aviator and a Pioneer Aviator. I'd always judged myself as a maverick pilot who often was too dumb to know when he'd stretched common sense beyond its limits, but here were these grand masters of flying (many of them with their pilot licenses signed off by one of the Wright Brothers!) and they were trying to tell me, "Hey, you ain't half-bad, son."

Anybody pats me on the back and calls me "son," well, I listen carefully to what he says because there aren't many of these people left. The warbirds passed by and their engine roar subsided into a comfortable rolling thunder. The old-timers lit pipes or cigars or tipped back a silvered flask, waiting for this one man to continue.

"You see, these little racers were *all* experimental. You wanted something small and sleek, like a fish, because the smaller and sleeker it was, the less drag it had, and the lighter it was, the better the engine and propeller could haul it through the air. So you had a machine cut down in every respect, and the pilot was shoved or jammed inside, sort of all scrunched up, and he had a tiny windshield to peer through, and he could barely move his arms and legs to work the controls. You really didn't horse those things around. They were too responsive. You know, just move the stick a hair and the damn thing would stand on a wing for you. So you had to think and *feel* the controls, sort of *think to your airplane.*"

He smiled. "You were asking me and the boys about test flying in those days." Abruptly he chuckled. "Anybody who was damn fool enough to fly those racers was a test pilot. Like I said, most of these things, well, they were hand-built. Designed on wrapping paper on a kitchen table and put together by a bunch of friends who dropped cigar ashes and beer over what they were doing, but they built some incredible little airplanes and they set world records for speed almost every time they went up.

"You'd fly her carefully for a while, find out what was wrong, like maybe one aileron was too heavy, or she was trimmed nose down; stuff like that. Or the engine heat came back into the cockpit and like to roast you from your crotch to the back of your neck, and that was sort of like flying right down there in hell, and you had to add an additional firewall and somehow close off the source of that heat. Or maybe the ground steering on landing would screw up an airplane that flew beautifully, but once she was on the ground she'd go mad, impossible to hold straight. A crosswind could tilt you up on one wing and you go cartwheeling down the field, and that usually meant the engine would come back into the cockpit or the whole thing would fold up, and either way, the pilot would be crushed so badly he'd be lucky if he was dead. And some of them burned, and that was the worst way to go. They were too small for parachutes, and we were all flying right down on the deck, so you really took your chances. They were worse than fighter airplanes, because in a fighter you want lightness and agility, but compared to our racers, a military fighter plane was like an old plug horse.

"You'd never know from where trouble would come. Sometimes a ship flew just great, and suddenly it would whirl out of control and tumble crazylike through the air, smash into the ground, and explode. There wasn't a thing wrong with the airplane, but the exhaust was somehow pulled around by the air curving about the airplane and all those exhaust gases ended up pouring into the cockpit, and the poor guy in there was getting poisoned by carbon monoxide, like sticking your head inside an oven, and it hit him so fast and so hard that one moment he'd be flying that thing, his eyes blinking, wondering what the hell was going on, and why were all the gauges fuzzy and blurry, and why, he'd pass out like he'd been whacked across the head with a brick. Well, he was already unconscious, so that when the ship just wheeled up and over out of control, of course it fell, also, and smashed into the ground with a hell of an explosion, I guess that was one of the best ways to go because the pilot, why, he was out cold as he came down and there wasn't no waking up between falling unconscious in the sky and exploding against the ground. It was sort of a gentle lights-out, you could say."

The old man leaned forward on his cane, hands folded over the curve, his chin resting on his hands as he flew back through the years. He harumphed quietly to himself, then sat up straight, a whimsical smile on his face. "You're going to write about the test pilots," he murmured. "In the early days I guess it really was impossible to separate the great pilots, you know, racers, test pilots, explorers; that sort of thing. You could always separate the wheat from the chaff, because there were so many of the young guys who died so quick. Flying the first air mail, why"—he snorted with indignation, and heads nodded in the group about us—"that wasn't flying. It was a slaughter. The thing was they needed the best pilots they could get so that the government would look good. And when they started flying the mail, well, the airplanes just weren't fit for the work. The point is, they pulled their pilots from everywhere. Or at least they tried to, but some of the best in the business took a look at what the government wanted, and they said, to hell with that! They'd rather take their chances with them crazy racing ships, or dive experimental models, or spin down from twenty thousand feet. Things like that. You had some latitude in that kind of test flying, but when they first flew the mail, you stuck your head in the icebox and your ass in the oven, so you got froze and burned all at the same time."

"When did that start?" A young newswoman, eyes wide as saucers, daughter of an airline captain, was reporting the gathering of the clan and she was awestruck. Just asking the question forced her to realize all this had taken place when she wasn't even a dream of being born yet, and her own father was still wearing knickers and kicking tin cans.

I answered the question. "It was 1934. It didn't last long, either. The President of the country gave the order for the Army Air Corps to fly the United States mail. There was a big drive in the Congress to put the airplane to work for the country. Give the taxpayers what they shelled out for."

"I'll say it didn't last long," another old-timer stepped in. We looked at him carefully. This pilot was a veteran of air combat in World War I and he was still flying, alert and strong and capable. "I flew Nieuports and Camels and Spads, even a few Samsons, in the Big World One. Some of them were pretty wicked. And I got into engineering with the army afterward. The word went out they wanted volunteers to fly the mail. When the pilots found out what they were up against, they balked, just like old granddad here." He jerked a thumb at his friend who'd held the floor. "Smartest thing there was to do. You see, the airplanes, well, they were junk. You had a better chance of living through a couple of dog-fights over Germany than you did flying over the Rocky Mountains in the dead of winter with the junk heaps we had to fly. It was like you just heard. It didn't last long, and people started dying off so fast they began pulling even the test pilots out of engineering to fly the mail."

A short laugh, with everything save humor, followed his words. "It was sad, young lady." He spoke directly to the woman. "Damn sad. Fourteen of the best pilots in this coun-try, all military, because the civilians knew better, were killed between February and June, back in 1934. A bunch more were hurt so bad they never flew again. We had transports that could barely get off the ground, we had bombers that maybe were good for carrying cucumbers on a nice sunny day, stuff like that. We even had single-engine fighters car-rying the mail. Or trying to."

We waited for him to go on. "Well, we were right in the winter of 1934 when it started. Ask anyone who was flying around that time and they'll tell you it was the worst winter any of them could ever recall. Up north in the Great Lakes country, we had blizzards coming down with blinding snow and the worst cold I ever knew. You got a fancy name for it nowadays. The Siberian Express, I hear. Good name, but what we called it I can't say in nice company. The storm seemed to go on forever along the Rockies, and when you got up to the northwest, it was like nature had gone plumb crazy. In the first three weeks everyone found out you just don't send rotten equipment into that kind of weather. Just like *that*"—he banged his cane on the floor—"there was nine pilots and passengers deader'n hell. Then came such a hulla-boo that for the next nine days, everybody was grounded. *Then* some genius figured out that with the planes grounded there wasn't *any* airmail going to get through. So they sent everybody up again.

"If we went up at night, well, would you believe our night deliveries were in single-seat fighters, open cockpit in them storms, and with instruments so bad a Boy Scout couldn't find his way out of his backyard. Some of the best airplanes in the world today, why, their pilots wouldn't even think of taking off in that stuff. Heavy snow from the ground going up as high as forever and gone. Winds doing forty to fifty miles an hour on the ground. Airplanes could take off just about right where they were when they went to full throttle, with that kind of wind. And then when you were in the air, you couldn't see hell from molasses. Not only dark, but you were in clouds and snow at night. So you used a flashlight, and you looked at your instruments, and *they* were covered with ice! It was a miracle that we didn't kill more people. Sometimes the pilots just eased back on power, let the plane come down as slow as they could, the nose up, and land absolutely blind. *Anywhere*. It didn't matter where. If they put down on some open field, why, they were *so* damn glad just to be alive. And they flew some real junk, like I said. Old Keystone bombers. Curtiss Condors, great big sailing ships of fabric the wind tossed around like paper toys."

The room fell quiet for a while. Gave me a chance to think about one of my best friends in flying. Robert L. Scott, pioneer aviator. The man who was too old for combat in World War II, and beseeched, lied, and did everything he could to get into combat against the enemy. Flew a P-40 against the Japanese. The old man flew often with the famed American Volunteer Group, much better known as the Flying Tigers. Scott wasn't a member of the AVG, but often he shared their air battles. Much more to his liking was going out on his own in a P-40 and attacking the enemy in the air, strafing troop columns on roads, ripping up enemy airfields and anything that might harbor Japanese. He got fourteen kills doing that sort of thing. The Japanese thought he was a whole squadron instead of one plane. He'd take off and rip up the Japanese in his P-40 with a nose spinner painted bright red. As soon as he landed, they'd fuel up and rearm his guns and they'd paint that spinner a bright color, just so long as it wasn't red this time. The Japanese kept seeing all these

P-40 fighters with different-color nose paint jobs, and Scott flew so many missions they figured it had to be a whole squadron.

He even performed a test flight of his own, without orders to do so, just to prove that our army wasn't using its planes to their best advantage. The Chinese were sent a bunch of Republic P-43 Lancers, radial-engined fighters that were forerunners of the famed P-47 Thunderbolt. *Our* army didn't think it was worth much, especially at high altitude, against the nimble Japanese fighters.

Scott, instead of throwing up his hands in despair, figured the best way to show the brass they were wrong, "borrowed" a supercharger from a British Spitfire, helped his mechanics install it in the "lead brick" P-43, and astounded everyone who found out what he'd done when he took that P-43 up to forty-three thousand feet and cruised high over Mount Everest!

But long before those days, when Scott also drove around the war-torn world in transports and bombers as well as fighters, he was one of those pilots who willingly (somewhat stupidly, he would admit later) volunteered to fly the mail. Bob Scott (who would one day write a smash best-seller, *God Is My Copilot*), was then a lieutenant in the Army Air Corps. And he was assigned to the infamous "Hell Stretch" that ran from Chicago to Cleveland and on to Newark, New Jersey. During the few months of airmail flying, Scott had two roommates killed and, finally, moved in with another man who had lost three of his closest friends on the airmail runs. They figured that after *those* losses all about them they would survive anything. Scott missed death by the barest margins. Several times violent weather forced him down to emergency landings. On two nights when other men were killed and he was hours overdue, Scott was given up for dead!

(At this writing, Bob Scott is well into his seventies and still flying. We've gathered with friends several times, and Scott some years ago returned to China to *walk* the Great Wall of China, over which he had flown so many times in combat. And then, just to keep in his hand, he bought a powerful floatplane and set off to fly the most inaccessible wilds of Alaska. Of such stuff are these pilots made.)

The young lady with us wanted to know more about the racing pilots, for they seemed to be test pilots, too.

"Well, it was more than just racing, because these people went all out to get the greatest performance possible from their engines and their airplanes. They were more than pilots. They were mechanics; hell, just about everybody in those days *had* to be a mechanic! They also knew more about airplanes than most engineers, so the races became one of the greatest proving grounds for advances in aviation. They designed and built airplanes that were incredibly innovative. They tried new things all the time to squeeze more performance from their ships. Not just speed. After all, these people had to maneuver against one another, go through some pretty hairy tight turns coming around the pylons, and they had to stay in the air long enough at top performance without their ships breaking down. So they broke the mold, you might say. They went for the Big One; anything to win. And a lot of them were military pilots."

Everyone grinned. One pilot broke in. "One of the few things the army did that really *was* smart. Put their own people and their own planes into the competition. Ships with wheels and on floats. Whatever would give them the best speed. Many of the army guys, and plenty of navy, too, did modifications that were against all the rules. The brass just looked the other way. You couldn't hardly get better publicity than a military man in a fighter plane beating out the best in the country."

They couldn't have hit the nail any more accurately. The big annual air shows and air races in the United States really began way back in 1920. That was the year the United States *failed* in the races. The French ran away with the trophy for the International Gordon Bennett race, leaving red faces from Washington to every little cow-pasture flying field.

This loss galvanized some heavy hitters into action. In 1920 the Pulitzer brothers, in order to promote the development of aviation in this country, put up the money and the organization to establish the Pulitzer Trophy Race, and this became air racing's bonanza competition for the next six years.

Despite the competition money and national plaudits for the Pulitzer winner-take-all contests, the civilian pilots quickly found themselves out of the running. In those days they lacked sponsors and they simply couldn't afford to pit the planes they *wanted* to build against the military fighters. So the Pulitzer, to the delight of military brass, became a highly publicized pitched battle between the army and the navy, which *had* the money (and private backing of Washington). For the next five years, victories seesawed between the two services.

Lieutenant Russell H. Maughan won the Pulitzer in an army fighter on October 14, 1922. Indicative of what these top pilots could do, and would do, was that Maughan would later make the first dawn-to-dusk transcontinental flight.

In that same 1922 race, flying a Curtiss racer (a Curtiss fighter with all guns and combat equipment stripped from the plane), Lieutenant Lester J. Maitland come in second. And just as Maughan went on to become a trailblazing pilot in noncombat roles, Maitland became world-famous for many aerial exploits, including the first flight from the U.S. mainland to Hawaii.

But by 1925 the grumbling from the civilian pilots reached enough congressmen to pass down the word: 1925 would be the last year for military competitive air racing. When that year ended, the army had its arms full of medals, trophies, and even more important, several new world speed records as well. To eclipse every other plane from every other country in the world was what pleased congress, the military, and the American public.

The 1925 competition allowed the army to break its own rules and order planes built especially for racing. They called in their best test pilots to smash old records. They gave these men several Curtiss R3C2 racers—and so did the navy, which meant the pilots with the greatest experience and skill would cop the honors.

These races startled the entire world. Lieutenant Cy Bettis of the army barely beat out the famed Lieutenant Al Williams of the navy by hammering out a new speed record of 248.9 miles per hour.

Several weeks later an enthusiastic Jimmy Doolittle (still a lieutenant), hauled Bettis's racer into an engineering shop and replaced its wheels with sleek pontoons to operate from water. Engineers scoffed that the pontoons would create so

Gee Bee Racer

much drag that Doolittle would lumber instead of thunder through the air. Jimmy Doolittle silenced all doubters when he took the pontoon racer through a difficult closed-course run with a new seaplane record of 232.6 miles per hour to grab the world-renowned Schneider Trophy.

For the record, Doolittle had entered the race against the best planes built by British, Italian, and two U.S. Navy hopefuls!

When you're on a roll, go for it. Doolittle took up the pontoon racer for a speed run on a straightaway course, holding a steady line, and brought in a new world seaplane record of 245.7 miles per hour.

The races were *on*. After the Pulitzer came the Thompson Trophy for closed-course speed runs, and the world-renowned Bendix Trophy for speed runs across the continent. All America thrilled to the competitions, and the pilots became household names the world over. Jimmy Doolittle, Roscoe Turner, Rudy Kling, James Haizlip, Harold Neumann, Jacqueline Cochran, Frank Fuller, Jr., and others sped to victories headlined across the country and in foreign lands.

In the 1932 Thompson Trophy competition, Jimmy Doolittle went into the fray in one of the most infamous planes ever built—the Granville Gee Bee racer designed by Bob Hall. The airplane was a stubby barrel, terribly short-coupled, unbalanced, needing absolute attention to its controls, and almost eager to fling itself out of control. Roaring into the ten-lap, ten-mile competition course, Doolittle came out at the head of the snarling racers with a new speed record of 252 miles per hour.

Most pilots judged that a combination of unexcelled skill and an enormous amount of luck brought Doolittle through the race—alive. Soon after, two of the best pilots in the world, Lowell Bayles and Russell Boardman, met violent deaths in other Gee Bee racers.

But from the uproar and the competition emerged what the designers, engineers, and pilots wanted most of all—new airplanes that could outperform anything else in the sky. Sleek engine cowls, better wings, retractable landing gear, high-octane fuels, propellers with increased thrust, and more powerful engines were only some of the benefits of racing. And these planes had to fly in rough air from the violent corkscrewing airstream of planes before and all about them, they had to pull powerful g-forces on men and machines, so that another issue arose from these invaluable competitions— building airplanes that not only proved structurally sound, but that could take a beating.

"What happened to, um, what was his name? Frank Hawks," the young lady said suddenly. "I mean, my father used to talk a lot about him."

"They called him the Meteor Man," a pilot offered from the group. "He broke records all over this country, and Europe as well. Like most of us, he flew with the army for some years. He quit to become a barnstormer. A wild man. He could do anything with an airplane. He got so popular an outfit called the Texas Company hired him to gallivant around the country. That would help them sell their stuff they made for aviation. If Frank Hawks flew it, they figured the public would conclude, it's good enough for us, too. So Frank, well, everywhere he went he went hell-bent for leather, and kept piling up one record after another. Um, well, back in

1931, for example, he took off from Los Angeles and pounded away for New York. Made the flight from California to the East Coast for a new record. Did it in twelve and a half hours.''

The pilot fell silent. An uneasy feeling seemed to go about the room. The young woman, sensing the discomfort, asked quietly, "What happened to him?"

The pilot with Wilbur Wright's signature on his flier's ticket sighed. "It's a crazy story. Crazy, because it was one of the dumbest ways to lose a great man that ever happened."

"Was he killed racing?"

"*No!* No way, miss. Not at all. They couldn't kill Frank Hawks in racing, and nothing ever took him down when he kept setting world records. We've got to jump ahead some years in time. Let me tell you, also, that people have designed some pretty weird airplanes in their day. Weird, but they seemed to work all right. And there are those times in life when a man's number comes up, when doing the simplest, easiest thing in the world will take down the greatest pilots that ever lived. That's what happened to Frank Hawks."

He took a long swallow from a huge coffee mug with the coffee well laced with brandy. "There was this designer, name of Joe Gwinn," he went on. "In 1935 he designed some crazy kind of ship he called an *aircar*. Wasn't a *real* airplane and it wasn't a *real* car, either, but a combination of both. Was supposed to make flying available for everybody, because you could fly this thing real easy. Looked like a giant bumblebee that was both pregnant and had mumps swollen up real bad, all over it. Some people said it looked unusual; I saw it myself and it looked *sick*. Short-coupled, like the tail was rammed right up against the cabin, like they forgot to put a real fuselage on it.

"You know how Gwinn built that thing? He took a whole bunch of parts from an Oldsmobile so he could make it cheaper than other planes. Now, he called it an aircar, not because you could drive it on a highway, but it had an automobile steering wheel for control, and when you turned it, it turned the airplane and for some reason, turned the nose wheel also, whether it was flying or not.

"You know how an airplane power is controlled?" He

watched the young woman nod. "Okay, then. No throttle in this mess like you find in other planes. Oh, it had a throttle you pushed in and out, but when you were on the ground, you forgot all about that and used a floor pedal, just like a gas pedal in a car. No one *ever* figured out why Gwinn did that. Just made everything more complicated.

"The man was bananas over floor pedals. There were two more of them. You shoved against one and the flaps came down. You shoved against another and you worked the brakes. So you had three pedals on the floor and you sure got mixed up real easy."

He laughed. "I saw this thing take off once. Couldn't believe it. You had to really run along until you got about sixty miles an hour or so. Then the pilot stomped on the pedal that worked the flaps, they came down, and the thing just jumped into the air like it was scared by a rattlesnake. When you landed, you came down, leveled off, pulled power, stomped that crazy flap pedal on the floor, and the flaps came down and so did the airplane. Just whomped right onto the ground. You couldn't keep it up with the flaps down and power back. Anyway, Gwinn ran around for a while in it. It had a Popjoy Niagara radial engine, and it turned this big clumsy four-bladed wooden propeller. It was a real bummer, but strangely enough, it seemed to fly pretty well, fat and clumsy like it looked.

"Gwinn couldn't sell that thing to save his life. No one would buy it after their eyes sort of swelled up just looking at it. But this Gwinn, he was a determined cuss. Pretty smart, too. This is where Frank Hawks came in. Gwinn hired him. We don't know how much he paid old Frank, but it must have been a hell of a lot of money for Frank to even be seen in that monkey airplane.

"About 1938, yes, it was 1938, Gwinn told Frank to pick up a passenger, some guy called Campbell, and fly on up to a big private estate in New York. Big muckamucks there. All millionaires. Gwinn had brought them all together to see Frank fly that thing, and make it look real good. So Frank, he picks up Campbell, and off they go to this big estate. Everybody was watching for them, and sure enough, right on time, there was Hawks coming down the slot on his approach."

Silence in the room. Finally the young woman couldn't stand it any longer. "What *happened*?" she pleaded.

"I told you about that crazy landing system. You level off, power back, stomp on the flaps, and it flopped down. Well, that's the way it was supposed to fly, and Frank, he flew it that way. When he shoved down on the floor pedal, the flaps came down and that piece of crap dropped like a stone.

"Right into power lines."

"My God . . ."

"Killed them both outright. *That's* how Frank Hawks died. It's amazing how many people don't even know that. I think, myself, they don't want to know."

Another voice from the crowd. "This Gwinn fellow, he also tried to sell that airplane on its stability. Said it couldn't stall and it couldn't spin. It was foolproof against that sort of thing."

Murmurs grew to heated conversations about unspinnable airplanes. "Sure. That damned thing was so safe it killed two good people. There's an old rule to this game. *Nothing* replaces skill and experience. *Nothing*. Frank could have been flying a hot racer or a fighter and he'd have slicked it right in. But when you get to airplanes that supposedly *cannot* spin, well, it's the same old story. To get something you have to give something. And airplanes that can't spin also can't do a lot of other things, like crossing controls or slipping into a tight field, or—"

Heads turned as one to another pilot in the group. He was in his seventies and he moved with the energy of someone forty years his junior. He'd held a proud name for a long time: Cloudbuster. Herbert Walker, best known as Tommy.

You name just about anything in flying and Tommy Walker has done it. He's been flying since he was barely able to walk, when as a kid his old man held him in his lap and they did loops and rolls and all sorts of happy nonsense in Cubs. Tommy went on to become a superb pilot in his own right. He became a barnstormer and did wild aerobatics all over the country and in a couple of countries with strange-sounding foreign names. In the barnstorming circuit he took up jumping. In a sort of way, that is. The man who owned an air circus asked him if he was an experienced jumper. "Hell, yes," Tommy told him. "Damn right."

Fifteen minutes later he made his *first* jump before the crowd. He made a couple hundred more. He also developed his own skilled technique for crashing airplanes before those same crowds. He crashed them into buildings, telephone poles, huge walls made of blocks of ice. He flew trainers, transports, fighters, bombers, and as a test pilot a bunch of machines he'd rather forget he ever flew. In the late thirties he was flying Vultees and Martin B-10 bombers with the Chinese against the Japanese, and then he got his hands on an old Curtiss Type III Hawk biplane fighter and fought some more. The Japanese overran their fields, or bombed them into ruins, and Tommy and his fellow pilots got the hell out of there before the Japanese made them guests for entertainment by torture. The Japanese loved etiquette, flowers, rock gardens, but most of all they loved torturing their prisoners.

But right now he was the center of attention in the clan. "Didn't you prove there wasn't any plane that couldn't be spun?" someone asked.

"That's what I heard," another pilot chimed in. "If Tommy couldn't spin it, he'd eat it."

Tommy Walker offered a huge grin with his memories. "Go on, boy. Tell the lady how it went." Tommy's grin widened. It's something special to be in your seventies, with every rating you ever had in flying for any and every kind of airplane, and be called "boy" by a man who was flying combat before you were born.

"Well, I didn't spin one of the Stinsons," Tommy said quickly, "and I didn't eat it, either."

"You back down, boy?"

"Hell, no," Tommy retorted. "If that thing was still flying when I got through with it, well, maybe then I would have chewed up on it a bit. I got a call from the Stinson people. They had trouble trying to spin their 105 model. This was in Oregon at the time I was testing a bunch of different ships. These people called me, and we talked about the 105 they'd built, and said it just wouldn't spin. I didn't really believe that, but it's the kind of challenge you just can't turn down. You know, I never found out *why* they said it wouldn't spin, or couldn't spin, but they'd also made this one of their big advertising gimmicks. This was about 1939 and the idea of an airplane that couldn't spin, or whip off into a spin no matter what you did with it, well, it had been talked about a lot, but the fact was that a lot of guys were killed in planes that people said couldn't spin and they spun right down into the ground. But I didn't know about the Stinson 105, and the company figured if they got this wild man, this hot-rock barnstormer and combat jock and test pilot, and if *he* couldn't spin their ship, they had some better advertising.

"The 105 had the seventy-five-horsepower Continental engine when I got my hands on it. The whole factory came out to watch the tests, because those people were really proud of the airplane. They had great hopes for it being a big seller.

"So I took it upstairs and I tried the regular spin routine. Full back on the controls so she pulled up as far as I could get her to go, and I kicked in rudder like crazy, and I was amazed, I mean, really amazed, because she just wouldn't spin. I could hardly believe it, but there I was, doing everything to dump into a spin, and she just mushed along.

"So I tried something else. Instead of pulling up, back, back on the elevator, I got into a steeper pitch attitude and I was about ten miles per hour above stall speed, and then I kicked her into a full-control-movement skid entry. I mean, I really booted that thing into the skid in the worst attitude I could get with that ship.

"For a few moments everything went crazy. I was trying to find out what in the hell the airplane was doing, because the controls were sloppy in my hands and the rudder pedals under my feet were like mush. I did everything possible to get control and then I turned to look behind me.

"Well, I still hadn't spun this thing, but I'd just about broken the airplane in half. I could see daylight where the rear half of the fuselage had just about busted loose. The connecting hinges were all broken and the back half of the airplane was slopping around like a flag in the wind. I could hardly believe it. I tried the controls again but it was a bad joke. This thing was falling out of the sky and here I am screwing around with the controls. Because no matter what I did the airplane was wallowing around and helpless. So there was only one thing to do. I kicked open the door and I bailed. In fact, that

P-38 "Lightning"

was my third emergency jump. The third 'caterpillar club' jump to save my life.''

Later, when Tommy was a lieutenant in the air force and doing some flight tests in the P-38, the big twin-boomed fighter with two Allison engines, he was all set to begin a series of spin tests. ''Jimmy Mattern came over,'' Tommy went on to the group and the woman who seemed hypnotized by all she was hearing. ''Now, Mattern was one of the really *great* test pilots, one of the top people over at Lockheed. He stood by the P-38 with me and he spoke quietly but earnestly. 'Listen, when you spin that ship,' he said, 'don't go over two turns. By the time you get to your second full turn, *get out* of the spin. Because if you don't, you'll find the thirty-eight starting to flatten out after the second turn. The nose comes up and you're going around just as flat as a pancake. By the time you're into your third or fourth turn, you can't get out of the airplane.'

''I blinked a couple of times and asked him why. He said to me, 'Because by that time the yoke is back full against your gut, and with all the dynamic forces holding it there, you'll never be able to push the yoke forward to get that nose down again. But if you *ever* do go beyond two turns, I'm telling you right now the only way you'll ever get out is with power. You'll find the rudders won't react, and then you've *got* to use power. By now you've got dead rudders and the yoke shoved against your body and that's when you go full bore. I mean everything you've got. Throttles *all* the way forward.' "

Tommy offered a half grin. "I took her up to twenty thousand feet. First shot in the spin, well, I always was crazy, I guess, so I let her rip right into the third turn. But with what Mattern had told me I was ready for this thing. As soon as I felt the back pressure increasing on the yoke, just like he'd said, I shoved the yoke forward and kicked in full opposite rudder, and bam, she came right out of the spin.

"So, what the hell, by now I'm hot snot, right? Hell, why not go for four turns? Back up to twenty thou and I kicked her into the spin, and let her go right into the fourth turn, and everything this guy Mattern had warned me about climbed right into the cockpit and crawled all over me.

"I eased the props forward so they could take—you know, they could absorb—the boost I was about to give them. I went to forty-five inches manifold pressure, and by God, it was just like the man said. Down we went spinning like crazy. The key was to go to full power with the *inside* engine. I was spinning to the left so I boosted just the left engine to full bore. That's the only way I ever came out of four-turn spins. I did it a bunch of times after that, but if Jimmy Mattern hadn't warned me about the problems I'd run into, and how to get out of them, I believe I would have had to leave that P-38 in the air, and I really wasn't looking forward to saving my hide with another emergency jump."

The silence didn't last long. "Dammit, Walker, did you ever fly anything you couldn't spin?"

"Or break in half trying?" another voice chimed in.

"What about the Ercoupe?" asked another pilot.

"Well," Tommy said slowly, "from everything I know, that's about the only ship that won't spin. I mean the original Ercoupe, that little job with twin rudders, but no rudder pedals in the airplane. It was crazy the way you flew it, but that design really worked. I mean, you don't have anything to do with your feet. No pedals down there. It was a real funny feeling. Like you don't have legs anymore. And the elevator travel was limited. But you *could* fly that little sucker through a really big barrel roll. I tried it again and again. It was sloppy, and when you came out, you dished out like crazy. I tried it with a whole bunch of these airplanes when I was testing them off the production line and I never did get one of them to spin. I even tried to loop." He laughed. "Tried it a whole bunch of times and they always fell down right between my legs.

"Let me say, as you people all know so well, that when you're doing a barrel roll the proper way, you're coordinating controls all the way through and that means you use your *feet*. Not in the Ercoupe. I'd get all the forward speed I could get and pull her up to the max and then bang over the yoke. Was it a real barrel roll? Well, it slopped around and sort of fell down like a sack of cement until you got the lift back to the wings. Not *my* kind of fun flying."

Tommy paused, then looked at the young reporter and back to me. "I'd like to add something that someone said before. It's not the big things that nail the experienced pilots. Almost always it's some stupid little thing you can't ever figure beforehand. It takes down the best pilots who ever lived."

The reporter regarded Tommy steadily. "Please," she asked quietly.

"Well, it was about Frank Hawks and the way he died. After he was gone we found out what had happened to an absolutely beautiful racing plane he had once had. Howell Miller had designed it and it was just a gorgeous ship. Big radial engine, a huge prop, gear came up. It was music and harmony and that sucker was built to *race*. It had over twelve hundred horsepower. They called it the *Time Flies* racer. They did their racing thing in it and a bunch of guys rebuilt it into a two-seat model, and then they called it the Hawks Military Racer HM-1. When they tested it on a straight and level run, it turned in just about 370 miles an hour at sea level, and that is some doing. Then Leigh Wade flew it in the 1938 Thompson race. It was a sort of vacation for Wade, because the ship didn't have enough fuel to fly the whole course with the throttle pegged all the way forward. He just put in an appearance.

"They wanted to complete some flight tests on the airplane and they brought in Earl Ortman to finish the job. Earl goes up to altitude and puts her into a dive, and at 425 miles an hour, that airplane came apart. I mean, it just about disintegrated, or exploded, whatever you want to call it. Earl got out okay; it was one hell of a jump, but he made it. Now, you know what went wrong?"

He looked about the room; everyone waited.

"There wasn't a damn thing wrong with that airplane. The engineers had stuck a fuel tank as a temporary move in the unoccupied rear seat. When Ortman got well into his dive, that airplane was way out of trim and that meant she was impossible to control from that moment on. The controls were literally jerked out of Ortman's hands and the ship ripped to pieces.

"A fuel tank in the backseat. That's all."

The talk turned to helicopters, with all the usual digs and nasty remarks about the rotary-wing jobs being "a bunch of loose parts in formation." Or "an optical illusion with sound effects" and the unkindest cut of all: "That whole thing is held together by just one big nut at the rotor. They call it the Jesus nut."

"Why?" asked the woman.

The pilot grinned at her. "Because if that nut ever comes loose, you can watch the rotor flying off, and right quick, you *know* you're going to meet the man upstairs. *That's* why!"

Laughter went about the room. "Hey, anybody here ever fly an autogyro?"

Several pilots stared at the speaker as if he was crazy. "Those things ain't airplanes," someone snorted.

"Ain't no helicopter, either," announced another.

"Then what is it?" came the expected question from the girl, writing furiously.

"It's a bastard stepchild, you might say," another pilot offered. "I flew one a couple of times. That was enough to add ten years to my age. Or take ten years off my life; you decide which. It's a Spanish design. This guy, de la Cierva, figures why build a machine that stalls? You know, like an airplane. So he takes off the wings—imagine that; he takes off the *wings*!—and he sticks a freewheeling rotor on top of what was a perfectly good airplane. He figures now he has autorotation *all* the time because that rotor is on its own. That means it can't stall.''

"Anything can stall," came the growl from uncounted throats.

"*I* didn't say it couldn't stall. This Spanish engineer, *he* says so. But do did Pitcairn and Kellet, and they built a bunch of them in this country, remember? Hell, back in 1939, they even started this crazy airmail delivery off the roof of the post office in Philadelphia. The pilot was a guy named John Miller. He fires her up and off he goes, and it's a real big deal, right? He flies six miles in six minutes, and you'd think the world was standing on its ear. From the post office to the local airport, right over the river in Camden. That's New Jersey.

"Now, don't get me wrong. I hate those things. Scare the hell out of me. They just don't *feel* like flying. But this John Miller, he's some kind of miracle man as a pilot. I mean, he did everything I figured the autogyro absolutely could not do. Miller was a test pilot and an airline pilot and I believe he could fly anything. But that autogyro, it tested him most of all. He was the first man to fly an autogyro clear across the whole United States, bless me if I know why—"

Fifty voices rang out as if rehearsed. "Because it was *there,* that's why!"

"Guess so. He also did aerobatics in that blamed thing. If I hadn't seen it with my own eyes, I still wouldn't believe it. That's when Wallace Kellet came along, and he's got this new autogyro, no wings at all. Let me correct something. The first autogyros, some of them, like the Spanish one, they had, well, sort of wings. Big stubs really, so they'd have extra lift. But Kellet, he went all the way. Not even a stub. By this time, Miller is all through running around the country and doing insane things in the older autogyro, he's flying for United Airlines, but Kellet talks him out of that job and says he *must* have him as his test pilot.

"They called the ship the KD-1. I mixed up some of the times here. It was this KD-1 that actually made the flights off the post office roof in Philadelphia. The government balked at this, but this guy, Kellet, he was a big shot and he knew the right people, and the government said, hell, give it a go. But not until you do dive tests.

"Miller said they were crazy as loons. Autogyros are *not* supposed to dive no more than a whale flies. But hell, he's a test pilot, and it's on the schedule, so he loads up the KD-1—they used to call her Katydid—with nearly four hundred pounds of sandbags and off he goes. It was stupid and he knew it. He comes down from about thirty-five hundred feet and that Katydid died right then and there. It looked like someone was throwing great big chunks of confetti through the air. It *disintegrated*. The rotor broke off in chunks and they went whirling around everywhere. And all this time, Miller is trying like mad to get the hell out of the thing. He's being banged around so bad he's cut and bleeding and every time he starts out the thing goes crazy in a different direction and slaps him right down again, and the ground is coming up awfully fast.

"This was dying time unless he got out. There was enough left of the rotor that Miller said later he was afraid the inner pieces, spinning like mad, was going to cut him up just like slicing a banana. And you know what was the most amazing thing of all? Since he couldn't get out to jump, he just sat back down again and he dove her steeper, he rammed the throttle just a bit forward, and he landed that damn thing! I never saw anything like it before and I don't expect I'll ever see it again."

Just about everyone in that room was wrung out; they were real-time listeners, and in their own way they were back in the cockpits with the pilots, living each experience. You can't help it. A man tells you how he grasps his control stick and your own fingers start to clench. Tommy Walker tells how he booted rudder to haul the big P-38 out of a dive, and legs started moving forward from the seated men. In their minds they were moving throttles and maneuvering; they were flying, with all the body English they could put into it.

Because they had been there, and they *knew*. Just about every one of them had in his time flown as a test pilot, and theirs was a brotherhood that didn't need talking about or explaining. You either knew it, understood it, loved it, or you just weren't part of the inner circle.

And this was just a part, one slice of the pie of test-pilot flying. They could have talked for days, for weeks, for months and they wouldn't have had to repeat a single thing, and still they would have left much of the test pilot story unknown.

Because by the period of the 1930s, the whole world of aviation had changed. Horsepower was way up over a thousand raging ponies in a single engine, and airplanes were flying with four, six, and eight engines, and their power was enormous. The fighters were tougher and faster. The big ships could fly thousands of miles nonstop, carrying huge loads of passengers and cargo. More and more men had come to brave the weather, to challenge the elements. They could communicate with one another now, they could fly along radio beams. They had pressurized cabins, and heat and air-conditioning, and bathrooms and smoking lounges in the big luxury ships.

But with all that they knew at this point, every step forward presented new problems, new dangers, and more demands for grueling tests in the air. The test pilot had been indispensable before; he was even more so now. Without the test pilot, trained and honed to unmatched skills and knowledge, progress in the air would have faltered everywhere.

No matter what the engineers did, or the scientists designed, or the production people built, there was always one acid test. You had to fly the airplane, and after you flew it and made sure it flew the way it was supposed to, and they fixed all sorts of things on them, *then* you got into the hairy side of flight testing, because you had to go beyond all the limits you had reached before.

Like dives.

The real killers of men.

Flutter Ain't No Butterfly

There are things in the sky eager and ready to punish pilots, to squeeze their bodies, stuff blood into their brains until their eyes are all red and ready to pop. Or invisible forces that grab a flier and squeeze him mercilessly until all of him turns to lead, like an elephant sitting on his chest, and he can't move even a finger. Those same forces drain blood from his head, because they make his heart and his blood so heavy the heart can't pump blood and the brain starts throwing in the towel, and a man loses his peripheral vision and everything goes gray and then black, and if he's lucky, the pilot lives to talk about it. These are the forces of gravity, and gravity, or its effects, can be increased enormously by centrifugal force. It's like being at the far end of a giant sling going around and around, faster and faster, as the g-forces load up on the pilot. You get this force when you make hard and tight turns in an airplane. You can do it in level flight by banging the ship over into a steep bank and hauling back on the stick so that the forces on the airplane increase the g-loading from "standing on the earth normal" to four, six, ten, or more times normal. That means that if you weigh two hundred pounds, when you're in a 10g turn you weigh two thousand pounds and you're really an unwilling passenger instead of a pilot. If you're lucky, you'll lose control of your body, because then your fist on the stick goes slack, like a rag dummy, and the airplane comes out of that crazy turn and the g-forces unload. The blood starts back up into your

188

brain and you come out with a headache, like someone stuffed a big cabbage inside your brain and everything hurts like hell.

In those days, when testing a new fighter plane—and the pilots were both military and civilian (company pilots or free-lancers)—you always took the airplane up high and nosed over and dove straight down, trying to get close to (but not hit) the planet below you. Faster and faster until the ship couldn't go any faster, and then you grabbed that stick, often with both hands, and you hauled back as hard as you could.

Well, the airplane was going straight down and now you were trying to bring it out of the dive, which meant you were really loading up on the g's. The pilot took a terrible beating from this sort of thing, blood might spurt from his nose and his mouth, the elephant was stomping all over him at this point, but it was doing the same thing with the airplane.

The trick was to see if the wings would stay on the airplane at the peak of the g-forces. Quite often they didn't. They would bust in half, or come apart in pieces, and then you were in a piece of junk in a berserk plunge toward the earth and your only hope of having dinner that night was to get *out* of that thing. Easier said than done. The air loads—the airstream winds screaming back—might pin you down like a fly jammed into a wall by a great big stickpin. There weren't any ejection seats in those days, so you had to try to fight your way out. And sometimes you couldn't. A lot of good men died that way.

More than the wings might come unglued. Those g-forces would break oil lines and fuel lines in the engine. The airplane's wings might stay on, but underneath that big engine cowl in front of the pilot, the lines were crumpling or snapping, and oil and gasoline dumped all over that hot engine and you had a hell of a fire on your hands—while you were still diving hell-bent for leather.

Engineers always tried to design and build their airplanes so that they were in perfect trim when the pilots went full bore. But aerodynamic loads were still largely a mystery, and what was like silk at two hundred or even three hundred miles per hour became madness at four hundred. The airplane is coming out of the sky like a shrieking banshee, and air loads up in front of it, and it can't get out of the way fast enough, so it applies tremendous turbulent forces on the machine. Shock waves bounce around like boulders, the wing and fuselage skin ripples like wind-driven water. Metal isn't supposed to do that, and often it crumpled and flew away from the airplane, and wings don't fly very well when their skin is gone and the ribs are exposed to the air.

Other times the airplane would build up the damnedest vibrations. Everything thrummed like ten thousand bass fiddles, a thrumming from a hundred thunderstorms, and it was scary music, because the pilot knew his ship was vibrating like mad, that the sound was resonating through the airplane and building up forces that were never meant to be. That kind of pressure could snap powerful metal like a brittle matchstick.

Then there was flutter. Innocuous-sounding thing, really. The airplane dove and everything was just fine and dandy, the wings stayed on, and the lines to the engine held fast, and the cockpit canopy (if there was one) didn't come unglued and fly away, the ship screamed down but the airplane was good and the pilot had control and by now he was grinning like a cat gorging on pure cream. Then the stick began to vibrate in his hand and trembling motions began to jiggle his feet on the rudder pedals. You couldn't *see* anything wrong, but it was there. It was flutter. That sounds like curtains blowing in a drift of air, or a flag waving idly in a breeze—and it's misleading. They should have called it something else. Like hammering, or anviling, or pounding, or just plain, *Look out!*

Because this kind of effect was the shock waves coming back from the propeller and the wings and they did curious things to the aerodynamic surfaces of the airplane. These are the ailerons on the far trailing edges of the wings. Also affected are the elevators hinged to the fixed horizontal tail, or the rudder hinged to the fixed vertical fin. These surfaces moved in flight, of course, because that's how a pilot controlled his airplane. But they were structurally weaker than the main body of the airplane, because instead of being an integral part of the structure, they were hinged, so they could move.

That was the weak point. Those hinges and connections. If there was any real kind of imbalance, the surfaces would begin to tremble and then to vibrate and then shake like mad. You never knew what was going to happen when you got into flutter. Oh, you knew you were in deep stuff, but *how* the ship would handle flutter was unpredictable, especially the first time. At times the ailerons, for example, would vibrate so violently the hinge connections became a sick joke, and the ailerons would rip off the airplane and vanish. They might also beat the hell out of the wing while they were in the departure mode, or whirl back and slam into the tail and do horrendous damage, and all the pilot could do was kill power and hope to slow down enough so he could crawl out of that thing and pray his parachute would open.

If the ailerons stayed on, the rudder might rip loose. Or the elevators. You never could tell. Sometimes the vibration and the flutter and the resonance all ganged up on that airplane and its scared-half-to-death pilot, and the whole tail would wrench violently, tearing off in a corkscrewing motion, and the pilot was trapped in his plane as it tumbled violently earthward. Maybe burning at the same time.

That's when the g-forces closed their traps again. Here's this test pilot in an airplane that's coming apart, he can't control it anymore, and he wants *out*. Despite the battering he's taking, he manages to get the canopy off the airplane (if it hasn't torn off, as many did); he still has to get out. But when the ship tumbles one way, it loads up on the pilot with 4 or 10 or 20g's and he's helpless because now that elephant has brought along some friends and a man can't do much when he weighs a ton or three. Then, suddenly, the airplane is cartwheeling or whirling, and the g-forces reverse. They go from positive g's (down from his head through his spine to his butt and his legs) or to negative g's (up from his feet to his butt and to his head and blood squashes like mercury into his brain). He's being banged around, and the g-loads are shifting so violently and so swiftly that inside his body he's being beaten to death from the weight of his blood and other body fluids. His stomach is a twisted mess and his lungs can't handle the loads, and now not only does he weigh whatever a man weighs when elephants are stomping hell out of him, but he's ripping apart inside of him and he can't get air into his lungs—

That's test flying. Or just one part of it. But it's enough

to make young men old in a matter of seconds. And more than one young pilot who went through something like this, and lived, would find, a few weeks later, that his thick, dark hair was just as white as fresh-fallen snow.

Take Jimmy Collins, for instance. Unlike many other pilots who flew for the military testing planes, or who were "company pilots" in the employ of big industrial firms, Collins was a free-lancer. He'd been an air cadet in the army, and he graduated way back in 1925, and he went through advanced flying courses, and one of his buddies who graduated with him was called by the nickname of Slim. His full name was Charles Augustus Lindbergh. After getting his wings, Jimmy Collins went on to fly pursuit ships (fighters) in the army and he honed his skills in this kind of airplane. Tough, powerful, agile; ships made to fly and fight, and be shot up and survive to fight some more.

After Collins left the military, he decided to work free-lance for the big aircraft companies. You needed a fighter plane, new and untried, with all sorts of vices cleverly concealed beneath its skin, you called on Jimmy Collins. You didn't have to tell him that he was hired to ride herd on trouble, because that's what testing new fighter planes was all about.

The way many pilots were picked out to fly for a company was to take it easy. They didn't send out stacks of résumés, because reputation was the big thing. The pilots would gather at favorite airfields and they all had two things in common as they slouched around coffee tables or sprawled in big chairs. The first thing was that they were skilled, experienced specialists. The second thing was easy to figure. While absorbing huge quantities of coffee and smoking cigarettes or cigars until the coffee shops and restaurants were blue with smoke, you knew they were unemployed. Sooner or later, they knew, something would turn up. If they got tired of coffee and the smoke got too heavy, you knew they hadn't earned any pay in a long time, and heads would often turn as the men instinctively looked at the telephone, waiting for word that a new and untried ship was looking for a pilot.

Jimmy Collins had gone a long time with his coffee mug before the telephone rang and the girl at the counter signaled to him. He grabbed the phone, and when he put it down, the quiet smile on his face told everyone else he'd nailed down a special job. "Big company," he said. "They build fighters and dive-bombers for the navy. They've got a new one for me."

"Fighter or bomber?" sang out one of the pilots.

Collins shrugged. "What's the difference? Its a demonstration deal."

Everyone laughed. There are a lot of meanings to the word "demonstration." This one was simple. Take up a new bomber to three or four miles, point it straight down, and keep on coming for at least ten thousand feet. What had Collins so relaxed was that they were hiring him to demonstrate an airplane already tested in its first models. This was their second model, it was on the production line, but they still needed to demonstrate to the navy that all the parts would hang together in the dive. The job was to take the ship right off the production line and do the dive test—oops, demonstration. That way the navy would know what to expect from the rest of the production line.

The company man on the phone, who hired pilots for these jobs, made it sound easy. And compared with other tests Jimmy Collins had done, it promised to be so. The ship was a stubby biplane with a reliable engine of seven hundred horsepower. In those days they called it a bomber fighter; today that same kind of design would be called a fighter bomber. No one really understands the twists in description, but it didn't really matter. Jimmy Collins liked the whole idea because he wouldn't be treading into ground never touched before. The airplane had been through its initial wringing out, and if it was in production, well, that was the icing on the cake.

Despite his experience and his skill, Collins would tell you right out he did *not* like test-diving experimental airplanes, especially fighters, for all the reasons (and more) we've just gone through. There was yet another reason. About six years before he got the call to do the dive demonstration, he'd taken on the job of putting an experimental fighter through its first dive tests. The designers raved about the airplane. "Strongest ship you ever saw. She'll take anything," they said.

Collins took her down and dove that airplane, as he later described the event, "to pieces." He said he'd never forget the "exploding crack of those wings tearing off." When this happened, his speed slowed like a truck crashing into a wall. The drag forces went clear out of sight and the deceleration was so abrupt that Collins's torso and his head snapped forward into the instrument panel. Still harnessed into the now wingless bomb (it wasn't an airplane anymore), he felt himself blacking out.

However long he remained unconscious, he came to with enough space beneath him and the ground to unbuckle and force his way out of the plummeting wreckage. He fell away, hauled on the ripcord, and loved the hammering sensation as the chute cracked open. But *this* trip wasn't over yet. As he began the drift to earth beneath the big white canopy over his head, his eyes widened and he looked up to see the still-disintegrating wreckage plunging right at him in the chute! He said that before he knew it he was into "heart-pound, breath-stop fear that that milling wreck" would plow right into his chute. The wreckage missed him by a distance he doesn't even want to think about and he didn't relax until he *heard* what was left of the airplane explode against the ground below.

On his way to do the "no problem" dive demonstration, Collins reviewed the events experienced by a friend, another "vagabond test pilot for hire," who'd gotten into one of those dive tests with a new ship. On his way down, the airplane held together—that is, the wings and the tail—but his propeller just went crazy. The prop tore itself apart and shed pieces like shrapnel and the pilot threw off his harness and struggled free of the gluelike grip of the screaming wind. He got out, all right, but he was still going so fast the wind snatched his body like a toy and smashed him against the tail of his airplane. He was a *very* lucky man. He broke both legs and one arm and banged hell out of his body, but despite the white-hot agony of broken bones he used his good arm to yank the ripcord. The opening shock of the parachute was like being dipped in molten iron. He hung, almost helpless in that chute, coming down, which gave him time to contemplate how the hell he was going to survive crashing into the ground with two broken legs, which could splinter the bones and turn his legs into scattered white sticks. But he made it, and he lay helpless on the ground, and people rushed to him, and he screamed in pain when they moved him. Then they did everything gently and got him to a hospital where he knew he was in for a long and painful stay, and that was *wonderful*. Because he was alive and his bones were knitting where they belonged.

What gnawed at Collins as he arrived at his new place of employment was the fact that this company had a whole bunch of very good test pilots. So why were they hiring *him*? The boss man laid it right on the line, said that their chief test pilot had already done more than a half-dozen steep dive tests and demos, and he was plumb worn out from it. The other men never had done the dives, and besides, if something went wrong this time, why lose one of their own? Collins nodded; from *their* viewpoint it made sense. It was lousy, but it made sense.

Very few free-lance test pilots—if any—made *real* money riding the dragon. For the ten days Collins would be flying the new bomber fighter, the company would pay him the magnificent sum of fifteen hundred bucks. If he went beyond the ten days, they'd slip him another thirty-five dollars a day. To sweeten the pot, they insured his life for fifteen grand so his widow and children wouldn't be left out in the street. And they'd also pay the insurance premiums so he could be taken care of if he crashed and they carried him off in a basket or a blanket, but still breathing.

At the factory where he reported, Collins detected a subtle but unmistakable smugness on the part of the company pilots who were *not* going to dive the new fighter. So he cornered their chief test pilot and asked him, "How come *you're* not diving this new ship?"

The chief test pilot looked him straight in the eye and admitted candidly that he'd managed to chisel his way out. Collins shrugged and asked to see the airplane. He liked what he saw. A stubby, powerful, sturdy airplane that sang strength. The bracing wires looked as if they could support the entire hangar that held the airplane. He talked with the mechanics who took care of the airplane and started feeling good about the whole affair. They believed in this ship.

The biggest change in the planes Collins had dove before

was inside the airplane. In his "old days," Collins and other pilots took up the airplane, shoved down the nose, and howled earthward. If the wings stayed on, they landed, got their money, and went home. Not anymore. Test piloting had gone through drastic changes. The cockpit, and other parts of the airplane, were loaded with recording instruments that registered just about everything that happened in the air. When the pilot landed, he didn't have to explain anything to anybody. The recording instruments had it all down, very pat. The fudge factor—a pilot holding back on one thing or another—was now history. The new systems recorded the times, acceleration, angle of dive, speed of dive, length of dive, and the times and g-force loadings during the pullout. It was like having Big Brother in the cockpit with you.

Collins checked the airplane thoroughly and then took her up for a familiarization flight. No fancy stuff, just getting the feel and heft of the tough bird. That went fine. With comfort in his mind, he began pushing the ship. He yanked and pulled and kicked and went through sharp control movements and maneuvers to see how she'd react when everything wasn't balanced so perfectly. He was alert for vibrations, rocking, oscillations, flutter, surging, sag, and delay—anything. After several days of these flights, pushing the airplane a bit deeper into the higher stress numbers of speed and abrupt maneuvers, he felt that both he and the new fighter were ready.

He did his first full dive from fifteen thousand feet, and then some more very careful dives, until he felt this thing was going to go as fast as it could, but still not in the vertical plunge. He dove at 320, then finally to 360 miles per hour. That ate up seven thousand feet of altitude. Pretty good.

Came the "big one" and he climbed to eighteen thousand feet. This time everything wasn't perfect. The little ship was a fighter and it climbed quickly. At eighteen thousand, Collins felt a bit woozy. He wasn't getting enough oxygen after the fast climb, he judged. And by now he knew enough about the airplane to figure he could get to its top diving speed without the engine howling.

He pulled back on power, rolled her over on her back, and pulled back on the stick to ease her into a vertical drop. She fell swiftly, and even with power well back, the engine thundered in his ears and the wind screamed past the struts and wire bracings. His indicated airspeed was just passing 380 miles per hour, but he was actually going much faster. At altitude, in thin air, the indications of airspeed are always less than the actual speed.

At an indicated airspeed of 395 miles per hour the needle pegged to a stop. He was now at nine thousand feet and had reached terminal velocity. The tremendous drag on the airplane wouldn't permit it to go any faster. But at 395 the noise was earsplitting. The wires were giving off a sirenlike scream.

He figured it was time to begin his pullout. He braced himself and caught a movement on the instrument panel. Not a needle in a gauge. *Something*. That didn't fit, but he had no more time to wonder because something else, he had no idea what it was, slammed into his face. For an instant an old fear stabbed icily through him as recollection of wings tearing off another airplane, years past, leaped unbidden to his thoughts. He turned a "fear-glazed" look at his wings. They were still there.

Sucking in air, Collins came back slowly and steadily on the stick to bring the howling fighter gently from its dive. Any abrupt maneuvers now, with pain still rocketing through his face and head, could take the airplane apart. Miraculously, the ship held together. He boomed upward, let the speed fade away in the climb, and leveled off.

Now he found out what had happened. The glass cover on an instrument had popped off from the tremendous vibration of the dive and the needle came with it, and either one or both of these "little things" had smacked him in the face. He took his time coming down, landed, and taxied back to the hangar. It *had* been that damn needle!

His job was done. The ship had held together and that was what counted. One more of those terrifying dives out of the way.

Jimmy Collins took another full-dive test soon afterward, another navy plane being wrung out for its manufacturer. He made that test on March 2, 1935.

He was killed in the test dive.

There are few fighter planes better known from the Second World War than the Lockheed P-38 Lightning, with its twin engines and big twin booms, and the honey sound of super-charged Allison engines that had the deep-throated purr of a seven-ton cat. The P-38 has so many "firsts" that simply to list them all would require a full chapter in this book. First American plane to shoot down a German aircraft during that war, it fought on just about every front where the American flag flew, and at war's end the big machine was the steed of choice for four of America's ten top fighter aces, including the two leading aces, Richard Bong and Tommy McGuire.

That's one side of the story. The other is that despite tremendous power, brilliant design, and the attention of a whole slew of test pilots—civilian, company, and military—the P-38 was one of the world's first airplanes to nudge its way into an enormous set of barrier reefs and baffling unknowns in the sky. It became the highwater mark for solving problems and led the way for later and superior fighters that owed their existence to the problems met by, and solved through, the P-38.

In 1937 the Army Air Corps cast a baleful eye on what was going on in Manchuria and China, where the Japanese military was slaughtering anyone who got in its way. Then they looked to Spain, where the Russians, Germans, and Italians were beginning a huge aerial brawl to serve as the testing grounds of their new air forces. The French and the British had also begun to spool up their war machines, and it was time for the United States to get off its duff and prepare for what a future enemy might throw *at us* in the air.

We want a new pursuit plane, stated the Air Corps, for "the interception and attack of hostile aircraft at high altitude." That was it. They wanted an interceptor that could get off the ground quickly, climb like a bat out of hell, and deliver withering firepower against incoming enemy bombers. The machine must be able to fly at 360 miles per hour at twenty thousand feet and, just over the treetops, bring in a guaranteed sizzling 290 miles per hour. And to top to the demanding specifications, the Air Corps added that once it reached twenty thousand feet the interceptor must be able to fly under maximum power for at least one hour—uninterrupted.

The Lockheed company in California jumped into the competition. Big move; Lockheed had never built a military airplane! Bob Gross, Lockheed president, gave the nod to H. L. Hibbard and Kelly Johnson. The designers groaned at the specs, decided right then and there that there wasn't an engine in the world that could handle the staggering demands, and opted for a revolutionary twin-engined design.

Right there the problems begin. You go to two engines and that meant weight. Weight meant high wing loadings and power loadings. A big fighter took a lot of pilot, so they added a tricycle landing gear to make ground handling and landing lots easier. The Model 22, as it became on the engineering boards, must fly so high and so fast that turbosuperchargers had to go in the airplane, and these could be placed in the large booms. Before they finished sketching and doodling, Hibbard and Kelly Johnson were looking at an interceptor (still called a fighter by most people) with a wingspan beyond fifty feet—not only revolutionary, to many people, it was crazy.

The weight of the machine kept going up, because if this thing was going to knock down enemy bombers, it needed massive firepower. Into the bathtub pilot nacelle between the two engines went four heavy machine guns and a wicked twenty-three millimeter Madsen cannon, and this combination would be many times more effective than most fighters with their wing-mounted weapons, because the P-38's terrific punch fired in a straight line from the nose, and it was firepower of the kind that not only could take a bomber apart with a short burst, but could punch holes in the sides of destroyers and cruisers at sea. Much later it did just that.

Bob Gross grabbed the blueprints and hied off to Wright Field in Ohio to sell his new product. It wasn't a record-breaking contract even if Lockheed prevailed, because the Air Corps was going to order no more than fifty interceptors from the competition winner. No one at Lockheed, including those who believed absolutely that Lockheed had the best design in the stable, ever thought Lockheed would build more than those fifty aircraft, which meant that the airplanes would be virtually hand-built.

In June of 1937 the army ordered the fifty fighters, beginning with the first experimental model. For a while Lockheed chewed on its fingernails, because the famed Grumman company on Long Island, New York, which had built one hell

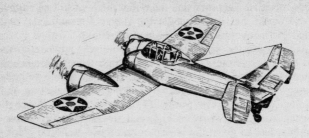

XP-50 (Navy Version)

of a lot of military airplanes, was also in the running with its XP-50 design.

Terry Treadwell, leading British aviation historian, in his superb book on the Grumman Ironworks, as the company was known, tags the fate of the competition to the XP-38.

Grumman's test pilot, Bob Hall, worked continuously on its development. Then one fateful day, Bob Hall decided to carry out some altitude tests. While flying over Long Island Sound, one of the turbosuperchargers exploded, cutting all the hydraulics to the landing gear. Although Hall managed to get the main gear down, he could not lower the nosewheel. After all attempts to get it down had failed, he decided to bail out of the aircraft, which he accomplished by jettisoning the canopy and sliding along the fuselage to the tail, then just stepping off! By doing this, he avoided hitting one of the projecting tail surfaces.

The army told Grumman to build another test model. But Grumman had Navy production contracts up the kazoo, and they told the Army, sure, "You give us a firm order for at least a thousand fighters and you've got a deal."

The Army told Grumman where *they* could get off, just like Bob Hall, and called Lockheed with the word to go ahead with the XP-38.

Anything as big, heavy, and complicated as the P-38 was going to have a rocky development road ahead of it. Even its first series of taxi tests, running the airplane back and forth on the runway to test brakes, propeller, and engine response to pilot controls and steering produced an ignominious halt to testing before the ship ever got off the ground.

The brakes had failed. It was that simple. You build an incredible, wonderful, powerful airplane, the best there is, and the damn brakes fail just moving from one part of the airport to another! It's one reason why designers and engineers almost always have prematurely gray hair or skulls as slick as billiard balls from tension.

On January 27, 1939, army test pilot Lieutenant Ben S. Kelsey, the appointed project test officer for the airplane, took up the XP-38 for its first test flight. *Trouble!* The control wheel vibrated wildly beneath his right hand. A flap linkage failed, and Kelsey brought the vibrating, shaking fighter back in for a hot landing sans flaps. Once again it was frustration time for the engineers (and the pilot): a piece of metal in the flap system had failed. It was that simple—if maddening to the people trying to get this hot new machine on its way.

In the next sixteen days the XP-38 spent just under twelve hours in the air, and the skies darkened, and the demons laughed as Kelsey took the P-38 on a record-breaking flight from California to Mitchel Field on Long Island. He refueled in Ohio. *And* he was holding an average of 340 miles per hour. He boomed out of Wright Field and was on final approach to Mitchel when an engine choked up at the worst possible moment. The XP-38 tore through a tree and whanged onto a golf course, ending the record flight in a ditch.

The XP-38 had the speed record, but the engineers and test pilots back at Lockheed were enraged. Tony LeVier, one of the greatest test pilots of all time, said it in no uncertain terms: "The Army grabbed our first P-38 to set a new transcontinental speed record. It was a grand idea, but the only

XP-38

thing a speed record would give them was some newspaper headlines for a day. . . . Instead of waiting a few weeks until we knew more about the airplane, they took it when it had hardly been tested . . . and the airplane fell short of the field and crashed. What did that do? It set the P-38 back about two years, because we had to start from scratch and build another prototype airplane and run a whole new test program, and as it was the best fighter airplane we had at that time, that incident may very well have lengthened the war.''

Big production contracts are mixed blessings. The XP-38 had crashed, but the opposition was at the bottom of Long Island Sound. Suddenly the needs of combat airpower heated up. The army ordered thirteen YP-38s for service testing. Five months later it wanted sixty-six more for operational service. ''I thought we were going to build fifty of these things,'' the engineers protested. ''If we build any more, we'll have to redesign the whole blamed airplane for a special production line.''

That's just what they had to do. In August of 1940 the

Army said change the designation. It's no longer an interceptor, it's a *fighter,* and we want another 607 of them.
Lockheed needed plant space desperately, and when in need
you take *anything.* The first production P-38s may well have
smelled like mash whiskey, because Lockheed bought a dis-
tillery and converted it to P-38 production.

At the same time everyone was wild about the new ship's
performance. The original specifications for a top speed at
altitude of 360 miles per hour went flying happily out the
window when Kelsey took the fighter up—a military airplane,
not a slimmed-down, souped-up racer—and turned in a blistering 413 mph.

The history of the P-38, as it would be with most new
high-performance fighters, is the running history of its test
pilots taking out the airplane for punishing maneuvers and
every test the engineers could dream up. The first real bear
were those turbosuperchargers. They surged and failed repeatedly, and Lockheed had fits with their manufacturer.

Then came the problem that drove engineers and pilots of
almost every really hot fighter mad with frustration. At high
speed, strange forces were hammering the P-38. Shock waves
bounced and flayed the airplane, and pilots came down white-
faced with reports of the tail fluttering so wild they could
hardly control the ship and were afraid of midair breakups.
The more flutter was encountered, the tougher became the
flight tests. The problems wouldn't go away. Diving into
higher-speed regimes, pilots found flutter and vibration so
severe that sometimes the airplane snatched control away
from the man inside.

So the engineers redistributed the elevator mass balances
by installing new fillets where the fuselage and leading edge
joined. They changed the angle of incidence of the entire
broad tailplane and sent the modified fighters back upstairs
for more tests. The changes had come none too soon.

Flutter had hammered the test ships so badly that several
P-38s diving at higher and higher speeds were literally torn
to pieces in the air. The replacement list for test pilots began
growing.

Flutter was a bitch to solve, but another gremlin showed
up as the P-38 moved into unexplored flight regimes, especially its tremendous diving speed. The second killer was

compressibility, also known as shock stall. These two effects were entirely unrelated. But to solve them meant putting test pilot lives on the line. The pilots were no strangers to flutter. As Lockheed compared its problems with the tests of other fighters, mostly single-engined models, they confirmed what they already suspected—that just about *everyone* was going bananas trying to solve flutter so violent it was ripping apart airplanes and killing pilots.

Few airplanes have ever been built as tough as the Republic P-47 Thunderbolt, yet it was already being looked at askance by its test pilots. When it went into high-speed dives, the pilots felt the effects of flutter, a rapid buildup of vibration, and before they could ease the Thunderbolt to slower and safer speeds, the rugged fighter would tear apart in flight.

There was the Curtiss SB2C Helldiver; in its SB2C-4 model it held honors as the toughest dive bomber of all World War II. But when the Helldiver started flying in its tests, flutter got so bad the airplane became notorious as a pilot killer. It was designed to *dive;* yet when it did, flutter and vibration ripped the aft end of the airplane away from the fuselage, literally wrenching it to shreds.

And there was the North American P-51 Mustang, a magnificent design with a sleek new laminar wing and stunning performance. The histories of these airplanes rarely discuss their bad times. George W. Gray wrote the outstanding study of NACA, *Frontiers of Flight* (published by Alfred A. Knopf), and set the record straight. "Several Mustangs had recently lost their tails. . . . Tail troubles similar to those that plagued the Mustang cropped up in other military airplanes. There was hardly a fighter that did not experience tail failure of one kind or another in the course of its evolution, as its speed was pushed up to and beyond the 400 miles per hour level."

As the P-38 variants came off the lines, there was one modification the Army refused to let Lockheed build into the airplane for its extreme-altitude operations—a pressurized cabin that would have eased breathing problems on very long-range missions as well as long flights where the inside-the-cockpit temperatures dropped to sixty degrees below zero and even lower. The P-38 was a magnificent airplane, but it had one of the worst heating systems ever put into *any* airplane. There were times when the ship flew beautifully, but the pilots were crippled by cold so severe they were forced to turn back from combat missions. Lockheed had the solution, but the brass refused the answer.

As the P-38 moved into combat, with its first mass operations in North Africa in the early winter of 1942, reports kept coming back to the States that the airplane was terrific; it flew as a fighter, escort fighter, reconnaissance plane, ground strafer, fighter bomber, and anything else that was needed. But amid these glowing reports were the disturbing notices that in high-speed dives, P-38 pilots found their airplanes uncontrollable and unable to survive the mysterious forces hammering the fighter.

General Carl Spaatz acknowledged the problems and dismissed them. Lockheed would get out the bugs. And in the meantime, he declared, ''I'd rather have an airplane that goes like hell and has a few things wrong with it than one that won't go like hell and has a few things wrong with it.''

Men stood on the flight line of Lockheed and looked to the sky. You couldn't mistake the sound. The eerie whine of the turbos, the howling of a P-38 moving *fast*. So fast that it was now in that ''hell envelope'' of a dive where the P-38 could become unpredictable. Then came a softer and infinitely more terrible sound: a dull, throbbing boom, an explosion, a rubbery crackling of noise. Hands pointed, and everyone saw a glistening in the sky, something twisting and tumbling as it fell.

Pieces of metal. What had been a full-bore diving P-38 rushing into what was now the dreaded *shock stall*. ''The dragon's claw of compressibility,'' some pilots called it.

''It resembled a giant phantom hand,'' said Tony LeVier, ''that seized the plane and sometimes shook it out of the pilot's control.''

George Gray in his NACA reports added: ''The behavior was new to pilots, terrifying, baffling. Several men, in putting this two-engine fighter through its diving maneuvers, underwent the experience: a sudden violent buffeting of the tail accompanied by a lunging and thrashing about of the plane, as though it were trying to free itself of invisible

P-38E

bonds, and then the maddening immobility of the controls, the refusal of the elevators to respond to the stick.''

Flutter would almost destroy the tail of any fighter caught in its grip. But compressibility was another kind of dragon. It would *sometimes* destroy the tail, or tear off a wing, or hammer the fuselage from the rest of the airplane, and sometimes it would do all these things all at the same time. And it had nothing to do with the structural ruggedness of the P-38, which was as tough a fighter as ever took to the air.

One P-38 in combat collided head-on with a Messerschmitt Me-109. When the shower of metal and flames whipped away, the Me-109 was a shattered wreck, wings gone, tumbling earthward. The P-38 was also a wreck, but it was a *flying* wreck—despite a dead engine with a prop ripped loose, despite severed horizontal tail, despite a shredded boom— and the pilot flew it home safely. After he landed, it was shoved aside as an unflyable wreck.

Yet even so rugged an airplane could be torn to pieces by compressibility. Lockheed knew that flutter wasn't the problem; that had been whipped. Long before its combat debut,

Lockheed had held its breath about the dangerous compressibility factor, recognized from the outset by Kelly Johnson.

Tremendous turbulence of the air hurled back from the wing at very high speeds was pounding the P-38 tail to destruction. The shock waves streaming back from the wing was locking the elevator in a steel vise from which the pilot was unable to free himself or his plane.

The Air Force told Lockheed to modify one airplane with a new tail. "Bend the booms upward," it said, "beginning immediately behind the coolant radiators, so that the entire tail will be thirty inches higher than the standard P-38. This will solve the problem."

Lockheed modified a P-38E as ordered. One of its chief test pilots, Ralph Virden, took the ship up to high altitude, pushed her into a dive, and "went for it." Compressibility grabbed him like a rat in a terrier's jaws. Ralph Virden died in that breakup.

The solution lay elsewhere. The tests had pretty well found the problem. Shock waves streaming back from the wing were *exceeding the speed of sound*. They distorted the air into raging rapids. At their worst these shock waves smashed into the tail with locomotive force. It was far beyond turbulence. The shock waves on the wing had become a standing force—as though they were made of steel—and air flowed about this force, whipped to frenzy and then slammed into the tail. Even the strongest metal built can take only so much. *Failure*.

A great many airplanes were lost, and literally dozens of pilots were killed, before Lockheed came up with the solution. And that was only after dozens of promising possibilities were studied by teams working seven days a week, hanging tight to the need at hand.

Lockheed had worked closely with NACA scientists in the great high-speed wind tunnel at Ames Laboratory. There, with a P-38 wing installed in the screaming gales, they tested a series of small dive flaps beneath the fighter's wings. The tests went on relentlessly, the underwing flaps moved from one position to another, and the forces of compressibility measured in exquisite detail. Finally they made their decision to install the dive flap permanently "thirty percent of the chord back from the leading edge of the wing." At

Lockheed, the flaps were installed beneath each wing, out-board of the main booms and just aft of the main structural beam.

To operate the flaps the pilot needed only to depress a button on his control yoke, and electric motors snapped the flaps downward into the airstream.

The solution was incredibly simple in its conception and implementation, as are the answers to most great problems, especially *after* thousands of people have worked day and night seeking the answer, and some of the best test pilots in the world, as well as combat fliers, have paid the ultimate price. And after the laboratory tests were completed, and after the dive flaps were installed, the test pilots took up the P-38s to high altitude and readied themselves for what could be their final dives. After all, there had been solutions before this moment, and they killed pilots just as quickly as the earliest days when the P-38s smashed into shock stall.

And it worked.

The dive flaps functioned in several ways, and one of the most important was that the system worked immediately, when the combat pilot needed it most.

The pilot, without moving his yoke, without moving the elevators in any way (and thereby not disturbing the angle of attack of the wing) could lower his dive flaps and instantly increase the lift of his wings. At high speeds this amounts to a tremendous force—the air-damning effect pushes more air down from the wing, and thereby increases the lift of the wing. The wing generates more lift without increasing the lift produced by the horizontal tail assembly—and the airplane is able to pull out from its dive.

An indication of just how serious was this problem—even aside from the P-38s that were lost in dives—was that experienced combat pilots in P-38s knew the tremendous dangers inherent in following German fighters in high-speed dives. For good reason, of course. Shortly after they raced earthward from high altitude in such dives their airplanes were ripped violently from their control. Some of the P-38s were in the grip of such terrible forces, they passed through the vertical into an outside loop at their greatest speeds, and total destruction was the inevitable result.

In those dives, when compressibility snapped its huge jaws

C-54

shut on the P-38s, the pilots faced three immediate problems: they could no longer maneuver in pursuit of the enemy, they could not hope to evade an enemy fighter after them, and they knew their airplane might suddenly and violently "come unglued."

Well, they had their answer in the dive flaps. It would solve *all* the problems remaining with control of the P-38 at any altitude.

Now, there's a final episode in this phase of the P-38's combat life that deserves our attention. The test pilots, dead and alive, had done their jobs. The scientists and engineers were proven completely successful. The factories were turning out the new dive flaps by the hundreds. But it was one thing to accomplish all the above and quite another to solve the problem with the P-38s already battling in Europe. *They* lacked the dive flaps, and they were still beset by the invisible dragons of compressibility. Lockheed put together several loads of dive-flap kits. The Pentagon ordered these rushed to England for installation on every P-38 in the theater. At the Lockheed plant, they were loaded into a waiting Douglas C-

Focke-Wulf Fw-200 "Kurier"

54 four-engined transport for the fastest possible movemen
to England. Once they were installed on the P-38s, the ai
combat situation would become a whole new ballgame.

Four hundred and twenty-five kits loaded in the cabin, th
C-54 began the long journey to England. It crossed the Unite
States, refueled, and began the final leg across the Atlantic

Messages don't always get through in wartime. Sometime
you pay grievously for that lack. Off the coast of England
a British pilot flying a Spitfire fighter was on high patrol. Fa
below him he saw a four-engined bomber with a single hig
tail. He knew the shape of that plane—a Focke-Wulf FW
200 Kurier, one of the four-engined German bombers so suc
cessful in sinking merchant ships. Down went the Spitfire
slicing in beautifully behind the Focke-Wulf. Heavy cannon
boomed from the Spitfire's wings and the big four-engine
plane burst into flames as it plunged into the Atlantic, alon
with the crew and 475 modification kits for the P-38.

By the time Lockheed was rolling its P-38J-25-LO mode
off the production line, with the dive flaps as standard equip
ment, approximately half of the nearly ten thousand P-38

built were either in service or in combat before that critical dive flap could be installed on the airplane.

Not too much later a new P-38L was rolling off the production lines at Lockheed and being rushed as quickly as possible to the front. The men receiving these new P-38L models thought the heavens had opened up to them and angels and sunshine had come to stay. For the pilots fighting over Europe, life had been as rough as any fighter pilots ever knew.

Art Heiden was a P-38 pilot fighting in Europe from the first dark days to the final ending of combat. Let Heiden finish this chapter:

Every airplane has one cross or another to bear. What happened in the early days with the P-38 in England, unquestionably, is that time when burdens were the greatest. . . .

New pilots made their attempts to go to altitude. This is what the curriculum called for and they gave it their best, but those early airplanes, the way they were set up, just wouldn't make it. There were disastrous incidents of ignition breakdown because of high-tension ignition leakage. The oxygen systems were woefully inadequate. This is what they put into the airplane and the pilot in the cockpit was stuck with what he had. It just wouldn't do the job. No one liked 30,000 feet anyway. There had been no training for it. There had never been any need for it. It was too cold and the windows frosted up.

All this piled up on the Eighth Air Force pilots, but there they were at 30,000 feet plus and sixty below zero. It was miserable.

Then things really started to come apart. Now, suddenly, superchargers were running away. They were blowing up engines on the basis of one engine blowup every seven hours. Intercoolers were separating the lead from the fuel and the result was lowered octane. Hands and feet were freezing; pilots were calling their airplanes airborne ice wagons and they were right. Frost on the windows got thicker than ever. The most disgusting of all was the leisurely way the German fighters made their getaways straight down.

Despite these revolting developments, the pilots of th
Eighth knew they could outturn, outclimb, outrun and out
fight anybody's airplane in the air, so they set about rect
fying their problems.

Every one of these problems was solved with the intro
duction of the P-38L.

Let me repeat this again and again. It can never b
emphasized too strongly! It makes up the gospel word.

The P-38L. Now, there was THE airplane.

Nothing, to those pilots, after the hard winter of 1943
44 could be more beautiful than a P-38L outrolling an
tailgating a German fighter straight down, following a spi
or a split-S or whatever gyration a startled, panicked an
doomed German might attempt to initiate. YOU JUS'
COULD NOT GET AWAY FROM THE P-38L. Whateve
the German could do, the American in the P-38L coul
do better.

It was easily among the greatest fighting machines eve
made.

Herb Fisher

For most of his life he was *the* man. Herbert O. Fisher, rotund and beefy with piercing eyes and a soft, laughing voice and the hands and senses of an angel come down to earth to fly with men. If anyone represents the best in what makes a test pilot, my lifetime friend Herb Fisher is that man. Likely he's not that well known to the American public weaned on high-publicity flights, and they never made a movie about him, but to the *other* test pilots, his peers, Herb Fisher was *it*.

The test pilot's test pilot.

Like so many in this game he learned to fly as a teenager. And like so many of the old-timers he got his first flight in an open cockpit with a barnstormer passing through Indianapolis, where he lived, and haunted the big open fields at the edge of the city where the barnstormers landed, and slept beneath the wings of their planes, and put on shows and gave rides before flying off to the next town. That's where it started.

No one could have predicted that this same excited kid would one day be praised by President Franklin Delano Roosevelt, who said: "God gave Herb the limitless courage, the steel nerves, the complete imperturbability in the cockpit that his job demands and I know his life will forever contain the undying love of the air."

I've known Herb Fisher for forty-six years. During that time everything they ever said about this man with the angel's touch on the controls and his way of making the most difficult tasks seem so easy is true. He *did* have magic in his hands. He could take the most cantankerous machine and turn it into an effortlessly soaring creature of the sky.

Shortly before I put these words to paper, Herb, well into his eighties, "went west." But he left a legacy I'm proud to bring to these pages.

To many people the test pilot must be a daredevil. Herb always looked and acted like a laid-back executive. The same man would shuck his business suit and make test flights with incredible ease; yet many of his tests were branded by other test pilots as "suicide." But Herb had more than flying skill. He was also a brilliant engineer and had a genius in things aerodynamic. Every move he made in the air was remarkably calm.

In his lifetime of flying just about every kind of airplane built, including some of the most dangerous high-speed fighters, Herb Fisher *never* had an accident. Just about impossible to believe, but true.

He followed the trail from awe-struck, barnstormer-riding kid to aviation cadet in the Army. Out of flight training he went straight into the 309th Observation Squadron, where he flew every kind of ship he could find. In between his military flights, he would rush off to commercial fields to take up private airplanes and commercial airliners. He was at home in anything he flew, and the siren song of flying the big airplanes—and getting into testing—brought him to the Curtiss-Wright Corporation in Buffalo, New York.

They sent him up with a check pilot to see how the new man would do. He came down with a job as production test pilot. Nothing sensational at the time. Production test pilot. You fly airplane after airplane, one after the other. As fast as they come off the line, untried and *maybe* true to their design, you take them up and run through the drill and do everything you can to discover and correct any problems before the ship goes on to the customer.

He was excited. He looked forward to production test flying, but just as quickly as he got the new job he was told he wouldn't be flying for a while. Dazed, he thought he'd been bounced. Not so; he'd have to wait a while. So Herb went enthusiastically into design, drafting, and engineering and got a terrific education in aerodynamics. He might have stayed in that job a lot longer, but the break came. A regular pilot called in sick. An airplane was behind schedule for delivery. An airplane? Good grief, it was a Navy dive-bomber!

"Can you fly that ship?" they asked him. Do birds sing? Do wolves howl? "Sure can," he said quietly. And he knew he could. In between his stints in engineering, after work and on weekends, Herb would sit for hours in the cockpits of different fighters and bombers, learning the controls, touching everything until he knew those airplanes blindfolded. Never mind that he'd never actually been off the ground in "that ship."

One hour after being called in from engineering, Herb had that dive-bomber at eighteen thousand feet for his first check-out flight. And as seems almost always to happen, on his *first* flight as a production test pilot, he ran into trouble.

The dive-bomber had a retractable landing gear actuated through a hydraulic system. A line had cracked open and all the hydraulic fluid was gone. No problem to Herb; this might be the first time he was flying this ship, but he *knew* the airplane. He released the emergency pump handle and began whanging away. He had to pump that blamed thing so many times to get the gear down he said "my arm ached for a week." But he brought that ship home for a feathery landing.

"Not many people really understand the production test work," Herb would explain patiently to new pilots. "It demands skill and patience. There's a tremendous responsibility here. One day a military pilot is going to fly in an airplane that one of us has tested. He accepts that we've done *our* job and this ship is safe for him to fly and a good value for the money our government paid for it. I want all of you to know what this really is. It call it the invisible responsibility."

We were flying one day in a warbird rebuilt from a World War II wreck, the kind of flying we both liked, which took Herb back to some of his most exciting times. "You know," he said casually, "those guys really had terrific enthusiasm. Most people don't understand this. Take the P-40 fighter, for example. Curtiss-Wright was turning out those things like they were doughnuts rolling off a conveyer belt in a bakery. And the P-40 was a powerful, big fighter. Our job was to make certain it was perfect when it left the factory.

"Everybody on our side in that war was in desperate need of those fighters. The British needed them, the Russians were screaming for them for ground-attack ships, and the Australians were beating down our doors to get them. So our pilots at the Buffalo factory flew P-40s *all* day. Often they flew them through the night. We all flew in sleet, rain, snow. You know the Buffalo weather, especially in winter. It's like Siberia, but we *had* to keep those fighters coming. No one had time to rest. We were bleary-eyed and exhausted, but there were always more planes to test."

In this particular job, Herb Fisher personally flew a total of 2,498 individual P-40 fighter planes, as a production and experimental (and combat) test pilot. Often he'd climb to twenty-five or thirty thousand feet in the airplane (without a supercharger other pilots said the P-40 just couldn't get that high: Herb did it as casually as an albatross gliding over the ocean) after his tests, and then, for the hell of it, he'd roll that P-40 over on her back, haul back on the control stick, and plunge for the earth with everything that P-40 had to give. You could hear his fighters screaming for miles.

There's an aside to this. Herb was ticked off that he hadn't reached 2,500 P-40 flights. We were together in Texas at a great annual bash of the Confederate Air Force when someone offered Herb his P-40. Herb snapped at the offer, and after years of never having seen the inside of a P-40, he took it off like he'd never stopped flying those things. That made 2,499, and still later, another pilot taxied up to where Herb was standing, in a Warhawk he'd rebuilt. "You want it?" he shouted to Herb.

He got Number 2,500 right then and there.

With Curtiss-Wright, Herb flew trainers, fighters, attack bombers, heavy bombers, dive-bombers, and transports. Strangely enough his only "real emergency" as a production test pilot came in an unarmed transport ship.

It was early 1942 and Herb was flying accelerated flight testing in one of the early-model C-46 Commando transports, a huge twin-engined job that had more power than a four-engined B-17 or B-24. Next to Herb in the cockpit was

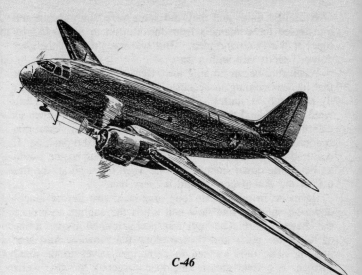

C-46

"Killer" Caldwell, a famed Australian fighter pilot who'd flown his P-40 in Africa against the Luftwaffe; Caldwell held down the copilot's job for this test.

The hydraulic system went kaput. Zero pressure. "We were able to get that landing gear partially down, but it wouldn't drop all the way into 'down and locked,'" Herb later reported. "If we touched down with the gear like that, she would have folded up like matchsticks. So we circled Buffalo for a while and tried every trick in the book to lock down the gear."

Nearly eight hours later they'd played out their bag of tricks. Herb had been flying the huge C-46 like a fighter. He made repeated steep dives and then pulled up sharply, hoping the g-forces would drag down the gear all the way and lock it into position.

Herb got on the radio to the company controllers. "Send me some tools up here for us to work on the hydraulics," he told them. They thought he'd flipped his lid. *Send up some tools?* Turns out it was a pretty good idea. They sent up a Stinson with a load of tools and another bunch of cans of hydraulic fluid, and they did some *very* fancy flying and transferred the containers from the Stinson to the C-46—by rope! It was a *terrific* idea. "But we never did get the gear down," Herb said with a grin.

When fuel began running low, Herb told the control tower that he was coming in because he *had* to. The C-46 doesn't fly very far on fumes. They rolled the crash trucks. Herb would try to land the ship with the gear 90 percent down as carefully as rolling an egg on the runway. As a last resort this sudden contact might bang the gear into its locked position. If not, and he was a better pilot than anyone dreamed, he would let her settle down smoothly. If he *wasn't* that good, the fire trucks and ambulances would be very busy.

He came in on a neat, long approach; just before touch-down he shut off fuel flow and killed the engines to reduce the chance of fire. The huge transport skimmed in over a line of telephone poles and floated along the runway. And kept floating. The tires seemed to paint themselves to the hard surface. A perfect grease job, done so gently the gear came up smooth and pretty right back into the wheel wells.

Metal scraped macadam. A howling screech burst through the air and sparks showered back like the Fourth of July. Thick clouds of smoke erupted from the engines. Men gasped. Someone shouted, "She's on fire!"

Not by a long shot. Herb wasn't missing a beat. Fully aware that the cascading sparks *could* start a fire, Herb yanked the fire-extinguisher handles the moment they touched down. Chemicals drenched the engines and sprayed back in a great mist. *That* was the smoke. For 750 feet the C-46 slid along on her belly as though this was the only way to land, and groaned to a halt.

"Herb brought that airplane in so clean and so smooth," related an amazed mechanic, "that there was hardly any damage. We could have just jacked up the ship, dropped the gear, hung two new props on that thing, and flown it away. Never saw anything like it in my life."

The Army took a long look at this superb pilot and judged his talents weren't being used to the fullest as a production test pilot. "Get him out into the field," the Pentagon said. "He can fly anything better than anyone else. That means he

can teach other people how to *really* fly their equipment."
Curtiss-Wright agreed. Besides, they'd been trying to figure
out a way to get Herb to the China-Burma India (CBI) Theater where the P-40 and the C-46 were in great use. The
C-46s were hauling supplies over the towering, dangerous
Himalayas, tallest mountains in the world and infamous as
the "Hump." They were proud to call themselves the Hump
pilots. They had a nonstop list of enemies. New airplanes,
Japanese fighters, terrible weather, god-awful mountains,
grievous maintenance, rotten airfields, even worse food—the
list seemed endless.

So Herb went off to Asia to become one of the rarest of
all test pilots—a civilian on military research missions in a
combat zone, with the Japanese enemy only too glad to shoot
at him. He made dozens of experimental flights (as a military
man he would have received credit for those flights as "missions in an enemy combat zone") in different C-46s over the
worst weather conditions in the world over the worst mountains in the world. The army had problems with the C-46.
She was a new and not-yet-proven ship, but had been rushed
to the combat zones where they needed her huge hauling
capacity. In between his "noncombat flights in a combat
zone" he personally trained hundreds of pilots in the big
transport. He showed them they were manhandling the airplane and were unaware of its best virtues. He taught by
demonstration. As fast as he completed his flights many of
the airplanes were modified at forward fields, and his recommendations went back to Buffalo to effect changes to the
planes still on the production lines.

Herb Fisher flew ninety-six "missions" in those unarmed
transports in skies infested with Japanese fighter planes, to
whom a transport was "meat on the table." He didn't receive
any ribbons or any medals or awards, but that didn't matter
to Herb. He was getting the job done, and all the accolades
he ever needed came in the skills he saw in the pilots who'd
been under his tutelage.

Flying and teaching in the huge C-46 was duck soup to
other jobs he tackled while in the CBI. Herb could fly a P-
40 with a skill other pilots considered nigh unto impossible.
So the army put the hand on his shoulder again, and Herb
was off to one Chinese airfield after another to visit P-40

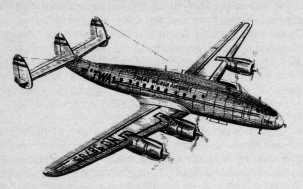

Constellation

fighter groups. He spent weeks telling the men what the P-40 could really do "if only you get to know this ship like the back of your hand. Then it'll fly for you like you never believed."

Talk was cheap. There were plenty of technical representatives from different companies overseas, most of them ground-bound. Herb figured the kids in those P-40s, against the sensationally maneuverable Japanese fighters, needed more than talk. He told the pilots he'd lead them into combat. Senior officers turned white. What Herb proposed was absolutely against every regulation they knew. If Washington found out, there'd be hell to pay.

"Don't tell them," Herb said, and climbed into a P-40. He flew another fifty missions in combat strikes against the Japanese in China. *Over* Japanese occupied territory.

A *civilian* fighter pilot!

If someone asked what was the most important thing Herb Fisher had done, likely they'd say that he helped to make life safer for millions of airline passengers (to say nothing about pilots and aircrews).

The war was ended just a bit over two years when Herb launched into a revolutionary flight test program that made the Himalaya circuits seem like duck soup. The "new age of air transport" was at hand. Douglas's C-54 was now the DC-4. Lockheed's Constellation, long and sleek, was in demand everywhere. Boeing had plans for big four-engined airliners to complement their huge Model 314 flying-boat airliners. Convair, Martin, and other manufacturers were rushing new designs, and the airlines were standing in line waiting for their desperately needed transports.

There was a major difference in the new ships. Many of them would feature pressurized cabins, enabling them to fly faster and more efficiently in the thinner air of high altitude. That paid its obvious dividends, but it also brought stark new problems to the fore. The most obvious was the possibility of sudden loss of cabin pressure, which in effect would "explode" the passengers from the low altitude of the cabin to the high altitude at which the airplane was flying. Being thrust from near sea level to twenty-five or thirty thousand feet is more than unnerving. To the elderly or the ill, it can be deadly. And there's no time to waste in getting down to lower altitudes.

The oxygen masks provided for each seat and passenger that we find in today's jetliners were a dream of the future. Getting an airliner down as quickly as possible was up to the pilots flying the airplane. And that created another problem. To get down quickly meant "dumping" the airplane, which meant dangerously high speeds for airplanes never intended to fly in fighter-descent fashion.

Herb Fisher and a group of engineers convened to discuss the problem and find its solution. When Herb finished his suggestions the assembled group looked at him as if he were mad. "Herb, you're crazy. You'd lose control faster than you could blink your eyes."

"You'd be heading right into an air breakup," added another.

Herb smiled, soft and gently. "It'll work. I'll fly it."

When they went their separate ways, two engineers stared

at one another in disbelief. "I can't believe he's really going to do this. *No* one's ever done it before."

"Yeah. For all the reasons we discussed."

"Can you imagine what it's going to be like up there when he reverses all four propellers at once?"

The engineers forecast disaster. But Herb was more than a pilot or even a test pilot; he was an engineer. He'd worked out the loads, pressures, deceleration, torque, and everything else that he and several other test pilots could envision. The top engineers at Curtiss-Wright looked at him in amazement. *They* understood all the factors he had already considered but their conclusion was different.

The major predictions were "out of control," "breakup in the air," and "she'll rip right out of your hands. What are you planning to do with a four-engine job—aerobatics?" But Herb had again and again studied propeller dynamics. The blades of a propeller "bite" into the air. The blades are set at such an angle that when the propeller spins rapidly, it creates a backward thrust that in turn pulls the airplane forward. With piston-engine airliners, the more powerful the engine and the faster the propeller blades turn, the faster the airplane can fly.

(After landing many pilots "reverse props." The blades twist around so that the thrust is sent forward to slow down the airplane, adding to braking power. But *never* in the air!)

A prop airliner like the DC-6 can descend only at a certain rate of speed or risk air-pressure overloads that can damage the airplane or even cause structural failure. By diving the airplane steeply with power cut all the way back, gear and flaps down, a DC-6 pilot can drop his big airplane between four and five thousand feet per minute. If an engine is burning, this means that from twenty thousand feet he'll need at least four or five minutes to reach low altitude, and he still has to get to an airport, make his approach and landing. Time runs out swiftly under those conditions.

But if this descent rate were speeded up, greatly, without damage to the airplane, and still under complete control, the time for descent could be reduced—and the safety factor increased.

The top brass at Curtiss-Wright listened to Herb and then

to the Doubting Thomases from engineering. They were torn. A vice-president leaned forward, nodding at Herb Fisher. "He's *never* been wrong." He smiled. "It's all yours, Herb."

The company got him a Douglas DC-4 airliner for the tests. Herb took the Douglas to high altitude and began nibbling at the effects of propeller reversal. He made more than 150 test descents, with varying power, angle of descent, and airspeed. Since he was in uncharted waters, he wouldn't dare just plunge in. He reversed one prop, then two, then three, always fighting the controls when the asymmetric thrust of different reversals tried to slew the ship out of his control. The engineers riding with him ran batteries of tests and recordings of aircraft stresses and other reactions to the rides that got pretty wild at different times, especially when the DC-4 would yaw wildly and try to throw its nose high.

After his preliminary tests ended—with Herb both sympathetic with but laughing at his green-faced engineers from the violent swaying motions of the DC-4—he moved into his own Phase II. He took the DC-4 to fifteen thousand feet. One by one he reversed and unreversed the four propellers to double-check. He was satisfied. He'd made every test he could imagine.

"Everyone in the airplane," he warned, "buckle up tight and hang on. We're going for the big one."

Herb took a deep breath, hands and feet poised on the controls, his body harness pulled tight, and in smooth motions hauled back on the throttles and slammed all four propellers simultaneously into full reversal.

For a strange, never-before-experienced moment, the big transport trembled from nose to tail, through the wings. Herb was surprised at the gentleness of the deceleration. Instead of an abrupt slam forward, the transport trembled, like a dog lazily shaking water from its body, and then began slowing, decelerating at a greater rate as though it were plowing into thick, molasseslike air.

The airspeed dropped to a comfortable, fully controllable 150 mph and Herb was on his way downstairs with a smooth, steady descent rate of seven thousand feet per minute, almost twice as fast as he had ever come down in a DC-4 prior to this test.

Behind him he could hear his engineers shouting with jubilation. The descent was perfect!

When the test ended, aviation had a powerful new safety maneuver available to its aircraft. The propeller-reversal maneuver became standard throughout the world as an emergency measure, and fully accepted practice after landing. An airliner landing on a slick runway was in trouble using its brakes, but with prop reversal the effects of *air* braking slowed down the ship without skidding out of control.

By 1947, propeller-driven airplanes were flying so fast that their propellers were actually getting in the way of additional speed. The big, whirling blades simply couldn't move air fast enough and it seemed the prop fighters had finally reached their limits.

Engineers designed new propellers—transsonic and supersonic props that spun so fast the blade tips were turning faster than the speed of sound. It helped (and created a terrific racket) to increase speed slightly, but few pilots wanted even to get into an airplane with the experimental propellers. No one knew what they would do under the tremendous loads of high-speed flight. Everyone remembered flutter and shock stall, memories sharp and clear of men dying.

There was only one way to find out—dive the airplanes with the new props as fast as they could possibly go. But most test pilots waved off the offers to take up the modified ships. The new blades were so thin and sharp that you could *see* them flutter when they ran up the engines to high power, standing stock-still on the ground.

The same message went through channels. "Get Herb Fisher."

Herb listened to all the dire warnings, then nodded. "I'll do it." That was his entire message. *I'll do it.* The mark of the gentle test pilot.

"The trick was to feed power to the engine *very* slowly and carefully," Herb explained to me. "On takeoff, if I accelerated the engine too rapidly, well, those blades would flutter and bend madly just like a handsaw. And if that happened, I'd never obtain enough forward thrust even to take off. I'd go right off the runway into the boonies. Sort of messes up your lunch. And when everything went right in the big P-47 we were using for the tests with the supersonic blades, well, I needed every foot of the nine thousand feet of runway we had available."

He smiled as he thought of the test flights. "There was another problem."

"Ain't there always?" I asked him.

Again that quiet smile. "Sure. The engineers figured that after eighteen minutes of fluttering, those blades would simply go to pieces. The metal would fail and the whole ball of wax would just disintegrate. That can cause you some unpleasant moments in the air. . . ."

The flight tests were intended to move the supersonic prop blades through the air at the highest speeds the fighter could fly. Herb and the engineers agreed that the safest way to run the tests was to go to full throttle as soon as possible after takeoff and keep the throttle cobbed all the way forward. This would impose tremendous loads on the propellers, and the test plane was packed with instruments to record the violence going on a few feet forward of where Herb would be sitting in the cockpit.

The test program called for Herb to make 250 dives at the greatest speed the airplane would give him. At the highest speed the big P-47 would be thrashing its way through conditions of severe compressibility, flying faster than it had ever been built to fly, and anything could happen. Normally, the big R2800 engines delivered 2,200 horsepower. Herb told his engineers to modify the engines to use a water-injection system to increase his power to 2,750 horsepower both during the level and the highest-speed dives.

Herb knew what might happen. Compressibility shock waves might snap off a wing or rip the tail from the airplane. Or those blades might disintegrate with such violence they would be screaming buzzsaws slicing into the airplane.

Herb listened to the dire warnings and nodded. The time for talk was over.

For these tests, Herb climbed out from the Curtiss-Wright Field at Caldwell, New Jersey, and headed for Allentown or Reading, Pennsylvania. Anywhere from thirty-five to thirty-seven thousand feet high, he would call Airway Traffic Control (that was the name then), already notified of the planned test, tell them where he was and that he was ready for his test run. All air-traffic-control centers were alerted and they in turn notified all aircraft to be on the alert. Not that *they* would be flying seven miles high, but Herb would be coming down to twenty thousand feet, and that *was* air traffic height, and if something went wrong, he might be coming down like a bat on fire through other traffic. In any event, once he was on his speed run, he'd be too busy to spend a second *looking out* from the Thunderbolt.

When he started a dive over Reading, Pennsylvania, by the time he completed his speed-power calibration test run, he would have raced back over New Jersey, flashed over New York, streaked across Long Island, and flown over Block Island. Just several hundred miles for the one test run.

One of the ruling factors that determined the height for pull-out-and-fly-level was the measurement of the speed of sound. It depends upon several variables, not the least of which is the temperature of the air. You can't just say, well, fly at an exact altitude of twenty thousand feet above sea level and you've got your mark. Real life (in test flying especially) doesn't work that way, because the pressure at twenty thousand feet is itself a variable. It changes with the temperature of air, and it won't be the same in winter as it is in summer. A fractional difference to be sure, but without exacting measurements the extraordinary and dangerous tests Herb would fly would lose their value.

So he had to determine the exact density altitude of twenty thousand feet as he climbed to start-the-dive altitude. This might on one day be 19,286 feet as measured above mean sea level. Once he had that number down pat, Herb would come out of his dive and level off *exactly* at 19,286 feet (if that was the measurement determined on the way up) and then *hold* that altitude as the P-47 went screaming through the sky. Never mind updrafts and downdrafts and bumps and eddies; to hold that altitude was everything.

On these flights, Herb had company in his cockpit. There were the normal instruments that told him of his flight performance, as well as instruments for engine and propeller performance. He also studied a new bank of instruments that ascertained by a hand-held computer (mechanical, not electronic), told him where, when, and how he was to obtain the measurements required.

We'll use that figure of 19,286 feet as the density-altitude measurement for twenty thousand feet above mean sea level. . . .

At thirty-five thousand feet, Herb leveled off and ran another complete check of his aircraft and instruments. Completing his checklist, he then activated the water-injection controls to pull maximum power from the engine, turbosupercharger howling at full speed. The throttle went all the way forward, he closed the engine cowl flaps to reduce drag, triple-checked his canopy lock, made a final radio check, turned on a photo recorder that would register just about everything happening to the airplane (and some of the things happening to the pilot). Now, if everything was right (and he was going to do this 250 times!), he would start down.

We can, with a bit of license, join Herb in the cockpit. . . .

Everything's ready for the dive. Herb calls mission control that he's checked everything, he's been holding level at thirty-five thousand feet and in thirty seconds he'll start down. The huge engine, along with the turbosupercharger and water injection, is screaming at full blast. The thirty seconds reach the countdown and Herb pushes forward slowly on the stick, letting the airplane nose over gently. His feet are as sensitive as a cat walking on hot coals, so he'll keep the ball center in the middle of his "no yaw, no skid" instrument. Finally, coming down straight and true and accelerating like a boulder falling off a cliff, he dives at a steady angle of exactly forty-five degrees.

The Thunderbolt winds up in a furious acceleration and a howling cyclone of wind about eight times the speed of a hurricane pounds him along with the explosive roar of the engine. The dials before Herb seem to have gone mad. The altimeter needle unwinds steadily but so fast it seems its spring has broken. His VSI—vertical speed indicator—holds steady, then continues to show increasing rate of descent. His airspeed indicator comes around the dial; other instruments show their reaction to the plunge. The needle indicates three, four, and five hundred miles per hour and still the airplane accelerates and the noise is now impossible, a constant roaring explosion about and within the airplane. Even through

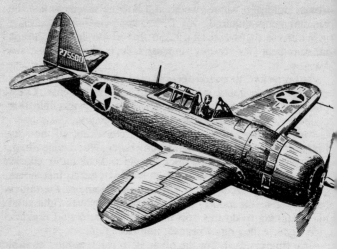

Thunderbolt

his earphones Herb hears, almost with pain, the screaming roar of wind.

Through the first five thousand feet of the dive, he's rechecking everything in the cockpit, including his engine instruments. Such references are critical—manifold pressure, RPM, oil temperature, cylinder head temperature, oil pressure, fuel flow. This is that period when he makes absolutely certain everything is "in the green" and its a *go* to continue the test. Now, at thirty thousand feet, he commits. If *anything* is wrong at this point, he'll come off the power and cancel the test.

Everything stays "in the green." Herb continues down, the P-47 still increasing its speed, the wind louder than before. Now he can *feel* the first touch of the dragon's mighty jaws, the sharp teeth of compressibility. If Herb could see the shock waves hammering against and hurling off the airplane, he would see steel bands of force that, if he makes a single mistake, *will* tear him apart.

The Thunderbolt is being shaken madly. It vibrates from nose to tail, and his body feels the effects of severe buffeting.

Herb is a big man and he needs all his strength to keep the maddened Thunderbolt from ripping away from his control. He feels he's in an old truck pounding along over railroad ties at a hundred miles an hour. The world has gone mad with vibrating, shaking, buffeting forces against the airplane. Somewhere between thirty thousand and twenty thousand feet the big fighter hits its maximum speed. Herb's eyes flick to the ASI (Air Speed Indicator) and he sees a frightening number—he's flying faster than 630 miles per hour!

Whatever he did before, Herb must now exceed with precise control of the howling Thunderbolt. When he pulls out of the insane dive, he cannot be more than fifty feet above or below the required density altitude of 19,286 feet as corrected on his altimeter. If he exceeds this margin and goes to fifty-one feet too high or too low, the value of the test is lost, and he must cancel. But he doesn't. He pegs the altimeter where it belongs and hangs on like glue.

All this has been but a prelude to an even more incredible requirement. After he levels out he *must* hold the Thunderbolt at maximum power while it loses some speed from the dive. This is a constant deceleration and adds more forces to the movement of the machine he's fighting to hold as steady as a rock. Now the speed is down and the airplane is flying with the greatest speed possible from the engine and the new propeller. This is *now* the critical test phase. This is when the photo recorder proves just how precisely Herb is flying this juggernaut because it is recording on film the readings of fifty separate instruments!

For the next two hundred miles Herb must keep this howling fighter from climbing or descending more than five feet from the start of the level run.

Five feet; not one inch more up or down.

That's like asking a racecar driver to speed at two hundred miles per hour over a winding, twisting, bumpy track and not lose or gain at any time more than one-one-hundredth of one mile per hour!

And he did this . . . this incredible test run . . . 250 times.

I knew the odds against going through this precision madness without *something* coming unglued, but it was almost as difficult as the test runs to get a report of any problem from Herb. Finally, he relented and admitted a few "tiny things went a bit the wrong way."

"Well, wait one," I broke in. "I'd like to hear from you what *you* consider the most dangerous incident in all your years upstairs. That includes China in the C-46s and the P-40s."

"The Thunderbolt dives," he said, nodding. "Had to be. We were really covering ground that no one had ever even thought of before, which means you can't prepare for what may happen. Aside from sitting carefully on the point of a needle so you *know* you're alert."

Herb had his own way with words. "Remember," he went on, "that these tests were really for testing those new props. Well, we had one instrument that measured the prop *thrust* throughout the flights. It was really amazing. The instrumentation was built into the engine. It was precise, it was absolutely accurate, it was a tribute to the men who designed and built it. It operated internally under severe oil pressure, oh, several hundred pounds every square inch. Well, one day, there I was, diving faster than six hundred miles per hour, when . . ."

That was a very calm "Well . . ." for what happened. He was coming down like Hogan's Goat when the only external high-pressure oil lines that led toward the propeller suddenly broke. Untold gallons of heavy black oil used for the measurements sprayed forward out of the engine, directly into that knife-bladed new propeller.

Nothing stays *forward* very long at five hundred miles per hour or so. Instantly, the terrific windblast and the propeller blast combined, hurled the jet of oil backward in the form of a solid sheet. It might as well have been liquid concrete. And just as quickly as it came back it smeared that oil thickly all over the canopy of the fighter, as if someone had painted the Plexiglas an opaque black.

Troubles amassed with explosive speed. Herb couldn't see out of the airplane; in almost the same moment he got his new canopy paint job the hot oil exploded back to spray *into the cockpit*. Immediately it smeared across all the instruments. Now Herb couldn't see out of the airplane, he couldn't see his instruments to control the airplane, and he was rocketing across Long Island at maximum speed. He had no way of knowing whether he was climbing, or diving, or rolling over on his back.

That's enough for any pilot to kill power and get the hell out of there as quickly as the airplane will let him. Herb knew he was on the thinnest edge of an erupting fire. But he stayed with the airplane, planning to hang on as long as he could—and in the next instant heavy black smoke poured thickly into the cockpit. Oxygen mask or no, in seconds Herb was gasping and choking. The smoke was so thick and being swirled about so violently it was getting under the mask. He knew he had to have fresh air immediately or he'd be unconscious. He started to come back on the throttle and his own body betrayed him. A violent wave of nausea had his arms and hands in a spasm of pain.

He had to have air—because at this moment he knew death had jumped into the cockpit with him. *But* . . . he was flying so fast that if he opened the cockpit canopy, the cyclonic force of the wind would blast with steel fists into the cockpit. Still, there really was only one thing to do and it was a last-ditch, desperate measure.

He yanked back the canopy. The explosion deafened him and hammered his body with a hundred heavy clubs. In an instant, the cyclone atomized the oil and whipped it everywhere about the cockpit. Thick oil was over *everything*—inside the cockpit, on his controls, the floor, and stabbing with agony into his eyes like burning coals.

By now he'd yanked back on the throttle and he was slowing rapidly. The canopy was still there. He slammed it closed so that he could try to clear his eyes.

It didn't work well. Whatever he saw was through pain and blur. He didn't dare start down with the plane. Whenever he turned the Thunderbolt and pulled back on the canopy, trying to see outside, oil again burst into his face and eyes. His eyes by now were puffed and swollen. They burned terribly. He held the controls as best he could and groped for his radio. By incredible good fortune he was over his home field at Caldwell. He got the tower on the radio, told them that he had an oil-line failure and would soon be out of oil, and he had to get down at once.

He could barely make out the field far below him. Twice he made wide circles around Caldwell, trying to regain his sight, flying more on instinct than anything else, able to snatch only glances out of the cockpit by looking backward.

He was on his third pass when his earphones crackled with a frightened voice. "Herb, you're on fire! *You're on fire!*"

He hadn't yet seen any flames but then he could hardly see as it was, and he didn't doubt that even the tough Thunderbolt might be burning. He was running out of time.

By now, in his descending turns, he was too low to bail out. He might climb to a higher altitude—in the Thunderbolt all he needed to do was haul back on the stick and he'd have enough height to jump. But his test pilot's instincts were calling him: *save the ship.* There was always the chance it might crash, pilotless, into homes and kill people. In the back of his mind was the thought that the loss of the ship would delay the program for months.

But he knew he was out of time. "Make your decision!" he shouted in his mind. All right; he'd belly in the Thunderbolt. He hated that choice but there wasn't any other.

Again, he yanked open the canopy. The wind howled in, tore the headphones from his ears, and flung them away from the fighter. Now he had no communication with the ground! His instruments were all still covered with oil muck as were the entire windshield and the canopy. He closed the canopy again.

"Time's up." The words came quietly and unbidden to his mind.

He called on every bit of his superb skills. Seeing through a black haze, he aimed the big fighter in the general direction of the field as he came around for the last time. He came back some more on the throttle and let the crippled airplane sink toward the earth. To eyewitnesses on the ground the Thunderbolt was a terrible mess, stained with oil, smoking, burning.

His instincts and experience told him by feel what his eyes couldn't see. His engine oil was all gone. Oil pressure was down to zero. He felt for the fuel selector and pushed it to off. He cut the ignition.

Now he was absolutely blind and he flew by feeling the airplane dropping. With some luck, he believed, he might be able to hit some part of the airport. Suddenly, on impulse, his hand shot out to hit the gear handle. He still rebelled at the idea of a belly landing. He felt the gear dropping, the airplane's shudders telling him what was happening, and finally he felt the solid bang as the two main gears locked down in position. He braced himself for impact, knowing it might be the last thing he'd ever feel in this life.

Seconds later the Thunderbolt lurched. Again he braced himself for the crash that would follow when the fighter hit again. *It didn't.*

He had made a perfect three-point landing and the Thunderbolt was rolling straight down the runway, with the disbelieving Herb Fisher working the brakes carefully; then aware that this was crazy, he slammed on the brakes. Was he heading straight anymore? He didn't know. Just get this thing to a stop!

The Thunderbolt stopped. Coughing and choking, he threw off his seat belt and shoulder harness, hauled back the canopy. Instantly he climbed from the cockpit, *feeling* the wing beneath his feet. He slid to the ground and ran blindly from the fighter, expecting the fiery blast of an explosion at any second.

He heard the scream of fire engines and crash trucks. Stumbling, running, he felt hands grasp his arms, people shouting at him, leading him away from the smoking fighter. He looked as if he'd been dipped and redipped in oil. Medics attended immediately to his eyes. His eyes still hurt, but he could see. And the first thing he saw was this enormous swath of oil, from *his* airplane, covering the runway.

He still couldn't believe—and these feelings were shared by everyone involved—that he was down safely and without a scratch to the airplane.

Herb Fisher went on from pushing heavy transports over the Hump to fighting the Japanese in P-40s and back to his beloved test flying and then diving Thunderbolts in the grueling propeller tests. He completed the Thunderbolt program to climb into the cockpits of our new jet fighters and bombers. He was one of the first pilots to test-fly the revolutionary British Comet jet airliner. Then he became one of the first pilots to fly the Boeing 707, Douglas DC-8, Convair 880, French Caravelle, and Lockheed Jetstar. He test-flew the Morane-Saulnier twinjet executive transport, the Vickers Viscount and Vanguard, Bristol Britannia, Lockheed Electra, and Fairchild F-27 turboprop transports. He made test evaluations

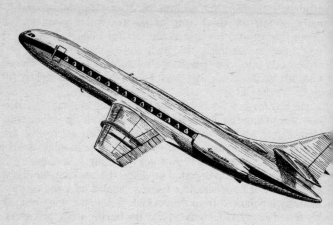

Caravelle

on almost every type of airplane that could fly, from lithe sailplanes to monstrous jet bombers, from his favorite P-40 to the Japanese Zero.

There was other flying. As a member of the famed Fireball Squadron made up of Herb Fisher and two close friends, skilled aerobatic pilots, he performed stunning aerial formation flying for millions of awed spectators. He did special aerobatic demos for the presidents of a dozen countries, cut sky capers for visiting international delegations, and once nearly blew away the shiny top hats of a Yugoslavian delegation visiting the United States. That scared the daylights out of the American officials—the Yugoslavs loved it.

When Herb Fisher made that last flight, gone west, and left this world forever a few months ago, there is likely one thing that he didn't do. I don't believe that even Herb Fisher could have counted that high.

Counted all the friends he left behind in *this* world.

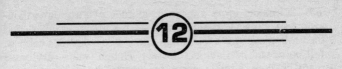

Nix Mach

It has been repeated ad infinitum that the P-38 and several other of the hottest fighters of World War II reached supersonic speeds by diving at full power from the highest altitudes possible. Such stories persist because so many men really believed they had performed the impossible. And impossible it was, no matter how skilled, how experienced, how believing were the pilots and other people involved. This was one chapter of aviation history about which Herb Fisher often beat me around the head and shoulders, and I guess it's time to once and for all set the record straight.

Because if anyone was going to take a powerful brute of a piston-engined fighter—with 2,750 horsepower and all the freedom to do whatever he wanted to in that airplane—it was Herb Fisher. So, for the record, it never happened and this is despite *official* claims issued to that effect by the Pentagon, by different aircraft companies, and by the pilots involved. There were pilots who believed they had smashed right through the sound barrier because people on the ground, watching as the fighter ripped overhead, said they absolutely heard the sonic booms created by the airplanes.

Pilots often referred to airspeed indicator readings of seven hundred miles per hour and greater, which "proved" that at high altitude, right after starting their vertical plunges, they had gone right past the speed of sound.

The first recorded instance of a "supersonic flight" took place when Colonel Cass Hough of the Eighth Air Force took a P-38G model up to a recorded altitude of forty-three thousand feet, cruised straight and level for fifteen minutes, and then rolled over for a maximum-effort dive—throttles cobbed, full bore, and into vertical descent. Hough was a *very* brave man; he dove straight down for twenty-five thousand feet, ran into the violence of compressibility effects, found the control yoke useless, and brought the fighter out by trimming madly with the stabilizer.

Now, it wasn't Cass Hough who laid claim to the supersonic speed. It was an enthusiastic public relations officer in the Pentagon who apparently didn't know the difference between Mach numbers (Mach 1 is the speed of sound, at any altitude) and the bow wake of a speedboat. In fact, the Pentagon official stated that Hough had pulled out of the dive at 780 miles per hour. Well, that's supersonic, all right, and at any altitude (on a standard day at sea level the speed of sound, Mach 1, is a rounded-out number of 764 miles per hour).

There was a real problem here. No one had any way of measuring accurately the speed of the airplane. The airspeed instruments, under the shock waves of compressibility, were a mess. Nevertheless, heartened by his achievement, Hough went up a few weeks later in a P-47 and, at thirty-nine thousand feet, started down again under full bore. And once again the "faster than sound" stories began blowing in the wind. This time Republic Aviation, manufacturer of the P-47, sounded the trumpet call by claiming a diving speed of 780 miles per hour.

There was more to come. The Army Air Forces reported that Colonel Ben Kelsey (who tested the first XP-38) had hit 750 miles per hour in *his* dives. By now the word was everywhere, but at Lockheed, Tony LeVier and other test pilots, who were doing some of the hairiest test dives of all time, viewed the reports of supersonic dives with open scorn.

Many years later, in 1971, a Colonel Yahne reported that he had barely escaped with his life in a screaming dive in a P-38, and that he'd ripped right through the speed of sound. In the process the effects of compressibility tore apart the airplane. Yahne managed to survive the complete disintegration of his P-38, fell clear, and waited until his body slowed in descent to open his parachute. Witnesses on the ground

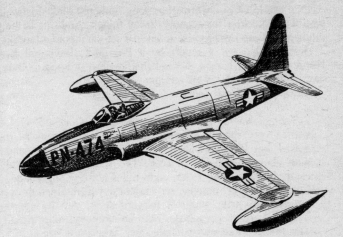

P-80 Shooting Star

confirmed the "sonic booms" of his diving airplane. But at that time just about the only sonic booms being heard anywhere in the world were from diving V-2 rockets into London and Antwerp and those were at speeds of 2,100 to 2,400 miles per hour.

No one else had ever heard a sonic boom and it was begging the issue to believe that even the sharpest crack of thunder from a diving fighter was, in reality, a supersonic shock wave. Once you've heard that sharp, explosive cannonade of the sonic boom and its characteristic double-boom crack, you don't forget it.

Not even the P-80 could exceed the speed of sound. Indeed, those pilots who tried it in the P-80 either survived the violence of compressibility or died in the attempt. The tail twisted wildly and the controls stiffened into concrete. The solution? The same type of dive flap as had been developed for the P-38.

But never faster than the speed of sound.

• • •

This whole can of worms had long bothered Herb Fisher, who was a stickler for accuracy in all things. And this is the moment to keep my promise to let *him* set the record straight.

Herb handed me a report by a P-4 pilot, Raymond E. Hurtienne of Wisconsin. "Read this," Herb ordered. "One day we'll set all this stuff straight."

Hurtienne's report states:

There I was at 40,000 feet in the AAF's latest P-47N, with a very specific purpose in mind, mischievous as it was. I was 19 years old, a recent Air Force graduate, and with about 100 hours in type. The weather was crystal clear. It was Spring 1945, eight miles above Long Island. I rolled her over, pointed her straight down, retarded throttle, full left trim and full forward stick. As the speed increased, control responses became more and more rigid. The airspeed indicator became stuck against the peg at 575 mph. Vapor trails were forming at both wingtips. The stick seemed like concrete. I had both feet on the left rudder. The altimeter was unwinding at a terrific rate. This was it! I was confident in my own mind. I had hit Mach 1.

There wasn't much time left. My arms felt like they weighed a ton. I pulled back on the stick. It seemed like it barely moved but the plane gradually raised its nose and I blacked out. Estimating the proper point in my arc, I released back pressure and when I again could see I was pointed up at about 20 degrees past dead center (pardon the pun). The altimeter was again winding up at about 5,000 feet. The G meter was stuck at 14-g's where it had been many times before. I estimated the bottom of the arc at about 2,000 feet. The entire maneuver lasted less than a minute, but will live in my mind forever. What a grand and glorious feeling. There wasn't another plane in the skies that could touch me and I had just flown Mach 1.

Herb Fisher wrote directly to Hurtienne:

Dear Ray: At a recent meeting of the Executive Council of the P-47 Thunderbolt Pilots Association at our Headquarters in the Wings Club, New York City, I was re-

F4U Corsair

quested to respond to your Pilot's Report, entitled MACH ONE. After reading the details of your flight, I concluded that it must have been very exciting for you during that one or two minutes of flight.

After analyzing your flight report, I would like you to know that no WW II propeller-driven fighter aircraft ever attained Mach One. This is due to the particular aerodynamics of the wing and other surface designs, plus the monumental drag of the aircraft and propeller once it began to reach 575 to 600 MPH. This was due basically to the state of the art in those days of aerodynamic design of aircraft, wings and airfoils during the WW II era. Supersonic velocity was not possible until fuselage and wing design and adequate thrust power was developed to attain Mach One.

It might be of interest to you that even the Lockheed P-80 Shooting Stars and two or three of our very first jet fighters were not Mach One aircraft.

Also, on a P-47 and other WW II propeller aircraft, if

14G was attained as many times as you indicated, first the pilot would be incapacitated and structural failure would probably occur on either wing or tail surface, or both.

I have no desire to criticize your paper, but I have 4,010 Flight Test Hours on a P-47 and as Chief Engineering Test Pilot for the Curtiss-Wright Corporation for 25 years, I have some understanding of the velocity limits of the P-39, P-40, P-47, P-51, P-38, Navy F4U Corsair, etc., etc. Curtiss manufactured hundreds of P-47's in Buffalo, New York for Republic Aircraft Company during the war and we ran a complete engineering flight test program before it entered the Curtiss production line. In 1945, I transferred to the Propeller Division of Curtiss at Caldwell, New Jersey, and had a C-46, C-54, B-17, B-29, Convair, DC-6, DC-8, P-47 and a Grumman F8F Bearcat doing extensive propeller tests (excepting the DC-8, of course) on all these aircraft. One of the test programs on the Thunderbolt I had for six years, was making high-performance dive tests, evaluating Curtiss transsonic and sweepback-type propellers.

During that period on one program, I made well over 100 High Mach number dives on our P-47 from 38,000 feet at velocities up to Mach .82, which is around 600 to 615 MPH. At this speed the aircraft will start to become uncontrollable and in a few recorded cases the pilot dug a big hole in the ground. . . .

And then there was a letter dated September 8, 1980. On that day, Clarence L. Johnson, the famed Kelly Johnson of Lockheed's Skunk Works that developed the fastest aircraft in the world, from the P-80 right on up through the triple-sonic SR-71 Blackbird—wrote to Herb Fisher. Herb passed the letter on to me with instructions to "get that thing published."

Dear Herb: It was nice to hear from you in your 1st August letter. . . .

I am surprised to hear that some World War II fighter pilots are still maintaining that they dove their airplanes through Mach 1 in the war. When Colonel Cass Hough reported his P-38 incident, I checked into the matter immediately and found the solution.

Pilots were indicating very fast dives, particularly at high altitudes, with various aircraft at the time, including the P-38, P-47, P-51, and Spitfires. The reason that they saw these false data on the cockpit instruments was very simple. It had to do with the fact that the static system was generally hooked to a pitot tube and had a substantial delay in its reading in a dive, giving false values of the airspeed indicator and the altitude. The lack of sufficient port size and the large volume in the various static instruments including the airspeed indicator, altimeter, rate of climb indicator, and the lines themselves could not vent fast enough to measure true static pressure in a screaming dive. The thing that happened then was the same as applying suction on the static side of the airspeed indicator which gave those erroneus readings.

After the war, when I was investigating jet airplane designs, I built a solid-steel, six-foot span model of the F-80A and dropped it from a P-38 at altitudes close to 40,000 feet. In spite of the heavy weight of the model, which was over 600 pounds, in a vertical dive, the model would not exceed a true airspeed of higher than Mach number .94. This value was obtained between 15,000 and 20,000 feet and decreased as lower altitudes were reached. With the full-scale F-80A, these results were confirmed and there was no recorded case where this jet fighter, as clean as it was, and with no propeller, could ever exceed a Mach number greater than .90.

I thought you might be interested in the above. Considering the fact that our SR-71 strategic reconnaissance aircraft cruises at Mach numbers well over 3, we have come a long way since World War II in high-speed aircraft design.

> Best personal regards,
> Kelly Johnson

And a final few comments from those in the know, because they were "up there":

"Anyone who ever reached Mach One in a WW II propeller aircraft ain't here to tell about it" (Tony LeVier).

"Anyone who claims he pushed a 'Jug' over Mach One is sucking on a jug of pretty potent stuff" (Scott Crossfield).

"No way to reach the speed of sound in any WW II fighter aircraft; even some of our first jet aircraft couldn't reach Mach One in a dive" (Herman "Fish" Salmon).

Seven-Oh-Seven

There is one characteristic that almost everyone involved in, or watching, the first flight of an airplane always shares. When the power builds up and the winged machine begins to roll for the very first time, no one breathes. You're too busy hoping that the machinery accelerating down the runway is going to keep right on rolling until the wings perform that always-miraculous and invisible curving and grasping of air so that the airplane leaves the ground behind. And keeps right on flying.

That sort of reaction started way back when; like 1903 at Kill Devil Hill. Fifty-one years after the Wright Flyer bobbled along over the Carolina sand dunes, along the runway of the municipal airport at Renton, Washington, the human emotions remained much the same as spectators regarded the great sleek shape into which the Boeing Company had poured just about every dollar and dime it could gather in one of the all-time gambles of aviation.

At fourteen minutes past two o'clock on the afternoon of July 15, 1944, Boeing Chief Test Pilot Tex Johnston advanced the throttles of the Boeing 707 jet airliner prototype. It was a beautiful day with clouds washed in sunlight, and a gentle breeze at seven miles per hour drifted out of the west-northwest.

Thirty seconds after the four jet engines reached their maximum thrust output, Johnson released the brakes. Sixteen million dollars of private enterprise began to roll. The 707 was light, down to a bare 110,000 pounds for her flight debut.

Boeing 707

It was an enormous gamble. Aviation companies do not invest sixteen million dollars in a single airplane as a matter of course. If the gamble paid off, Boeing could look forward to a tremendous production future of the greatest airliner ever built. The United States would enter the first phases of the commercial jet age. The U.S. Air Force would commit itself to the purchase of more than *five hundred* speedy jet tankers, the KC-135, and inject powerful new combat strength into its strategic air arm.

Sunlight glistened off the brilliant yellow paint as the prototype pushed eagerly forward. Speed built up quickly. Faster and faster sped the fifty-five tons of airplane—and then *the* moment was at hand. Seventeen seconds after Johnston released the brakes, a bare 2,100 feet from the start of the takeoff roll, the great airplane broke away from the runway, reared high her nose, and rushed into the sky. The time was exactly fourteen minutes and forty-seven seconds past two o'clock.

That was the beginning. Eight days after the first flight, the 707 prototype had logged fifteen hours and forty-six minutes flight time in seven separate flights. Flown with superb sensitivity by Tex Johnston, one of aviation's all-time great test pilots, the sleek ship touched her nose above forty-two thousand feet and split the skies at better than 550 miles per hour. The nation's first jet transport had quickly reached close to the speed of sound—Mach .8, and accomplished this feat in level flight. It was truly remarkable: only nine years before, the hottest jet fighter planes in combat couldn't match this performance.

Boeing wanted results quickly with the 707, and Johnston worked hard to provide them. In that first week, he put the Stratoliner prototype through a grueling series of climbs, banks, and stalls. The longest test flight, the sixth, kept the prototype aloft just short of four hours. A typical test operation, it went like this:

Johnston climbed to operational altitude, maintaining maximum-climb power setting so that the flight engineer, and a battery of flight-recording instruments, could obtain data on engine cooling and pressures. Engineers in the cabin took sound-level measurements. In various orders, Johnston shut down, and then restarted the four jet engines at operational altitude. Everyone looked hard for trouble, for malfunctions, for any inconsistencies.

There weren't any. The Pratt and Whitney jets operated in superb balance; a flight engineer's dream. Johnston dropped the prototype through the skies at five thousand feet per minute while engineers checked the fuel-tank vents. He extended the landing gear and the dive-brake spoilers on each wing. Other engineers studied the airspeed indications and measuring system with the aid of a "trailing bomb" static source, extended by cable far behind the airplane.

The test program progressed steadily. All systems worked satisfactorily, including the air-conditioning and pressurization systems. Satisfied engineers wrote that the Pratt and Whitney JT-3P engines were "excellent in all respects." Thirty-four hundred pounds of test equipment, mounted securely in the forward part of the passenger deck, steadily collected data for later meticulous study and evaluation.

Johnston made one more flight, Number 7, and then the engineers really began to pour it on. They stowed aboard the airplane heavy lead ballast, in lieu of cargo and passenger payload, and began to run the prototype through the grueling tests of maximum loads, and then overloads.

Like all other large, new airplanes, the 707 prototype didn't escape its growing pains. "This development is of course of extreme importance to the public, to the industry, and all of aviation," Johnston explained at the time. "It didn't just happen. And it wasn't easy or simple to achieve. We encountered many problems, and the solutions weren't simple. The jet transport that finally goes into production by the many hundreds won't be entirely the result of engineering and testing of this particular model. We had other people and aircraft to lean on. We got some really great engineering know-how resulting from preceding programs on the B-47 and B-52 bombers; what we learned from them we plowed into this airplane."

On August 5, 1954, after a normal landing, a faulty hydraulic system was revealed under the worst possible circumstances—as the plane rolled down the runway. Earlier in the day's test program, Johnston went through numerous braking tests prior to his first takeoff. With these satisfactorily completed, he took off and flew the specified air maneuvers, then returned to the field and landed normally. Immediately upon touchdown he applied the brakes—with no results. "In fact," he reported later, "the airplane seemed to accelerate. The copilot's brakes were applied immediately, and *they* didn't work. The emergency braking system wasn't working either."

At once Johnston rolled the 707 off the runway, moving to the adjacent turf in an effort to gain as much deceleration as possible before he ran out of airfield. Sinking into the ground, the airplane began to slow its rush down the field. As the 707 reached the north end of the airport Johnston felt it had reached a safe speed where he could ground-loop— turn the jetliner rapidly within its minimum turning radius. He turned the nose steering wheel, whirling the airplane about on its gear.

Then fate slipped a joker into the deck. What would have been a perfect recovery turned into the airplane's first accident. Airport personnel had dumped surplus chunks of concrete on the ground; the nose gear plowed into the jagged concrete and collapsed. The prototype 707 slid to a stop on its nose, minus its gear. "Considering the circumstances," explained Johnston, "the airplane suffered very little damage. The subsequent investigation yielded some rather interesting information. During the brake tests prior to takeoff, the temperature of the hydraulic fluid was appreciably increased, which resulted in considerable expansion. During the cold-soak period at altitude the fluid cooled off and contracted. The hydraulic fuses interpreted this flow as a line rupture, and actuated. As a result, after landing, even though the hydraulic system was full and the pressures were normal, no pressure could be metered to the brake cylinders. Unfortunately, those fuses were common to both the pilot's and the copilot's braking systems and so was the accumulator-actuated emergency system. Needless to say, this system was revised.

"A new nosewheel assembly had to be manufactured. While the airplane was laid up, our engineers modified the brake system to correct the deficiency. That's why we build a *prototype*—so that the bugs will be ironed out before we go into production."

Four years later the advance in braking ability of the 707 was proven in dramatic fashion. It was the summer of 1958, and Boeing experimental test pilot Tom Layne had just taken the third production 707 airliner through functional and reliability tests, with a pilot from the Civil (now Federal) Aeronautics Administration in the right seat. In the passenger cabin were powerplant engineers. Layne chose this moment to impress the government inspector pilot and his passengers with the performance of the Boeing-developed jet thrust reversers.

On its final approach to the field the 707 grossed out at 185,000 pounds—more than five tons above its maximum landing weight. A light breeze from the north drifted across the runway. Layne carried out a normal approach from the south and eased the airplane down onto the main runway of Boeing Field in Seattle. The airliner flashed over the runway threshold, and Layne deliberately held her off. Then he flared out, and eased the ninety-three-ton ship to the concrete—1,500 feet beyond the threshold.

Immediately he pushed the control yoke forward, dropping the nosewheel to the runway. He placed the spoilers in their full-up position of sixty degrees, grasped the thrust reverser controls, and applied full reverse thrust from all four engines. Responding to the sudden power, the airplane decelerated rapidly. At a speed of sixty knots, Layne sharply reduced engine power to prevent the reversed exhaust gases from being ingested into the engines—which can cause a surging, or backfiring, effect. The giant airliner continued to decelerate, and began to back up! Out the window could be seen the runway marker indicating eight thousand feet. Without once touching the wheel brakes, reverse thrust from the 707's engines had stopped the airplane and backed it up—within 6,500 feet of touchdown.

A new, large airplane has never been tested without its hairy moments. In this kind of flying the test pilot goes out of his way to get the airplane into trouble—after all, the time to discover the unexpected is during flight test, and not when the airliner is cruising cross-country with 112 passengers aboard. As part of the 707's grueling checkout marathon, Tex Johnston went through high-speed flutter investigation— to determine exactly what happens at extreme speed, when the airplane nudges the speed of sound. During this phase of the tests, he made several flights at a high Mach number without incident. Then, on a subsequent flight, when he was checking out another pilot, he exceeded his previous flight maximum number by exactly .001.

"Instantaneously we got severe rudder flutter," Johnston related with a dry smile. "Power was reduced immediately and up elevator applied. As the airplane decelerated the flutter condition stopped. Even though no structural damage to the airplane occurred, I can tell you there was an appreciable vibration." This could have been the understatement of the year. What Johnston shrugged off as "appreciable vibration," as brief as it was, ripped the flight engineer's panel from its mounting.

Engineers immediately located the cause of the trouble, a mechanical stability tab. Further tests were shelved, and with a potential trouble source pinpointed, Johnston took the 707 back up for some more serious troubleshooting. Time and time again he pushed the prototype over into a dive to reach Mach numbers considerably in excess of that at which the difficulty was encountered. No more flutter or vibration. Up to 95 percent of the speed of sound, at which time a definite buffeting (which serves as a warning device) takes place, the 707 remained free of all difficulties.

Slowly but surely the 707 ran through every possible range of flight as the Boeing engineers brought the airplane to that point where the first commercial—production—model could be given the green light. Once again Johnston experienced trouble with the brakes, this time not on the ground but at twenty-two thousand feet. After accelerated braking tests on the ground, and after the ground crew assured him that the brakes were not excessively hot, Johnston took off and established a steady climb to reach an altitude of 35,000 feet. He never got there.

"At twenty-two thousand feet there was a terrific explosion—a sound similar to someone shooting both barrels of a twelve-gauge shotgun in the cockpit—and I knew immediately the brake pressure had been too high. About this time the F-86 chase plane pilot reported black streaks appearing in the vicinity of the wheel-well doors. The gear was immediately extended, and sure enough some of the tires were on fire and obviously blown out. When the airspeed was increased, the fire was extinguished and the airplane returned to the airport. On this particular landing I can assure you no brakes were required as we rolled to a stop, and power was required to taxi off at the 3,500-foot taxi strip. Investigation revealed that this particular type of brake was a very good heat reservoir, storing the heat in the internal portion of the brake, and later radiating it out to the rim.

"All new airplanes have had their growing pains," Johnston sums up, "and they have undergone certain modifications as a result of their early phase of testing. This has been the history of the advance of aviation. This is why every airframe manufacturer and equipment manufacturer maintains and operates a test division. The high-performance airplane of today requires even more testing than its predecessor, not because of its complexity or its size but because of the efficiency required of its engineering."

Well, Tex Johnston spoke those words quite a few years back. In 1958 the 707 commercial airliner was rolling off the production lines. There had been jet airliners before of limited

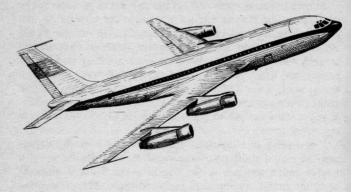

Boeing 720

size and power, but the 707 brought the jet age to the commercial passenger world with a thundering rush and an ovation never seen before or since.

That was more than thirty-three years ago. In the years following the first commercial 707s, the airplane spawned a seemingly endless series of models, and even entirely new airplanes based *exactly* on the cabin fuselage of the first commercial airplane. Soon after the first 707s were in service, the 720 model appeared. Same wings and engines and the same fuselage, but the latter was shortened in length to make it more efficient on shorter commercial flights. Then came a steady series of major improvements and model changes in the 707 itself. Much more powerful engines and an extended fuselage meant that the 707 could now make transoceanic flights anywhere in the world. Some models used American engines, others flew with British-made engines. Whatever the modification, the new 707s carried far more than double their original passenger loads and tripled their nonstop range.

But it didn't stop there. Everybody wanted Boeing on their airline, and to meet the demands of different routes and staging, Boeing soon produced its famed 727 series, a three-engined model that, again, retained the 707 fuselage but carried all three engines clustered in the tail. Production went on at a frantic pace until there seemed to be more 727s than 707s.

Then there was the 737 series, looking for all the world like a squat, stubby wrestler or boxing champ. One engine beneath each wing, an airplane designed to carry its passengers in the same comfort as its bigger 707, 720, and 727 brothers—and the same basic fuselage, but shortened even more than the others, and with amazing get-in-get-out ability in small, rough fields that seemed impossible for a solid jetliner. One of the first customers was up in Alaska, and the 737 proved a world-beater in operating during the worst weather and from some of the world's worst airfields.

The saga continued. The U.S. Air Force ordered many hundreds of KC-135 aerial tankers for refueling its fighters and bombers on strategic missions. Then the Air Force ordered still more of the dash 135 series as AWACS, the military 707 with a huge rotating radome as an airborne radar surveillance, interception, and control aircraft. Other military 707s were configured with tons of electronic communications and control equipment for air command and control—their latest performance in Operation Desert Storm termed as nothing less than "spectacular, unprecedented and overwhelming to the enemy."

The story didn't end there. Other 707s were modified as Air Force One to carry the president of the United States and his staff throughout the world. Then, more 707s were either modified in the field or built new with still-secret electronic equipment for military and space research.

It might seem that this was enough. But then, as the airplane aged, there came incredible advances in jet engines, with each engine having the power of all four engines of the original 707. At once airlines began re-engining *their* airplanes. It was a miraculous transformation. Fuel efficiency became a dream come true. Operating weights went up, take-off distances were shortened, as were minimum required landing distances. And range increased so greatly that airplanes formerly used mainly for overland flights were suddenly lofting across oceans with ease.

Then the Air Force took a long, hard look at its aging fleet of KC-135 tankers. They had billions of dollars invested in those airplanes. The decision was made: update the 135s. The ships were completely revamped, first with the immense power of four new engines, then with electronics, automatic control systems, and the latest advances in aeronautics applied to the tankers.

Presto: a whole new air force of modern, far-ranging, highly efficient jet tankers equal to any in the world.

Then came the great colossus of the commercial skies—the huge, magnificent 747 series. I flew one of the original 707 commercial airliners when researching a book on American Airlines. It was dazzling and incredible *then*. Later, when I had my shot at the 747, the difference was, well, it was like comparing raw cotton to the finest silk.

Now you can count the new numbers. The 757 and the 767, in service throughout the world, among the most fuel-efficient and reliable jetliners ever built. And there's a new iron bird on the line, now in its advanced design stage. The 777—or Triple Seven as it's already being called—the next adventure taking us into the twenty-first century.

It's going to be quite a ride.

14

We Call Him Saint Nicholas

It was one hell of a question.

We were gathered beneath the wing of a huge Lockheed Constellation at Miami International Airport. Not the glitzy side with the airline terminals and the huge central building with thousands of people milling about. Nope: we were on the north side of the field. On *our* side of the field were men with grease-stained overalls and jeans and heavy boots and sneakers, and almost all of them had skinned knuckles and healing scabs on their heads, the unmistakable signs of mechanics, repairing airplanes—like the grand old Connie beneath which we had gathered for a break. The Lockheed had been relegated to hauling cargo. The paint was peeling, the names had been scrubbed off to be replaced by new names, and she was *tired*. She would never fly again. The Constellation had been drained of all fuel and oil and she was chained to the ground because she was being cannibalized, picked clean of metal parts, engine pieces, instruments and wiring, and anything else that was still in good working condition or could be rebuilt for installation in other planes.

The sign on the hangar, fencing in the airplanes about us, read AERO FACILITIES, and within that fencing you could find ships like the Constellation, or Convairs, Curtiss cargo haulers, old twin-engined Martins, a swarm of Douglas DC-6 and DC-7 cargoliners (banished from passenger hauling by the faster, glitzier and newer jetliners). You'd see Lockheed

DC-3

Lodestars, belly down to the ground, and the ageless DC-3, and the indomitable Beech 18.

And there was one ship that was starkly different from all the others, a great corrugated-metal, slab-sided, ugly-beautiful, paint-peeling three-engined Junkers Ju-52/3m. *My* airplane. I'd flown her here, shaking and throbbing, rustling through every rib and spar, abandoned many years before in the high jungle fastnesses of Ecuador. I'd flown her like this with her original German engines from way back in 1935. Now we would rebuild the airplane German troops in World War II had christened *Iron Annie* because of her incredible structural strength. There comes that time when you put down the old girl for a complete rebuilding. I had some ideas about modifying the ancient, powerful wonder, and I had met with Nick Silverio, boss man at Aero Facilities, to plan the resurrection.

"We can do it," he said quietly. "We can do it better than anyone else. When we get through with this airplane, and we rebuild and add your modifications, and a few we'd like to recommend, she'll fly better than she ever did."

I shook hands with Nick Silverio. He had a terrific crew working for him, he was an engineer, an aerodynamics whiz, an air transport pilot, an instrument instructor, a fighter pilot, a pilot of trainers and transports and bombers, he held an airline captain's rating, and he was also a longtime test pilot. He added to that list a bunch more stuff, including being an airplane mechanic and an engine mechanic, *and* a federal inspector, *and* a federal examiner for other pilots. Most important of all, when Nick and his crew finished their work and I paid them more money than I could carry at one time and I was ready to do some test piloting of my own, why, Nick Silverio was in the right seat with me. Also coming along for the ride because he could fly anything, had all the ratings like Nick, was another miracle man, would be Frank Ray.

If the man who works on your airplane won't test-fly it with you, don't let him touch it. There's simply no sense in having someone on the ground screw up your airplane and you find out you're up to your butt in alligators at fifteen thousand feet while that mechanic is on the ground three miles below, grinning like a mule eating tree bark.

Like I said, we'd gathered outside, away from the riveting and hammering of air guns and hydraulic lines and lathes ripping metal with the shriek of a hog having its throat cut. We sat around with sandwiches and coffee and cigars, and it was a time to talk. You see, in this group there were a bunch of test pilots. Not the kind you read about in the Sunday supplements because they've gone high zoom in some billion-dollar experimental rocket ship, on which a couple of hundred people have worked day and night to make ready for a brief but always exciting ride. Those people have had their pictures on television and in newspapers and magazines, and their teeth are bright and straight and they wear shiny uniforms, and they deserve all the praise they get, but if you count the numbers, there's really but a few of them and a hundred or maybe a thousand times as many of those other test pilots, who do their thing day in and day out, month after month.

Like Nicholas Silverio. Behind his back we called him Saint Nick, because, among other things, he flew like an angel, and in a field where gruff people guzzled beer and spat tobacco juice, Nick stood out as if he were swathed in golden-white robes. There was a radiance about him.

A gentler man there never was, and a better pilot there never was. In this business, if you wanted to make your living as a test pilot, you had to be a lot more. You needed an academic background, and you had to be an accountant and a straw boss and you needed to know your business inside and out, because if you didn't—why, you went broke. The aviation business is littered with the debris of manufacturers, rebuilders, maintenance shops, and airlines that have all gone belly up and put hundreds of thousands of skilled people back on the streets.

So in Nick Silverio, and the others like him, we have the test pilot you never heard about. But he's also the kind of test pilot who makes our vast industry work. Without Nick and Frank and others like them, the aviation industry would be faltering and stuttering along.

Back to that gathering beneath the wing of the tired old Constellation waiting for her bones and ribs to be picked clean. There was a young crew chief asking that question: "At what age are you finished as a test pilot?"

Finished? That's like belching loudly in church or at a wedding in the middle of the ceremony. Heads turned to Terry Ritter, big and young and husky, crew chief now, a genius with automotive mechanics and things electrical, working for his aircraft mechanic's ticket and learning to fly so he could earn his commercial ticket so he could test his own work upstairs, not just here on the ground.

"You crazy?" Frank Ray stabbed back. "You're *never* finished because of age. Jeez, man, you fly until you drop, *period.*"

Terry pulled his shoulders together as if he'd just said something blasphemous, but Nick Silverio came in, nice and easy, "You don't drop out because of age, like Frank said," Nick offered in that gentle, disarming tone. "So long as your medical ticket is valid, you keep right on doing what you always did in life. But you can't ever lose what brought you into this work in the first place."

Nick didn't make speeches. Not very often, anyway. The sounds of rivet guns and air hammers and screeching metal and roar of jets overhead seemed to fade away as everyone listened to "the man."

"Every flight you make," he said, "is just as thrilling as your first flight, and just as thrilling as the last flight you made. This is really a love affair, this committing yourself to aviation. And this business of being a test pilot? Well, the longer you're at it, the more experience you put beneath your belt, and the more experience you have, the better equipped you are to meet the unexpected when it drops like a burning coal in your lap. The thing you *never* want to lose is the right mental attitude. Tex Johnston always pounded the table on that point, and he's right. He told me and a bunch of other pilots one day that it's losing the mental attitude that finally grounds most of the older test pilots. *Every* flight has got to be your best, and the best flight you're ever going to make is always your next one. Your body may age, and maybe the old eyes will need glasses, and you get aches and pains you never knew you had, but you're always becoming a *better* pilot."

Frank Ray grinned. "There are a dozen pilots on this field right now, in their seventies and eighties, and they're out there testing and hauling even the big four-engined jobbies. And that includes the piston jobs and the jets."

That answered the question, but another pilot jumped right in. This was too rare an opportunity to miss. Nick Silverio had salt-and-pepper hair and he was a gentleman of the old school, but his eyes always had that glint of fire and steel in them. If you knew how to look, you saw the pilot in there.

"What got you started, Nick?" came the inevitable question.

We knew Nick would dodge anything like that. "I'd always wanted to fly," he said, and smiled, as if that was answer enough for anybody.

So I'll let you in on a history filled with backbreaking work and skill. All such stories begin the same way. A kid is born, grows up with or without a family, goes through schooling, excels in this or that. Some want to be doctors or lawyers or sailors or mountain climbers, perhaps a scientist, and there are those who want to *fly*. For Nick, there was high school, like millions of other youngsters. Ho-hum. But that's where it ended, and Nick's path in life became an unbending arrow in unending flight.

As he told a packed throng in 1986 at the annual gathering of Silver Wings, where he received the award of Aviation Man of the Year: "This honor makes me grin a lot because it is for something that had made my working life a joy. *Aviation.* I've lived many phases of it since 1938 and I still find it new, exciting, and thrilling. To receive an honor for the pleasure that has been mine is, to say the least, 'frosting on the cake.'

"That's why I can tell you, from my experience, why I so sincerely believe the quotation, 'Whatever a man soweth, that shall he also reap.' This is *not* a sermon. It's also more than a way of life. It is life itself. . . ."

Nick did some very heavy, very serious, very dedicated sowing. He went straight from ho-hum high school to Aviation Trades in New York, where he spent seven days a week to become an aircraft and engine mechanic. When he had put behind him the scraped knuckles and bloody forehead, he sort of flowed into Erskine College in South Carolina. There, he buried himself in geometry, algebra, trigonometry (and a bunch of et ceteras). He took a heavy-hitter course in physics, then loaded up with laboratory work, history, cartography, meteorology, geography, engineering, aerodynamics, English (you got to be able to write comprehensible test reports), government air regulations, and added medical training to the rest. *All* to prepare himself for flying. And when he departed Erskine, it was straight into the waiting arms of the U.S. Army Air Force's Aviation Cadet Program.

This was more like it! But there seemed to be as much classroom work as ever before, because Nick had been marked as a pilot-to-be by the AAF. They gave him a heavy grind of textbook learning on the ground but also control-stick learning in the air. In May of 1945 he wore silver wings as an Air Force pilot. His new orders took him to the University of Ohio, where, during the day, he was required to pass a full accounting course (he's still not sure why, but it paid off in spades years later). When the sun went down, Nick started the really serious sessions, which continued throughout his career.

Purchasing, management, Spanish, Italian, English composition (again), all aspects of aeronautics and aerodynamics, engineering, advanced mechanical engineering, aircraft inspection, welding, flight safety, air-ground operations . . . From then on, with classrooms behind him, he plunged into flight-instructor revalidation, high-altitude indoctrination, recertification as a fighter pilot, weather radar, multiengine and single-engine seaplane courses (and licenses). He worked his way up through the civilian ratings of private, commercial, and airline transport. He got his tickets as a flight instructor, then as an instrument flight instructor, then as an airline check pilot, and a few dozen other specialized fields.

That's the routine, essentially. For the record, he went on to check out and get his ratings in a whole family of small, medium, and humongous-sized piston and jet aircraft, and in between he also learned to fly gliders and then became an instructor in just about anything with wings. Nick judged his future in aviation depended on a foundation of everything mechanical, engineering, and testing, so he did his best to go without sleep as long as he could and work some nine days every week. Early in 1941 he was inspecting fighters and dive-bombers as they rolled off the lines of the Brewster Aero Corporation in New York. The Navy asked Brewster to assign him specifically to check their fighter planes before accepting them for service.

That stint behind him, Nick was off and running to Truax Air Force Base in Wisconsin, and also put in a stretch (August 1941 through October 1943) at famed Wright-Patterson Air Force Base in Ohio, where he mixed with and worked with the best research teams, ground and air, in the Air Force. Soon he was running several special test projects and learning the nuts-and-bolts routines of pilots beating their airplanes half to death in the test-flight program.

Someone in Luke Air Force Base in Arizona, struggling to cope without enough men who knew what they were doing in servicing, repair, and flight test, had heard of this go-getter named Silverio, and Nick found himself on an Air Force transport headed west. He loved it. More than 120 top specialists worked under him in the daily chores of maintenance and rebuilding, but it was Nick who got the top job

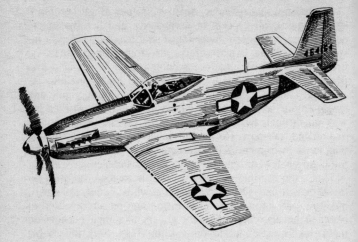

North American P-51 Mustang

as test pilot on the hot North American P-51 Mustangs after they'd been taken apart and put back together. He put in several hundred hours as a Mustang test pilot.

For the next four years he "took it easy," returning to the classroom for specialized courses while flying as an Air Force reserve instructor pilot and test pilot in single and multiengine trainers and transports. Somewhat of a comedown from the hot Mustangs, but he made up for that missing fun time by instructing in seaplanes, which to Nick were a real gas. In the interim he managed an assignment to Mitchel Air Force Base on Long Island, New York—more intensive maintenance and flight tests of military aircraft. Nick couldn't do all the flight testing himself, but the men he sent up to fly rebuilt and experimental airplanes (and you better believe that most rebuilds are experimental as all get-out!) knew, and understood, that the man at the desk behind the sign that said NICK SILVERIO had already done everything they were going to do, and had he the time, would have preferred to be behind the control stick than the mahogany desk.

When Nick ran Aerodex, Inc., for example, in addition to a thousand other tasks, he was overseer for the overhaul and rebuilding of more than fifty thousand piston and jet aircraft engines, and literally millions of aircraft components. By the time you're done that kind of work for nineteen years, you've got a sense of *knowing* that sets you apart from almost everyone else around you. You become recognized as "the master."

There were more than 6,500 employees at Aerodex, and the word was that just about any one of them could recognize "the man" on sight. Because every chance he had, Nick was off into the cockpit of anything that needed testing or flying. Finally it dawned on the executives of Aerodex that to have Nick Silverio pilot their personal business jets was to increase considerably the odds of their safe arrivals.

That cut Nick loose from the reins of management. Not only was he committed to Aerodex and other military-contracting firms for a nineteen-year-period, but he was again chief pilot and supervisor of all flight testing. More than five hundred Douglas C-47 transports as well as dozens of other types of planes passed through his hands, without so much as a single accident to mar his perfect record.

Finally Nick just bought the sprawling hangars and workshops and flight line of Aero Facilities at Miami International Airport (where our paths first crossed some sixteen years ago). Now he was performing maintenance and modifications on everything from small single-engined aircraft to huge jetliners. He expanded to a global import-export business, working with aircraft from all over the world. And he made certain he kept his hand in as a test pilot or copilot, for he had first call on every airplane that went aloft; either as the chief test pilot, or yielding that seat and flying as copilot to check out the pilot in command who now occupied the left seat. Being "signed off" by Nick Silverio had come to be judged as a highwater mark in the life of *any* pilot; it was perhaps their most coveted signature and explanatory note in their log books.

Frosting on the cake came with an Air Force contract to rebuild, equip, and flight-test transport planes, because the government contract specified that Nicholas Silverio must be the chief test pilot for the program, and they meant with his hands on the yoke of each aircraft and not resting on his desk as president of the company.

Remember Herb Fisher? We haven't come that far since Chapter 11 to forget that incredible saga. But what concerns us now is that both Herb Fisher and Nick Silverio followed basically the same path. Each was an army pilot, each was an instructor, each took a backbreaking load of academic and scientific courses throughout their careers, and each flew both their airplanes and, so to speak, their desks.

There's far more than pushing a throttle to aviation, as both Fisher and Silverio knew. Even as a young man, Herb Fisher worked as a secretary of the Indiana Aircraft Trades Association, became a state governor of the Indiana Aeronautical Association, and was director of aeronautics for the Indianapolis Chamber of Commerce for eight years. Later, he became chief of the Aviation Development Division of the Port of New York Authority—which sort of tied up Herb because this outfit operated the busiest aviation terminal in the world, which includes the famed Kennedy International, La Guardia, Newark, and Teterboro airports, as well as a far-flung network of heliports.

Both Nick and Herb Fisher served with innumerable aviation groups and organizations, civilian and military. In addition to the groups they shared such as Silver Wings, Quiet Birdmen, Air Force Association, Aircraft Owners and Pilots Association, Army Aviation Association, National Business Aircraft Association, Quality Control Society, Confederate Air Force, Valiant Air Command, National Aerospace Service Association, National Aeronautic Association, OX5 Aviation Pioneers—well, we could fill several pages just with the list. My favorite is an area we haven't yet touched on—business and corporate flying.

In a 1979 book called *Corporate Flying* by Jack King, there's a photograph of the key professionals of Corporate Aviation's "Hall of Fame." In that book you'll find the photographs, next to each other, of Nick Silverio and Herb Fisher, two men whose paths crossed as executives and pilots.

"You can always wrangle more time test-flying airplanes if first, you work your way into a position of authority."

Nicholas Silverio grinned at his audience of pilots—the group of civilian, military, test, American and foreign fliers—who had gathered to honor him. "The trick is to understand the system. One guy on top looks over everybody else and pushes buttons as to who flies and who doesn't fly. Sometimes the choices are fair because everyone rotates through the system. Sometimes the choices are rotten because the guy on top may have a nephew in the crowd below, and nepotism is no stranger to any activity. I managed to get in so much time test flying so many different kinds of airplanes because I made sure I got my hands on the buttons, *first,* and that opened the way to the cockpit."

Heads nodded and laughter swelled about the auditorium. "When I was on active duty in the Air Force at Wright Field," Nick went on, "I did some pretty good wrangling, and *very* quickly I was on top of the administrative heap and I was negotiating all sorts of contracts. Everybody wanted everything done quickly, like overnight or even yesterday. Naturally, the goal was to be expeditious. Get cracking! Move it! *Fly!* So I set up the system in such a way that the contractors would land at Wright Field, sign their papers, and be ready to leave within one hour. Well, the only way to make certain their planes were ready was to test them. And since I'd already assigned all my pilots to very necessary work, out of sight, why, I *had* to volunteer to do the test piloting. It was really"—the shy, crooked smile reappeared—"very generous and considerate of me."

What Nick rarely ever admitted was that his wish to get airborne at every opportunity had no limits. The flight operations officers of engineering and flight test operations at Wright Field became close friends of his. He knew they were always running short of critical parts and special personnel. Most often it was the end of the day before they'd know precisely what they needed for the next day, but with their own operations shut down for the night, they knew they'd be wasting all the next day waiting for parts and people to arrive. Thus, late in the afternoon Nick's phone would ring. "We've got a real emergency on our hands, Nick. We've got the planes but no pilots to fly tonight. Could you give us a hand?"

Nick would have thrown them a bushel filled with hands,

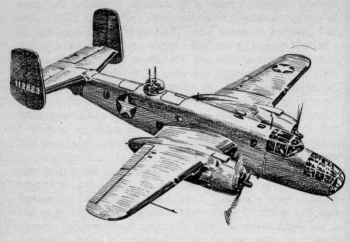

B-25

gloves, fingers, and elbows. The moment he hung up his phone he was on the way to the ops shack. It didn't matter what the weather was; Nick would save everything.

"It was terrific," Nick recalls. "They scrounged up aircraft for me anytime at night and always on the weekends. The system tried to keep me chained to my desk, but with *my* system I was flying almost constantly, and I maintained the kind of proficiency I demanded for myself, in a great variety of airplanes, but mostly in the AT-6 trainer, the C-45, the C-47 Gooney Bird, but the two I liked the most were the B-25 and the P-51. I loved to have an 'emergency' delivery run in the Mustang fighter. I flew those things through every kind of weather imaginable, including some of the wildest blizzards I'd ever seen, and I made so many instrument and blind landings under radar control some people thought I might be forgetting how to fly on a clear day."

He also arranged a special service for contractors to the air force, which called for him to fly *documents* directly to a contractor. If he timed it right, and the contractor would pore over the paperwork, why, Nick would be off and running for a visit home in New York. And he'd always be back on schedule in Ohio with the paperwork signed and delivered. (It's a good thing they didn't have FAX machines in those days. Nick would likely have spent much of his time disabling them.)

Nick spent almost twenty years with the giant Aerodex firm (just as Herb Fisher spent some twenty-five years with Curtiss-Wright), and Aerodex was more than willing to have one of their new top executives behind the controls. They knew that in this way Nick would never be a second behind the times. "During my time with Aerodex," Nick explains, "I flew the A-20 Havoc, ,B-23 Dragon, DC-3 Gooney Bird, Beech 18 twin, the Lockheed Lodestar, and the Jet Commander as Executive Transportation. I loved it. I worked and flew such long hours, including weekends, that at age fifty, I had become a stranger in my own home. My wife raised the children and handled all our personal obligations. In nineteen years with Aerodex I had one two-week vacation, and that was *it*.

"Finally I had to resign, as much as I loved being able to fly as much and as often as I wished. I wanted to smell the roses. I wanted to get to know my own family. So I stayed out of the business for a while, doing some free-lance testing and special flights, but that wasn't the way to go either.

"Then, in October 1972, the heavens parted. Dick Jordan was president of L. B. Smith, a huge corporate conglomerate, and offered me carte blanche in running the Aero Facilities rebuilding and flight testing outfit on Miami International Airport. I thought about some of the crazy things and close calls I'd had in the past. . . ."

Back in 1953 Nick was chief of flight operations for an outfit in Miami that overhauled and flight-tested rebuilt transports for the Air Force and also was deep into converting hot bombers from World War II for use as corporate and business aircraft. These conversions were tricky. The airplanes were designed essentially for combat use and that required its own special training, operation, and maintenance. Because the work involved so many unknowns, Nick gave orders that when anything "demanding" came up, *he* would be the test pilot.

He didn't wait long for one of the hot ships to make its appearance. "We had a Douglas A-20 Havoc light bomber on hand that was flown only by a single pilot. Nobody in the right seat in the cockpit because there *wasn't* any right seat. This ship was light but it had big engines. Nobody really wanted to mess with it, so that meant it was my job to handle. As a good idea of what this airplane was like, my boss told me to take it out over the ocean for the flight testing, and that if *anything* went wrong in flight, I was to dump it in the ocean and come home by parachute.

"I'd never flown the A-20 before. I spent the day and night prior to the flight reading the manuals and sitting for hours in the cockpit to familiarize myself with all the bells and whistles. The next day I took off and headed right out to sea. The A-20 was a real mover. It boomed right out and climbed like a fighter. Just offshore of Miami Beach (I wanted to stay as close as possible to Miami International, that 'just in case' nagging feeling in the back of your head) I went through my airwork procedures. Different speeds, full operation of the controls, testing her out. Then I ran through a stall series with the gear up, letting her go into full stall and catching her as she broke. Not so bad, so I dropped the gear. Or, anyway, I *tried* to lower the gear for the gear-down stalls.

"I worked that gear system again and again, but nothing doing. I had a clean airplane and it was determined to stay that way. Now I had some choices. Belly the ship in on land. Not the best shot. Then I wondered how this 'machine' would do if I ditched it in deep water off the coast. Ditchings have a nasty habit of either slamming the pilot forward into the instrument panel, or else the glass in front of you caves in and the ocean comes in after you.

"Never give up until you've exhausted *everything*. That attitude has saved my hide a whole bunch of times. Finally I found the *unmarked* emergency-cable-gear handle release (that's why I studied the manual and sat in that cockpit for so long before flight). I came back on power to ease the air loads and pulled with all my strength on the handle. It didn't take a genius to realize that handle hadn't been moved since the war—if ever. So I tried it again, and again and still some more, praying all the time that the end of the cable wouldn't end up in my hand while the other end wasn't attached to anything. That A-20 must have looked pretty funny to a lot of people; wobbling at low speed through the air while I flew with one hand and tugged and pulled with everything I had with my other hand on that cable.

"Finally, something in the system gave. I felt an easing of pressure in the cable system. There was a chance now that the gear uplocks had released. I put down the nose and let the A-20 dive steeply enough to get some really good airspeed, and then hauled back hard on the yoke for a sharp pullout to get some good g-forces on the plane, hoping that this would force down the gear.

"I was having a grand roller-coaster ride. Since the gear didn't come down, I climbed back to altitude and started all over again. Dive faster and faster, haul back as hard and sharply as I could until my head felt like a watermelon, and climbing steeply. I did this ten times until I began to sweat the fuel remaining in the airplane. I could almost feel myself getting wetter as it looked as if we'd end up in the Atlantic.

"Persistence, diving, g-forces—the whole lot—finally paid off. The gear just fell down and I got three green lights. Well, no more flying this ship today. I sure wasn't going to pull that gear *up* anymore. I called Miami Tower and went back to the field just as fast as that ship would fly with all the garbage hanging out. How was the landing? Uneventful. That's the kind of emergency test flying I like the most. You solve your own problems in the air and you come home with an airplane that's still in one piece."

Of course, at the time, Nick didn't know that nobody believed he'd bring the A-20 back "in one piece." They figured he'd make a short-lived seaplane out of it when he ditched, and emergency recovery crews were already on their way to pick him up from the water. . . . .

Sometimes a careless mechanic's slipshod work or poor memory can kill a pilot. . . . Nick's outfit accepted the delivery of fifty North American T-6 (also known as the AT-6) Texan advanced trainers, a tough machine with six hundred horsepower and flying characteristics *intended* to give its pilots fits. That's what it was designed to do: *train* pilots. The airplanes came with forebodings; they'd been stored for years in the Mideast and nobody knew what would be their condition. The Dominican Republic offered to buy them all, but only after Nick's group inspected and then restored every one of the fifty to perfect flying condition. That meant testing the fifty Texans and that Nick would get in a whole bunch of test piloting.

An inspector waited for him by a T-6 ready for flight, assured Nick everything was ready. Nick climbed in, adjusted his harness and parachute, and took off. He began to go through his test checklist and then to perform a full aerobatic routine—a requirement he'd personally written into the contract. An airplane isn't ready to be signed off, if it's an aerobatic ship, until you've flown it through the whole routine of loading up on powerful wind and g-forces and come back in one piece.

The checklist went smoothly, and Nick started the aerial ballet with a steepening dive prior to pulling up into a high loop. He never made it. Without warning, everything in front of him went dark. The world disappeared before his eyes as a large maintenance plate on the T-6 nose broke free and slammed back against the windshield. Nick pulled gently out of the dive, tried to shake the plate loose. No deal. Well, that's why there are pilots and why there are test pilots. To Nick it was a no-sweat deal, and he came back to Miami enjoying the view through side windows only.

He discovered the mechanic who'd removed and then replaced the access plate had left most of its fasteners in his toolbox. "So I relearned an old lesson." He grimaced. "Walk around the ship myself, look at and touch everything myself, and *don't* accept the word of anyone who just tells you everything's okay."

That plate could have smashed the windshield, sending chunks right into Nick's face and eyes, and that would have been a *very* different ending to a "routine" test flight.

On many of the major overhaul contracts, Nick's outfit used a Beech 18 they'd rebuilt themselves to carry company officials around the country. It not only gave Nick the flying time he wanted, but it also demonstrated that they believed in their own work. Nothing like putting your own hides on the line in the equipment you've resurrected.

"Nick, we've got an important one tomorrow. We fly from Miami in the Beech, full passenger and baggage load. We've *got* to get there on schedule. Big contract. Be ready to launch first thing in the morning."

Routine. But the weather wasn't, and as his passengers trooped aboard, Nick had his first misgivings. He'd been given a passenger manifest that kept the Twin Beech within normal loading and center-of-gravity limits. But in the morning a huge weather front hung over the area. Everything was zero-zero, fog right down to the ground. Weather so bad even the airlines shut down all operations. The passengers on his manifest came aboard, but right behind them came "three more people who were all tall and very heavy. They looked like football centers or wrestlers. *Real* big, and they came aboard, and as soon as they sagged into their seats, some more people began loading boxes of files into the airplane. I wondered what in the dickens was going on. One look outside made it all fit. Nobody else was flying so it was up to me. But I didn't like it, and by the time everybody and everything was aboard and they shut the door, I groaned to myself. I figured we were already a thousand pounds over gross weight. The Twin Beech could handle it, but it was stupid. Because the right way to say the Twin Beech could handle it was to add the fillip 'just so long as both engines worked perfectly.' And I was breaking my own rules to never let yourself be set up for a situation your airplane can't handle."

Nick fired up, taxied out *very* carefully, and the tower cleared him for takeoff—with full instrument conditions on the runway as he started to roll. Nick kept up power and climbed out in the blind to ten thousand feet, and began cruising north.

"We were level between West Palm Beach and Vero Beach when the right prop ran away. It overspeeded and was at a high scream before I even had the chance to pull back on the propeller control. I pulled it back, all right, but moving the control was an empty gesture. The prop was really howling now and I knew we could be overheating or the whole thing might come apart, tearing apart the prop and the governor and perhaps even the right engine.

"This was full-adrenaline time. I had to feather the right prop to prevent disaster out there—but now the prop refused to feather. In those few seconds we had gone from comfortable cruise to critical emergency. We still had that tremendous overload *and* our full load of fuel. Now I had no choice but to reduce power, so I came back on the right throttle to prevent immediate disaster, hoping that now the prop would go into feather.

"No way. I was now as alert as I'd ever been and flying with every bit of skill I'd ever used. I couldn't get sufficient power from the right engine to keep our altitude. We were slowing down steadily and it was only a matter of time, a very *short* amount of time, before I wouldn't have enough flying speed to keep us in the air.

"These are the times when you make your own decisions and *stick with them*. I radioed control center, told them what was happening and that I was turning ninety degrees to the right, off the airway and we were descending. Center came back with those incredibly dumb words to 'maintain altitude.' I could hear them, but the airplane couldn't, obviously, and no matter who said what, it simply wasn't going to hold altitude. If I tried that, we'd run out of airspeed with just one engine giving us our best and that meant a complete loss of control. So you don't argue with either the controller *or* your airplane. You follow the first rule: Fly your airplane the best it will fly.

"Down we went. I didn't ask center for clearance; I *told* them maintaining altitude was impossible and that was that, and we were coming down. Center got the message this time and cleared me toward Palm beach and 'cleared to descend to two thousand feet.' Nice of them, since we were headed that way no matter who said what. I put the nose down and that gave us the extra airspeed we needed to keep flying under control. As requested, I called out each thousand feet of altitude in the descent; I had the left engine at max power. On the way down, center advised that Miami had lifted a bit with its weather conditions with a ceiling of three hundred feet and one-mile visibility.

"Forget it, I told them. We'd never make it to Miami. The only field I could reach with safety was Palm Beach and *they* were still zero-zero. Terrific. A heavily overloaded airplane, my right prop shrieking like it had gone insane but not delivering any thrust, and the right throttle pulled all the way back, and an airplane that couldn't maintain altitude on just the left engine—and the world was totally blind before us.

"But there was that ace-in-the-hole. I knew the Air Force still had a GCA system at Palm Beach—ground-controlled radar approach with experienced men who could paint you on their radar screens down to inches of accuracy, and they could talk me in. Like walking blindfolded on a tightwire, but I'd done it before, and in fact, had practiced blind landings with these same people. It was a terrific insurance policy on which I hoped to collect right now.

"The GCA man was on the horn with me almost at once. He was *great*. He led me down the airway with only minor corrections, and from what he'd heard from center, he must have known that I didn't dare bleed off my airspeed. I had to keep descending *all* the time. My second engine now was called gravity. The GCA controller gave me a gentle turn so as not to increase my stall speed, and lined me onto final approach.

"Now, for the first time, I could ease back on the left engine just a hair, because it was threatening to overheat. If that happened, we'd be a lead brick on the way down—descending without power in the blind. *Not* the way to go into a heavily populated area.

"That GCA man talked to me all the way down, and I heard him saying when it was time to put down the gear and the flaps, gravity still giving us the minimum speed we needed. 'Start your flare . . . *now*!'' he called out, and I eased back on the yoke, and we slowed, and I felt the first nibbling touches of the wings approaching a stall. But in this kind of situation you absolutely trust that man in the GCA truck. He was *beautiful*. Just seconds before the wheels touched I caught my first sight of the pavement and before I could even blink my eyes we were rolling on the runway.

"I'd made the entire descent at a constant rate. If I had been farther north of Palm Beach, or if that GCA hadn't been operating at that field we would have all been statistics.

"Who to blame? *Me*. Nicholas Silverio. Nobody else. I was the captain of that airplane and I'd done a whole bunch of stupid things. I *knew* what can result from overloading an aircraft. But to accept that overload in blind-flying conditions was stupidity heaped upon stupidity. I never made that mistake again; never. I don't care how important any appointment was. Never put yourself and your airplane into a situation where you can't see or fly it out by yourself. *Never.* If we had been within weight limits, we *could* have kept on flying long enough to get up to Georgia or South Carolina and make an emergency landing—with the field, *any* field, in full view before us.

"But that wasn't possible, and it took a bunch of small miracles to keep us alive."

"The first unbreakable rule in our business of rebuilding and flying the airplanes we handled is that *every* flight, especially with new or untried equipment, *is a test flight.* I was preparing to fly a full load in the Twin Beech, the D18, out of Miami, across the Gulf of Mexico to San Antonio, Texas. But this flight wasn't just 'another hop,' because we were testing a new type of spark plug in the engines. The new plugs, so went the sales pitch, were modern miracles. They would last longer than any other plug ever built, give us lower fuel consumption, they were cheaper to buy, they'd make the airplane happier—right; sure. My boss told me to install them in our engines for this flight.

"I didn't like it and told him so. These were *new* and, to me, untried, and that meant a test flight with all precautions up to full speed and always keeping a way out of trouble we couldn't figure out before any trouble started. So I nodded to the boss man, but I made sure our mechanics installed the new plugs in *only* the right engine. I wanted to know what I had working for us in the left engine, which under any normal circumstances alone could keep us flying.

"On the way out to San Antonio that right engine purred like a fat cat. Perhaps my misgivings were the result of being overcautious. We finished our business in Texas, refueled, checked out the airplane, got a perfect pretakeoff engine check both left and right, and launched for Miami.

"Overcautious? Uh-uh. *Dumb,* for breaking my own rules. We were 150 miles out from Tampa, cruising at nine thousand feet, when suddenly the right engine shook madly, vibrated like it wanted to tear itself right off the mounts, and backfired like a battleship broadside. Immediately I shut down the engine and feathered the prop and we chugged along on the left engine only. Tampa Control launched a Coast Guard amphibian immediately to escort us into Tampa, and if we had to ditch, they could land in the water to pick us up. We made it into Tampa safely and I ordered the right engine opened up. My mechanic, who flew right seat with me, pulled those so-called super plugs from the engine. They were an absolute mess, fouled and some of them were broken. I always carried extra sets of plugs on these flights, the kind we'd used for years and I knew were reliable. We installed them, did a thorough check of the engine, and cruised back to Miami.

"Let me say right off that this constituted the only two times—my first and my last—that I ever let anyone talk me into trying any unknown parts on any airplane where I carried passengers."

"I'll *never* understand why so many people in our business, with all the stark statistics to warn them, are so convinced you can try something new and that it will always work as advertised. My flight this time was in the venerable D-18, and once again we were given the swan song to try something that a Beech service center in Dayton said was so reliable that a test flight was just a waste of time. That was warning enough; again my suspicious character asserted itself but fell short of saying no.

"The idea was to use a fuel tank in the nose baggage area of the airplane. The tank had always been there, but I'd never used it before to carry fuel. It was certainly simple enough, even innocuous. The Dayton service people said they'd used the system for years without any problems. But I had misgivings about flying back to Miami with the boss man on board without *first* checking out this 'absolutely reliable system' on a test flight. The boss said to launch, I didn't put my foot down, and off we went. But at the least I'd use the main tanks until we were cruising at high altitude, so if anything went wrong with that new system, I could always switch back immediately to the main tanks.

"Naturally, the weather is *always* lousy at such times. The cloud tops were at three thousand feet, so we'd cruise in the clear, but down below the clouds hung at only three hundred feet above the ground, and the airports all had visibility of only one mile or less. Well, that extra fuel now would be a real winner. With that fuel used in the air, I could fly all the way to Miami and then switch to the mains for the descent into blind-flying conditions.

"We climbed out in the soup and let our speed build up, and learned immediately we weren't going anywhere down south. As soon as our speed increased I saw liquid flowing over the side of my windshield and I smelled gasoline. That's when your nose and your brain scream at you that you're on the edge of a fire, and when the fire hits all the way into your electrical system, airplanes have a habit of exploding rather violently.

"Immediately I turned off all electrical power and that left us without radios or any navigation equipment. I continued the climb to three thousand feet to break through the top of the cloud layer. Terrific; no comm or nav and that gasoline was still pouring back from the nose, and we had to get down as quickly as possible. Which meant a full-instrument approach back into Dayton. And *that* meant turning back on the electrical power for radio communications or the instrument landing systems. I expected that when I did *that*, we might make a very bright light in the sky.

"I switched off everything, held my breath, turned on one radio, and as clearly and quickly as I could speak, told them of my problem, that I would make an ILS approach in ten minutes without any further communication. I didn't ask; I told them what I was going to do, snapped, 'Over and out,' and shut down the radio.

"I'd been circling on top, so I knew we were still close to the field. I turned on one nav to determine my exact position, turned it off immediately, and began my circle to line up with the ILS runway heading. Now I had no choice but to keep my nav approach system on; I turned on the ILS equipment and went directly onto final approach. I'd had enough time now to *think* and I'd decided to *not* lower the gear electrically. Gasoline was still pouring up over the windshield and the smell was overpowering in the airplane. My mechanic, who wasn't a pilot, listened to my instructions and started hand-cranking down the gear. I also told him, 'Don't touch the flaps. We won't be using them.'

"Talk about the saints flying with you! I broke out at three hundred feet with the runway dead ahead, shut down the electrical systems again, landed, and headed in a steady taxi toward the tower.

"What had nearly turned us into a fireball was that during installation of the nose fuel tank the mechanic had cut the scarf on the end of the tube that was in the slipstream. Being cut in exactly the wrong direction, this siphoned out our fuel as our airspeed increased and sprayed it back onto the airplane as if it were coming at us from a high-pressure hose.

"I guess my flying the airplane—once again without my own personal test flight without passengers—goes into the file of *never again,* because I never repeated that mistake. Once is enough."

There are so many more incidents in all these decades of testing and flying. Nick has had swift jets snap out of control from runaway autopilots that wouldn't shut off, had more engine failures than he can remember, had his propellers run away, airplanes burn in flight, and all manner of equipment fail. In many ways testing rebuilt airplanes to their maximum performance envelope poses hazards not too many pilots want to tackle.

Come back with us to that night in 1986 when Nick Silverio, the man who represents "the test pilots nobody ever knows," and hear what he told that assembly of grizzled veterans when they honored him with their Aviation Man of the Year award. "One day at Aero Facilities," Nick related, "two men in a Cessna 401 asked our shop foreman, Bob Reed, to check scorched paint on an engine cowling. Bob discovered the main exhaust manifold burned completely through. He told the men their next flight, unless they repaired the damage, would certainly be their last, and it would be as a fireball. They wanted immediate repairs and asked, 'How much?' Bob said he'd check parts costs and labor. They told him they couldn't wait. 'Just give us a damn number and we'll pay it.' Out of the blue, Bob snapped, 'Five hundred bucks.'

"They told him to go ahead and they'd be back in a week with the cash. The job cost us nearly twice as much, but when the two men returned they handed us five hundred dollars. We would eat the rest of the cost; then I asked them what names they wanted on their receipt. They glanced at one another and the first guy said, 'Thomas Jefferson.' His friend grinned and added, 'Ben Franklin.' So I figured that two can play this game, told them we'd spent another four hundred on their ship, and would they pay it? They nodded but added they had no more cash with them. 'We'll take your check or you can use a credit card,' I told them. They laughed at me. Checks? Credit cards? They thought that was hilarious, said they never used those, and they had to have the airplane *now*. They told me they'd be back the next day to pay the rest.

"Well, since Ben Franklin and Thomas Jefferson rarely show up more than once, and these two dressed in a funny way to be Ben and Frank, with colorful sport shirts open to their navels, showing chests festooned in heavy—and I mean, *heavy*—gold chains with huge gold eagles, I figured that would do nicely as collateral. They looked like they'd wandered off the set of *Miami Vice*. I estimated those chains as worth at least three to four thousand dollars and heavy enough to tie down their airplane. 'We can hold those for you,' I offered. They laughed again, whipped those chains off, and handed them to me. No receipt; nothing. Ben Franklin and Thomas Jefferson were sure some trusting souls. Twenty minutes later they were gone.

"They didn't return the next day and I was wondering how I'd look in a loud sport shirt with all that collateral on my chest weighing me down. Ten days later their Cessna barreled onto our ramp, they hopped out and handed me four hundred-dollar bills, took their chains, waved—and we never saw them again.

"I had one of the greatest trips in my life in a most unexpected way—like something out of a cheapie version of a James Bond movie. A big company that brought many planes to us for complete overhaul and flight testing parked a four-engined DC-6 on our ramp. At the time, in early June of 1974, I'd finished my workday and was in bed reading. The phone rang, I ignored it, but it kept ringing. It was the owner of the DC-6 and he had a question for me.

" 'Nick, you got a pilot to fly my DC-6 for me? I've got

to have that ship in Cyprus by Wednesday or I lose a couple hundred grand on the airplane.'

"I told him this was Sunday night, finding a pilot on such sudden notice would be just about impossible. It was crazy to even try. Well, this guy *was* crazy. Almost but not quite as crazy as myself, it turned out. 'Nick, all we need is a warm body to be legal. I've got a qualified captain and a flight engineer and we need someone in the right seat. Dammit, man, *you* make the trip!'

"Well, he was a good customer, I thought it over for at least two seconds and said I'd be at the field in one hour flat. The deeper I got into this caper, the more I realized just how crazy I really was. I met the captain and the flight engineer. 'How long have you been with this airplane?' I asked.

"They gave me a strange look, said they'd both been hired a few days before and *all* they knew was to get the airplane to Cyprus as fast as they could. Since I was there for the right seat, they'd leave immediately.

"My brain said, 'Whoa! Stop!' What are you getting into, Nick?' Because this pilot did not have any charts. *Nothing.* No en route flight charts, no approach charts, no radio or navigation frequencies; nothing. The captain rushed off to the Pan American flight shack where he borrowed everything he could get his hands on, and when he came back, he borrowed *my* pen! Meanwhile, I was giving this airplane a real looking over. While the captain was stealing—I mean borrowing— whatever he could from Pan Am, I was kicking tires, looking into the engines, working the control surfaces *and* reading that flight manual as fast as I could, and noting, especially, what switches *not* to touch. The captain finally got his act together and I began to appreciate what a smoothie he really was. I also began to appreciate how much he did *not* know.

" 'Nick,' he said with a huge smile, '*you* file for Gander.' Okay; I did. I listed all the HF radio frequencies the captain said were on board for crossing the ocean and into Europe and on to Cyprus. Suddenly we had company. The man who owned the airplane was Lebanese. He introduced himself and handed me a thousand dollars in cash and said, 'You're in charge. He flies'—he motioned to the captain—'but *you* run things.' Then he also gave me a check for a thousand dollars drawn to a Miami bank.

"I explained to him I didn't know too many people in Gander, Newfoundland, or Ireland, and maybe I had a few relatives in Italy who'd trust me with a check for an even grand, but that was it. 'I'll need five thousand cash just to cover expenses,' I told him.

" 'Nicholas, my friend'—he smiled, holding my arm—'it's Sunday. Where am I going to cash a check for five grand on a Sunday?' He was right. He also told me he had absolute faith in my getting that airplane to Cyprus, post-haste. I told myself, what the devil, you've got your American Express card with you, so I knew that in an emergency I *could* pay the bills.

"Sometimes I *know* I'm crazy.

"Two o'clock in the morning and we thundered into the air. We were climbing out steadily, just north of Miami and over Palm Beach when the autopilot quit. Good Lord; we'd be flying all the way to Canada, on to Europe, and across the Mediterranean with hands-on flying the whole trip. Oh well, I welcomed the practice. We'd also fly at nine thousand feet, so that meant we'd likely be punching through weather. *Very* good practice. En route to Canada I tried to call New York Overseas Radio on HF to report our position. All we could raise on the HF was the emergency frequency and we didn't want to do *that*. Too many questions. So we cruised on up to Newfoundland and finally got Canadian control on very high frequency (VHF) and descended into Gander.

"That's where my past sins came home to roost. I used up the thousand dollars cash in nothing flat and charged a lot more on my credit cards. We bought supplies and food and we charged that to my credit cards. We paid the necessary fees and charged *those* on my credit cards.

"We boomed out of Gander and overflew Greenland and put down across the Atlantic (*lots* of hands-on weather flying) in Ireland. The whole way across we Mickey Moused our communications, using our VHF radio to relay position reports to the many jetliners miles above us.

"And here we were in Ireland with the only money among us my last three hundred bucks in cash. That paid for three beds, a few bags of potato chips, and loads of Irish coffee.

Then I went to the operations shack, held my breath, and told the Shell dealer in my best debonair manner to 'top it off.' How I was going to pay for all that fuel was an interesting question, but I'd learned from my own customers in Miami to fill it up first and answer questions second.

"We were almost ready to leave when we were informed by the Irishman at the fuel pumps that he did not trust an *Italian* pilot, nor would he accept any kind of check from a *Lebanese,* drawn on a *Miami* bank by a bunch of seedy-looking characters on their way to the *Mideast.* What that meant was: You fly *after* you pay, not before.

"So I got on the phone and called the airplane's registered owner—whom I found finally in Beirut!—and told him to pay Shell *there,* and have Shell telex the people in Shannon to get their guards away from our airplane. *His* airplane. 'And while you're at it,' I added, 'have them remove the fire trucks in front of the airplane, and have them take the chains off the wheels.' While we waited for all this to happen, we met some marvelous Irishmen who were determined to spend the night drinking us under the table.

"Lo and behold, the miracles had come to pass by morning, and fire trucks, guards, and chains were gone. We lost no time in firing up all four engines and beating a hasty path out of Shannon. I could hardly believe it when we landed on schedule in Cyprus, where the new owner looked proudly at *his* airplane.

"Would I care to fly Pan American back home? I looked at him carefully and said: 'Ahab, I learned long ago that when you're in an Arab land, do as the Arabs do. You don't attract too much attention that way.

"How naive! Ahab booked me on the Arab line Mideast, being flown by British pilots. Ahab also thrust a heavy package into my arms, loaded with Lebanese food, including some overwhelmingly fragrant salami for his friends in Miami. Thank the Lord it didn't fit under my seat. I'd never have lived that long. I grabbed the package when I saw that my airliner was leaving much too soon for comfort. So there I was, dashing wildly into the terminal, checking in, and then rushing to the airplane. That's all it took. I heard my name on the loudspeakers as I climbed aboard the 727, and they ordered me back down to the ramp. There a mob of suspicious guards, all heavily armed, studied my personal luggage, the life raft I'd borrowed from my own company, and that enormous salami package that would have bowled over anyone carless enough to stand downwind of it. They checked everything, including the strange assortment of luggage and packages. I sagged in my seat with relief when we took off.

"Less than one week later war broke out in Beirut and the airport became a vicious battleground. I hate to think of my having been stuck there, but at least I wouldn't have starved. Not with all that salami.

"When I arrived back in Miami, everyone in my office stared at me and held their noses. We sent the salami off in a cab by bribing the driver with a twenty-dollar bill, and he rode off with his windows open and leaning out into the fresh air.

"The next day they pointed to several rebuilt bombers. The work order called for me to take those things up and wring them out to the absolute limits of their performance. I loved every minute of the peace and quiet as I climbed, dove, and beat up those airplanes as best I could. I'll take flight testing any time against that salami!

"It's been a terrific life. I'm still flying as a test pilot, I'm well into my sixties, and I can still pass my first-class physical for the air transport rating. I'm teaching new pilots more than ever before. They'll carry the banners from now on.

"When you add it all up, there's no question left. The Lord has been good to me, and no man can ask for more than that."

$\overline{(15)}$

Hi-Ho!

"Nobody ever wanted to fly more badly than I did. There were uncounted people who wanted to be pilots with the same intensity that drove me, but the problem was that year after year, every time I busted my gut to get my pilot's wings, something interfered."

Harold Silver leaned back against the corrugated side of the Junkers Ju-52, glancing across Gainesville Regional Airport in Florida. For a moment we suspended conversation as a Messerschmitt Me-208, with our good friend Jay Hinyub at the controls, whistled smoothly down the runway and departed in a smooth curving ascent. Silver gestured at the airplane. "I used to dream about things like that. Just busting down a runway and soaring into the sky. Sounds like something out of a movie, doesn't it? But it was real to me, so real I could taste it, and every time I gave it my best shot, like I said, things would get in the way."

Hal Silver grinned. "Do mothers who were terrified of flying count in the history of a guy who finally made it? Who went beyond even his best dreams?" Laughter shook his big-bodied frame. "Because I had a mother who thought all airplanes were the work of the devil. Because back in the Second World War, I had two brothers who were overseas in combat, and another brother was all set to go, and here was her youngest, me, chafing at the bit to enlist in the air force and go kill Nazis and Japs." He drifted back in memory for the moment. "It was really like that. Wanting to go so bad it hurt. But you couldn't tell that to a Romanian mother who thought her sons were going to die and she wanted to hang on to the last one as hard as she could.''

Memories drifted in and out. ''But I'd had this thing under my skin as far back as I could remember. Living in East Harlem in New York was hardly the kind of place where dreams of flying ever had a chance to get off the ground. We lived in that no-man's-land between White Harlem and Spanish Harlem, and when you get right down to it, it was a worse battle front for most of us than going off to war. And then my mother got to blame my father.'' Hal chuckled. ''When I was sixteen and talking about how bad I wanted to fly, my father looked at me in a strange way and told me something he'd never mentioned before. Way back in 1910 my father had taken photographs of Orville Wright. *Orville Wright!* I could hardly believe it. *My* father, this quiet man who lived a life without excitement, had actually *seen* Orville Wright fly? And had spent time with him? And never said a single word to me all those years?

''I wanted to hug him and kill him at the same time. How could he have kept this to himself? And why? Of course you don't get answers, even with the torrent of questions I threw at him. What you get is a monumental shrug. That was a good lesson. If I was going to become a pilot, I'd have to break the mold. I'd have to get out and *enlist*. We were all full of razzmatazz to join up. And there *was* a way.

''The army air forces needed all the pilots they could get at the time. We were taking heavy losses in the air on all fronts. So they set up a deal where you could volunteer at seventeen years old and you went on the list as a potential aviation cadet. *After* you passed the physical and a tough written exam. It was made to order for me. Still wound up like a drum every time I thought of Orville Wright clattering around the skies, and *my* father taking pictures, I tried to sign up. You know what's tougher than the army to get going? Your mother. *My* mother. What sold her finally was my solemn promise that if she didn't sign permission for me to enlist in the aviation cadet program, as soon as I was eighteen I'd enlist in the infantry and I'd probably end up in some damned foxhole and a tank would run over me or some big Nazi would run a bayonet right through my stomach and it would be all her fault.

"She signed, I went down and passed the physical and the written and then I had to go home and wait. I was already in the City College of New York in mechanical engineering, and my mother was praying every day the war would end before I could go off and be the hero I was determined to be. Heroes are a very big thing when you're seventeen. It's all patriotic and romantic and you go see these movies about the Flying Tigers and what the fighter pilots are doing and you go crazy waiting.

"Then we got word that one of my brothers had been wounded in combat. *That* did it. Hair pulling and hysteria. Well, my brother lived through his wounds, but the army didn't send him home. And we never did tell my mother that after he recovered from his wounds, the army put him in the military police, and being an MP after a battle wound could be terrific. He went to Paris, where he was stationed outside a whorehouse, and his job was to keep the long queues straight. You know, when the GIs would line up by the hundreds to get theirs."

Hal shrugged and turned to the big three-engined German bomber. "Hell, man, let's *fly*."

He'd had enough talking for a while. Getting Harold Silver to say the things he'd just been telling me was a rare event. He's one of those people who would rather *do* what needed doing than just talk about it. We did our walkaround to pre-flight the Ju-52, and I watched Hal checking, scanning everything. He had the practiced eye of the professional. Hal Silver was my attorney. What's *that* got to do with all this? Well, he's a *flying* attorney, but that still doesn't place him in a chapter in a book on test pilots.

Ah, there's the rub. Hal had been one of the best test pilots in a game few people ever hear about. A test pilot for the *Army*. Not the Air Force or the Navy or some big company, but the good old-fashioned United States Army. He was also a skilled and combat-proven engineer with hard-won experience in Korea and Vietnam. He was a commercial airplane and helicopter pilot; he was an instructor, and an instrument pilot, and an instrument instructor as well. He had been a leader in project engineering, flight test engineering, aerospace safety engineering, human factors engineering, and, well, he set records building airfields for jet fighters while combat raged in Korea, and he built them in record time that amazed his superiors.

So I didn't see my lawyer doing the preflight for my airplane. I saw an Army pilot who was more than a test pilot; he'd been a master army aviator in fixed-wing aircraft and in all sorts of helicopters, and he'd been one of the top men for our Army and for NATO all through Europe and parts of Asia, and he had been in command of field troops and forces that handled every kind of weapon in readiness against the Russians, including a wicked variety of nuclear weapons and airplanes and helicopters and guided missiles and—

I put all that aside for the moment as I followed Hal, for we had agreed never to trust just one of us when we went flying. We always tried to find something the other guy had missed or screwed up. Just so one of us could give the other holy living hell and that way we felt comfortable before we ever started an engine. We took turns in the air checking each other out, and there the yelling got pretty good sometimes if one of us was just a hair too light or heavy on the rudder or did something sloppy.

Watching Hal peering into the engines and studying the brakes and the hydraulic lines and the tires, draining fuel from the sumps and running skilled fingers along the propeller blades, looking for anything that might be out of line, I again had to remind myself that this was the same man who, years before, had also been a safety officer and a safety investigator for the army, that he'd been a key member of the U.S. Army Aviation Center Accident Board, and that he'd also been as tough as a keg of nails with the men who flew for and under him.

When Hal got near an airplane, you forgot he was a brilliant attorney. You dismissed everything about him beyond his flying and his experience as both a test pilot and an operational pilot in the army. What could drive you nuts was that he had so many qualifications.

I mean, the guy so casually doing his preflight on the big airplane had just about done it *all*. He had excelled in every aviation and engineering field I could list. Even his educational background, if you want to call cramming three dozen separate careers almost all at once into a single skull, demanded special attention. Not satisfied with his initial engineering degrees, he went on to become a master of aerospace operations management at the University of Southern California. During his career as a test pilot, project engineering test pilot, field operations commander, and a few dozen other commands, he'd gained for himself the Army Commendation Medal—a fact I had to drag out of him with pliers. He got it for putting up hangars or buildings and setting still-standing records for building huge runways in combat territory. Lots of good engineers do that. Hal was better and faster than anyone else.

Hal Silver busted a bunch of Army regulations to get what he wanted in rotary wing operations in the Army. Now, busting regulations is a great way to get yourself busted, because the Army has always been infamously intolerant of people who don't play the game the way the brass and the regulations call it. But Hal Silver, already wearing master-army-aviator wings, had a record of doing the impossible—keeping pilots from killing themselves, and their crews, because of poor training, worse operational command from their superiors, and an organization that kept busting out of its seams with helicopters howling and spinning down from the sky and smashing into fire-ripped wreckage. That meant dead pilots, dead crew members, and an appalling loss of valuable, expensive aircraft.

So the Army tapped this lieutenant colonel on the shoulder and sent him forth to straighten out this unholy mess. Off Hal went to the U.S. Army Aviation School at Fort Rucker, Alabama. His orders, in effect, were to "design, implement, and supervise an aggressive safety program in the Department of Rotary Wing Training." All that matters here are the results.

One of the ways Hal gets things done is to *show* his people how it should be done, and he did extraordinary things with helicopters—light, lithe, skittish as dragonflies in turbulence—how *not* to kill themselves. During this period, and here is where the *numbers* have paramount meaning, *he achieved a fifty-seven percent reduction in helicopter accidents*. The army brass was stunned. He had more than cut in half deaths, injuries and loss of helicopters at Fort Rucker! By the time he was through with this assignment, he had changed forever the flying practices of two hundred instructor pilots who were training 4,500 helicopter pilots every year, and who were flying an average of 125,000 flight hours per year.

But let's back up just a bit. What Hal Silver represents are those people who do incredible service to their military branch and to their country, that you just never read about. They don't make headlines, and they have to fight every inch of the way out of city tenements. These are the unsung among the rest of us pilots. The dream of this man—when he was still way back in his teens—was to earn his wings to fly and fight. Hero time, the grand stuff we shouted as a nation to enthusiastic youngsters who'd heed the call of the bugle and the drum and go marching (or flying) off to war.

Finally he got the call. But long before you got near the cockpit of a military aircraft, when those machines were still under the direct control of the army air forces, you had to get through all the exams. Ninety-three young hopefuls gathered for the rigid screening process, and when it was over, only thirteen were left, and one of those thirteen was this eager-beaver kid named Hal Silver, who felt he had his own special mission because *his* father had met with, spoken with, and photographed one of the giants of aviation—Orville Wright.

Off they went, this little band of potential pilots, to Keesler Field in Biloxi, Mississippi. At last—flying! No way, José. More written exams and the first of intensive psychomotor tests to see if all this fresh meat had the stuff to train as pilots. Hal went through the drill and the competition and became not an aviation cadet, but a preaviation cadet. And from the time he was sworn into military service in November of 1944, until a year later when the army handed him his honorable discharge papers, he never once had the chance to get into the air. Those preaviation cadets wrote down answers to questions and were put through rigorous physical tests, while the sound of roaring engines and wind whistling past wings and cockpits drifted all about them from the airfield and drove them crazy with frustration.

Back to college, back to mechanical engineering, aeronautical engineering, and anything else he could learn about what this flying was really going to be all about. When he clasped his engineering degree in his hand, he had something else to show his growing knowledge of how the system *really* worked. Along with his degree went an officer's commission in the Army Corps of Engineers. *Now* he really had his foot back in the door. His record was so outstanding the Army told him they'd make him a regular (e.g., permanent Army) commission instead of being a part of the reserves.

But—and it was the kind of but he kept his eyes open for—that meant he couldn't transfer into the U.S. Air Force as a second lieutenant to be assigned to flight training. So he turned down the regular commission, knew he had a battle on his hands to transfer to the Air Force, and discovered there was a new program for pilot training in the *army*. The stolid, old-fashioned, ground-pounding army, which, as the Air Force was created as a separate service, had been left virtually without pilots and airplanes. The army greeted his application with its own zealous response—and then Hal Silver and almost all officers selected for flight training in the army got tossed aside when massive budget cuts just about killed the Army's flight training program.

Hal bided his time, studying every possible way to circumvent the obstacles that kept springing up in his path. "I figured my golden opportunity was at hand in June of 1950 when North Korea came pounding across the Thirty-eighth Parallel and we were getting the hell beaten out of us by Communist forces. Right after that invasion from the north, my outfit was called up and assigned to immediate active duty for Korean service. Now I was in the 969th Engineer Construction Battalion. Once you're that far up the ladder, you've got the right to hammer on the door for flight school—*again*. I was young, I had my college degree, I was lean and mean and eager and almost flapping my arms I wanted to fly so badly.

"Everything was perfect, except somebody higher up figured the army needed engineers right *now* in Korea. We had been battered so badly and pushed back so far in South Korea that new airfields for fighters and bombers were needed desperately. Off I went to Korea, muttering under my breath, and now a member of the 822nd Engineer Aviation Battalion.

We were to build a runway 8,000 feet long by 150 feet wide and deep into the ground so it could handle heavy jet fighters and bombers.

"Well, we outdid ourselves just a bit. We built that field with a length of ten thousand instead of eight thousand feet, we did the whole thing in concrete, and we also did the job in thirty days flat. Apparently it was quite a record; we were getting commendations and awards left and right."

In every man's life there comes *the* moment of opportunity. It happens at the right time, and when you happen to be in the right place, you react instinctively. Hal Silver was inspecting the runway. Still not officially complete, it was already being heavily used by American jet-fighter bombers. He looked up from his work as a Republic F-84, heavily loaded with machine-gun ammunition, bombs, and powerful rockets, started its run-up. The pilot locked his brakes and moved his throttle forward to get maximum power from his jet engine. The F-84 wasn't exactly the greatest takeoff fighter in the world; it needed every foot of runway available; it had well earned its many derogatory names, beginning with Lead Sled. Everyone paused as the jet engine built to an ear-piercing scream, the fighter straining for release, when flames exploded from the airplane. The engine was taking fuel through its systems like a huge geyser and the flames ballooned upward. Immediately the pilot cut power, but the flames spread swiftly. If the fire reached the high explosives in that airplane or its fuel tanks, the blast would level the area.

The pilot got his canopy back and Hal saw he was struggling wildly to get the hell out of that cockpit before he was engulfed in the spreading flames. Whatever had short-circuited in that airplane had also boomed through the cockpit, and the man, despite his efforts, was trapped. He was as good as dead, until a young officer, weighing all of 150 pounds, dashed madly across the runway, climbed up through intense heat and whipping flames, reached into the cockpit, and with all his strength literally lifted the pilot, weighing well over two hundred pounds with all his gear, helmet, survival kit, and parachute. Not *helped* him out; he *yanked* the pilot clear of his seat and over the side of the cockpit, dragged him onto the wing, jumped to the ground, and half carried, half dragged the man from the burning fighter that threatened to explode at any moment. Well off to the side of the runway, now safe behind the protection of construction equipment, Lieutenant Harold Silver hauled the pilot to a sitting position, checking him over, as crash trucks doused the F-84 in foam and a medical team rushed to the pilot.

Then they looked at Silver—all 150 pounds of him if he were sopping wet—and shook their heads. "How the hell did you manage to do that?" asked an incredulous officer. "Just a few more seconds and this pilot would have been a cooked goose. Didn't you see the flames tearing up the cockpit?"

Silver shrugged, even embarrassed by the questions. A man was in terrible danger and at any moment could be killed, and he did the *only* thing there was to do. Other engineers crowded about him, amazed by what they had seen the skinny officer do.

The Army awarded Harold Silver the Soldier's Medal for that terrifying episode. The Soldier's Medal is a rare award. It's not given for combat. It can only be awarded when the man involved has ignored all risk to his own safety and life by acting in an extraordinary and courageous manner.

Well, that was done and behind him. "I did what I did because it *had* to be done," was all Hal would say. But it was *that* moment, and he lost no time in going to topside command and applying again for flight school. He figured by now, with all that had happened, he'd breeze his way through the doors that had been closed to him so many times.

Wrong. He was already being recommended for special commendations for his work as an engineer, and an engineer he would stay while he still had his duty tour to complete in Korea. After two years of day-in-and-day-out construction work, he was rotated back to the States. He still hadn't gotten off the ground.

Well, back at Gainesville Airport, and Hal muttering, "Enough of all his jabber; let's fly."

"Okay, let's go," I told him. "You want left seat?"

He looked at me as if I were a drooling idiot. Did he want the left seat? The captain's seat in this three-engined ironmonger of an airplane? An airplane that *demanded* to be flown with skill, because it was a huge ship with main gear and a tailwheel, not a machine with gussied-up tricycle gear and everything made as easy as possible for the pilot. Big tail-dragger airplanes are infamous for their wicked behavior on the ground, and the Ju-52 had cut many a smart-ass pilot down to size. This was *my* airplane, and I was the federal examiner on this ship to check out other pilots, and if I didn't believe that they could handle the ironmonger, they did *not* get into the left seat. I'd had to take away the controls from too many pilots who were hurtling into a crash, and I didn't relish that thought.

I also entertained no misgivings about this guy Silver. "Okay, Hi-Ho, you've got it." We climbed aboard and closed up the ship and fired her up, went through the checklist of some fourteen pages, worked the control tower, and taxied out to the run-up area to work the engines, fuel flow, propellers, and the forty-odd other items on the checklist. The tower told us we were number one and cleared to go; Hal wheeled Iron Annie slowly and expertly to the runway, settled the tailwheel straight and true, locked it, rechecked all the gauges and controls for the fourth time, turned to me, and I pointed down the runway.

"Hi-Ho!" I shouted above the engine thunder, and Hal grinned and kept the yoke full back and poured the coal to the three big engines, released the brakes, and we were rolling and into the air in eleven seconds flat. We climbed up to 6,500 feet, where the air was smooth as glass, and throttled back to comfortable cruise; this guy next to me might have been in a rocking chair in his living room.

"Let's go look at Disneyworld," I told him.

"Great," he said, and off we went following Highway I-75 and the Sunshine State Parkway. Who needs charts and all that stuff when you've got the Yellow Brick Road to follow? Hal synchronized the props into a smooth purring, and I eased off my seat belt, slid open the window hatch above us for fresh air, and lit up a cigar. For a while we flew in silence, and then I figured, hey, there's no better time than now. I thumbed the intercom.

"How'd you finally get in?" I asked him. What he wouldn't talk about on the ground, he gave free rein to in the air. Sneaky of me, but it worked.

"Two years in Korea and I came home and those bird-brains had me scheduled for discharge," he said, shaking his head. "All I'd ever wanted to do was *fly*. To hell with the awards and commendations. I'd trade everything in the world for my wings, so it was decision time. If I couldn't get into flight training, I was getting out of the army for good. I went straight to the Army Chief of Engineers in Washington and said either send me to flight school or I quit. The odds are what you get for pulling a stunt like that is to get tossed out on your can. But now the guy on top looked at me and smiled. 'Silver, we're running short of aviators who'll serve their time in the engineer corps. I've looked over your record.' He stuck his hand out and said, 'Welcome aboard.'

"I was *in*. One week later I had my orders and I was off for basic flight training in Texas at San Marcos Air Force Base. It was Air Force training, not Army. Terrific! They started us off in the military version, the L-21, of the civilian Piper Super Cub. Compared to the stuff I'd seen in Korea, it was sort of dinky with a 125-horsepower engine, two-place tandem seating, no radios—we shouted a lot at each other in those things—and it was squirrelly.

"But I was *flying*. I'd be the best. I'd be an *ace*. I'd fly like a bird and then some. I was so damn good I nearly pulled out my shoulder patting myself on my own back. Then we got into stalls and spins, and my instructor had a stomach made of cast iron and he gave new meaning to the word 'spin.' He threw that L-21 around like it was a rag doll. He slipped and he skidded and he'd stall while we were standing on a wing with the nose at some crazy angle, and suddenly my hero—*me*—couldn't tell up from down or my stomach from my throat, and we'd whirl around so fast I didn't know where we were, and he'd pull out and grin at me and shout, 'Okay, Silver, you've got it, now let's see you do your stuff!'

"Boy, I sure showed *him*. I doubt he'll ever forget it. I yanked my beautiful baseball cap from my head and I puked, and gagged, and threw up again until I had the dry heaves and sagged in that seat like a sick dog. The instructor slapped his knee and chortled all the way back to the field. I could barely walk and I was embarrassed as hell.

"I slunk into the barracks wanting to die. Then I passed out and boy, talk about your crazy dreams. All of a sudden I was in an airplane again, spinning like crazy, but now I was in a single-seat Spad fighter in World War I, and I could hear the wind screaming through the wires and the earth whirling around, and suddenly Jean Harlow is in that airplane with me, her arms around my neck and singing out, 'My hero!' I nearly threw up again, but this time I awoke with two things: a cold sweat and a grim determination to learn everything I could about spins and other maneuvers. If I couldn't hack the flying without puking every time we went into aerobatics or spins, they'd cut me from the program. So I stayed up all night and crammed, reading every instruction book on flight maneuvers we had until I *understood* the aerodynamic forces working on the airplane.''

Hal gave me a sheepish grin. ''There's nothing like being a damn fool at the wrong time—like your instructor watching you throw up like some schoolgirl—to straighten you out. Well, I cut the flying instead of being cut out.''

Hal was among the first of his class to solo *and*, despite that gagging scenario in the air, finished his initial flight training with what the Army classifies as ''superior skill and ability in flight n:aneuvers.'' He went off to Fort Sill in Oklahoma, stepping up to heavier and more powerful airplanes, and soon after they made the dream come true by pinning Army aviator wings on his tunic.

And he didn't throw up.

Several years later Hal Silver was highly skilled as both an airplane and a helicopter pilot and was selected to create a new program that would enable an entire engineer topographic company to move from the continental United States to Alaska. The test program was to determine if the unit could meet emergency military needs and, on twenty-four hours' notice, be on its way with the helicopters and cartography experts to provide up-to-the-minute maps and charts for military operations. If the new system worked, the army would be able to react to emergency military situations with greater speed and efficiency than ever before.

Hal moved with the Thirtieth Engineer's Topographic Group to Alaska in record time, the helicopters flying day and night while their combat troops, specialists, and equipment were flown into remote areas by army transports—and then the group "left to fend for itself under conditions of extreme difficulty."

"We had those Hiller H-23 choppers," Hal related. "Among the helicopter family these were the 'weak sisters' of rotary wings. They had little two-hundred-horsepower engines that made every flight an adventure. That was for just flying around. But taking those things with people and equipment to rugged mountaintops, and then trying to land on uneven ground, often on steep slopes and crags, was more nightmare than fun.

"We'd load them up and you knew before you ever left the ground that you had a giant-sized load of trouble on your hands. Those ships needed twice the power they had, and you could feel the heaviness in the machine even as you started to lift. They were sluggish, as if they were trying to fly through thick soup. We had to be alert every second of the time not to lose lift, and we flew with the throttle wide open, using every trick in the book to keep going."

Down low, near the ground, it wasn't so bad. But they had to fly those anemic choppers to between five thousand and eight thousand feet above sea level. In calm air with nothing to slam into, it wouldn't have been so bad. But now, climbing with the heavy loads meant the choppers were straining every foot of the way, and the pilots found themselves suddenly out of power and with no reserves. Rotors thrashing, engines running full tilt, controls set for climb, the choppers were just *sagging* in the air. No matter what the pilots did, they'd lose altitude, and keep on coming down until they were in air dense enough for the rotors spun by their gasping engines to sustain them in flight.

For a while the program went slowly. Hal Silver studied every aspect of helicopter flight aerodynamics. He went out alone in a heavily loaded Hiller to duplicate the problems his pilots faced—and found himself falling out of the sky. One way to get those things up to altitude was to strip everything nonessential to the mission out of the machines, and that included the gear the pilots wore. Every pound counted. If the choppers had to be flown in skeletal form, that's the way it would be done. If the mission called for forty minutes of flight, then the Hillers would start their flights with no more than forty-five or fifty minutes of fuel aboard. At six pounds a gallon, that could make the difference.

"The only way to convince my fellow pilots of what could be done," Hal related, "was to *show* them. I was almost flying the Hillers in my sleep in the field test program. Up at the crack of dawn, because the air was colder and denser, and the machines had thicker—denser—air in which to operate, and that gave us an extra edge. We learned that if we tried to do the job on days when it was warm, let alone hot, the Hillers just couldn't hack it. Like I said, something with more power could have made life easier, but,"—he shrugged—"you use what the Army gives you and you make it *work*."

He ordered an end to vertical lift-offs, because they placed the greatest demand on the lift capability of the Hillers. They would barely get off the ground when the pilots were already translating into forward lift so they could fly an upward swooping curve toward their mountainside destinations. That way they were burning fuel as they went, and that meant eliminating those crucial extra pounds from the Hiller.

That completed the first round of tests: to prove that the Hillers *would* get to the heights needed to carry topographic gear and specialists to their lofty perches to do their work. "The first part of the test program was relatively easy compared to what came next," Hal said with a distasteful grimace. "If we were going to get to some mountain, let's say at six thousand feet, and we had a level place to land, well, there are techniques that let you come in hotter than usual, and between flaring at a certain attitude, your angle of attack, and using ground effect—that cushion of air beneath the chopper—you can do things that aren't in the book, and you can do them safely.

"But that wasn't the problem. We didn't have any level places where we could land using all these fancy, tap-dancing techniques. The army wanted *realism,* so they gave us a bunch of mountaintops and high crags that would give fits to a goat. And the army told us to *land* on those sites. Half the guys believed these would be the last flights they'd ever make.

"It wouldn't have been so bad if we'd had some sort of guidance from some poor sucker who'd done this before us.

But *we* were the poor suckers who'd prove whether or not it was possible, so a lot of people stateside watched everything we did. The stickler was setting down the chopper on its skids and shutting down the engine. If you've got a steep slope or a ledge, you can put the bird down on one skid and keep it 'flying in a standstill.' It's resting on that skid, so that what you've done is take the full weight of the chopper from the rotor lift, and once you've done that, it's the same as holding your position by 'elbow-leaning' on the mountain with the one skid.

"Which is what we had to do. *All* of us. That meant we became one hell of a team. No one wanted to see a Hiller go tumbling end over end down a mountain, spitting out pieces of chopper and people while it was burning and tearing itself apart. Okay, baby, we'd come in with that tap-dancing approach and work one skid down on loose rocks and gravel, ease off the demand on the rotor. Once we got to that point— my God, the Hiller people would have cried if they'd seen what we did with their product—we would move the chopper in such a fashion that the skid dug itself a trough. Slightly forward and then slightly backward, and from side to side, all the time *flying* that thing like a very expensive shovel. That's exactly what we did with the skid against the mountaintop slope. We'd dig a trough with it using a helicopter that was about to gasp its last, and when that trough was deep enough and wide enough, we could slowly lower the other skid so that the angle of the dangle—the way the chopper would slant on that slope—was just shallow enough to let it rest on its own weight. Then we'd cut the power, and there'd be a lot of crossed fingers and praying and cussing and everybody wishing for a very big shot of whiskey.

"We did it. We never lost a chopper. We met every demand of the Army and we went way beyond what they expected. Our favorite landing—it was *the* challenge for all the pilots—was what the guys called the Jewish Mountain. There was a cone-shaped peak, it must have been an old lava formation, and it formed a perfect cone at the top, with smooth sides on the slopes all around. By now we were grasping at anything that might even have some humor to it. The cone-shaped mountain became Mount Cohen, and you were considered a graduate of our school-on-the-spot if you could bring your chopper down perfectly, with the winds really knocking you around, with each skid on its own side of that rounded cone, which itself was only an inch or two from the belly of the chopper.

"I wish I had movies of those scenes. Because here was this little helicopter, balanced perfectly atop the mountain, and it looked like some kind of dragonfly that just laid an egg that was, literally, as big as a whole mountain!"

If it took being high in the air to get all this from Hal Silver, it was worth it. We continued south in the Ju-52, following the Yellow Brick Road, and worked our way through the thickening traffic of the Orlando area. There's something great about being in the midst of all these super-glitzed, multimillion-dollar jetliners while you're flying one of the great ancestors of the breed, and all the controllers know your radio call sign, and the real heavies are willing to give you the right of way so that they can see you in the air and know what their daddies flew. We went into Orlando Executive Airport (which for a long time was simply good old Herndon) and taxied up to the Ninety-fourth Aero Squadron, which is not a flight operations shack or an aircraft shop, but a terrific restaurant. Time for a thick steak and back into history.

"What did you do when you finished your chopper madness in Alaska?"

Hal tapped his knife on his plane. "We went to Europe, where you can get schnitzel and food you just can't get over here." He smiled and waved away the waiter determined to sell us some wine—very good wine but we'd soon be flying again. "Oh, in between the Alaskan program there were all sorts of special assignments, but they didn't last long. I became top dog for aviation in a combat engineer group in Germany, working closely with NATO teams. Then I supervised missile site construction, buried myself in heavy engineering and construction, all the time chafing to get back to full-time flight work. I wanted more testing. I loved the challenge, the risks, the rewards of achievement. Life gets dull without that."

Things picked up when Silver became a top aviation officer and aviator for the NATO commander and flew off to Izmir,

Turkey. He didn't get his flight testing assignment, but it was close to it as he flew American, Turkish, Greek, Italian, British, and Canadian military teams throughout Europe— mostly into oddball places where *everyone* was regarded with suspicion. "You never knew when you'd be fighting your way back to your plane." He laughed. "For all I know they were asking us to stay for dinner, but waving knives and guns in the air often gave me the urge to look down on all those people as we accelerated our departure mode."

Then the wheels turned again and Hal was back in test work. Very unglamorous test work, but vital. This was hands-on grease-monkey stuff, improving the performance of various types of helicopters, flight-testing spark plugs to destruction, hammering engines at full power under the worst conditions to define their limits. "Nothing to write home about, that's for sure," Hal confirmed. "But it's the kind of testing that goes on *all* the time, and no one gets medals for it, and hardly anyone recognizes it, but the people who do that work year after year are what enables the rest of us to fly with a feeling of safety."

"You stay in that long?"

Hal grinned like an old hound dog with fresh possum in its jaws. "Couple of years." He shrugged. "Then the gods smiled on me and it was tap-dancing time when I received my assignment to the Army's Aviation Test Board at Fort Rucker in Alabama. The sole purpose of this outfit was to test military aircraft. It was absolutely the dream assignment. They tested military aircraft to determine their potential use in the military arsenal—period. That's a fancy way of saying, 'Here's this airplane, we want to know everything about it, so go upstairs and beat the living hell out of that thing, study every part and piece and everything it does or fails to do in the air, don't get killed, then come back with a *very* detailed report.' They might have added that if your report, single-spaced, wasn't at least an inch thick, they looked at you as if you were a slacker."

"They really turned you loose like that?" I pushed.

"Boy, did they ever. Gave me my own test pilot program for the NU-8F, which was the prototype of the Beech U-21 twin-engined turboprop utility ship. This actually was the ancestor to the civilian job everyone knows now as the King

Air. But the best thing is that I was to flight-test the prototype, the first ever of its kind. In fact, the two new turboprop engines were numbers one and two PT6A powerplants from the Pratt and Whitney factory. It was a whole new ballgame, and when I got my orders specifying an absolute minimum of 110 flight-testing hours, well, this is what I had always wanted.''

The moment the army gave him the nod, Hal was winging his way to Wichita to accept delivery of the first experimental NU-8F. ''We stayed at Beech long enough for me to go through the official checkout so that when I put Kansas behind me I'd be not only the test pilot but the official instructor pilot as well. That was a neat position to hold. Man, I was king of the hill.

''Now, the airplane that eventually became the King Air was a very civilized bird. It traced its ancestry back to the Twin Bonanza that you used to fly. Didn't you have your own airlines with a couple of those things?''

''Sure did. We covered the Bahamas with them,'' I confirmed. ''Operated out of Merritt Island, right close to Cape Canaveral.''

''Well, the Twin Bonanza was also an army airplane designed to army specs that called for operations out of the worst rough airfields one could think of. Out of the T-Bone came the Queen Air with the bigger cabin, but it still had the T-Bone wings, tail, and other structural elements. Beech then improved the whole arrangement with structural mods and the turboprop engines and created a new airplane that was a world-beater.

''But we weren't going to fly it in a safe, sane, and sober manner. My job was to fly it smoothly, but to beat the hell out of it. So we did what very few pilots ever do in the King Air series. We often wore parachutes. Sort of raised my eyebrows to do that, but when I got into the real wild stuff in that ship, I appreciated having the packaged nylon strapped to my carcass.''

Hal Silver's flying had been, for the most part, down low. If there were mountains, he expected to fly through the ravines and the saddlebacks and the passes, turning and twisting and flying down valleys. He liked that kind of flying in both fixed wing and helicopters. Suddenly the test protocol leaped out from the program pages at him. High altitude? He'd *never* flown to high altitude in a test or operational program before.

His copilot on some flights was considered to be the cream of the crop in flight engineering—Captain Ivar W. Rundgren, Jr. "How high do we go?" he asked Hal.

"As high as this thing will take us." Hal shrugged. "You got any ideas?"

"Damned if I know," Rundgren replied. "And don't ask me what the book says. Those engines out there haven't been taken all the way up before. What's your guess?"

Hal Silver stared Rundgren in the eyes. "High," is all he would say.

Hal drove the new ship all the way up to twenty-eight thousand feet. He couldn't believe it. What the hell am I doing up here? he kept asking himself. The army was pleased with the ceiling he'd reached because the airplane was still climbing. "Can you take it higher?" they asked him. He stripped down the airplane and took her up. How high? "Don't know," Hal said. "Recording instruments froze or just plain failed. But I'll tell you this: We were *way* up beyond what Beech or Pratt and Whitney said that thing could do. It was great."

The stall tests were *not* so great. The more Hall considered the nature of the airplane and the severely altered airflow from the earlier Queen Air derivatives, the more convinced he was that the sleek engine nacelles of the NU-8F could hide some nasty surprises. So he set his minimum altitude for his series of stall tests at eight thousand feet. Other pilots told him he was being an overcautious old woman. Hal didn't deign to reply.

There's an old rule in our game. You can blow all the smoke you want to people about what you do in your airplane. You can spin tall tales until the cows home home and it doesn't matter a whit. But if you lie to your airplane—it will kill you.

"So this overcautious old woman"—Hal laughed—"stayed with the safety rules above all else. I knew the Queen Air was a sweetheart in the stall regime. It had been tested and proven thoroughly. But we were entering virgin territory with the NU-8F.

"Up to eight grand above terra firma and I put her through

the first full stall tests, and *BLAM!* Talk about the unexpected! She came up with her nose as I kept the yoke coming back toward me, and walked rudder to keep her headed straight and true, and then we were into the full stall. She shuddered and shook her fanny in full warning as lift spilled away from the wings. Now, in the Queen Air the nose will drop and you can recover with very little loss of altitude.

"NU-8F apparently hadn't read the book on its predecessor, because when I kept her at the very edge and then into full stall, that airplane kicked like a mule that's just sat on a hornet's nest. The nose stayed on heading, but the left wing snapped down violently. The next instant the airplane was standing on its left wing—the wings were vertical to the ground—and in this attitude, and sans airspeed, that was all she wrote. It took me just about three thousand feet before I got full recovery from that stall.

"Well, maybe I'd screwed up. Back to eight grand and let's try this again, baby, and the stall was worse than the first time. I went through this drill at least ten times to be absolutely certain, and the results were the same every time. This airplane had a *problem*. I wrote a detailed report to that effect.

"My boss was Lieutenant Colonel Robert J. LaHaie. He was one of the old-timers from the air force, a pilot forever, and for some reason shifted over to army aviation. He really didn't believe my report. The blue-suiters are like that. You can't tell them a damn thing. He glared at me, grabbed his cap, and said, 'Let's go, mister. I'll take the left seat.' Well, at the time he outranked me, and so . . .

"He took the left seat, we went to eight thousand feet, and the know-it-all blue-suiter let his jaw go slack when that new turboprop reared wildly and this time swung the nose violently as the left wing ran for the ground. What he said in exclamation I won't repeat, but he turned the air as blue as his suit. He repeated the stalls several times, and every time the airplane tore itself out of his control. I had that famous old mule-eating-tree-bark smile on my face. To LaHaie's credit he told me he respected a man who stuck to his guns, and I'd done that, all right.

"We also found the necessary fix. We called Beech and I gave their people some rides out of that violent wing pitch-down out of the stall, and they were hanging on for dear life as we ended up diving for the ground. The Beech engineers corrected the problem by installing stall strips on the inboard section of each wing, and just like *that* we had an airplane as docile as the Queen Air in the stall regime. But without these tests, and repeating them so many times all questions were banished, we'd have put an airplane into service which, had it been stalled by an unwary pilot closer to the ground, could have killed a great many people.''

Everybody who flies military missions needs to know how their airplane will handle severe weather conditions, and that means ice. Ice increases your weight tremendously, blankets out the windshield, and so corrupts the airflow over the wings that in a very short period of time the airplane is no longer able to fly. Every year airplanes crash because of this problem, and that includes everything from the small single-engined jobs to the four-engined heavy iron. Hal flew a long series of icing tests. Since the idea was to find out how the NU-8F handled in ice *before* it became uncontrollable, they worked with another airplane, a large de Havilland Caribou that made instant icing weather.

Caribou and Beech went up high enough so that the outside air temperature was down to about zero degrees Fahrenheit. The Caribou held a huge tank of water colored with yellow dye and released the water in a heavy stream—into which Hal flew in the Beech. Immediately ice began forming on the wings while cameras and instruments recorded what was going on and Hal determined the deteriorating flight characteristics of NU-8F. As the tests continued Hal would let the Beech ice up on one side, end the tests, let the ice melt off, and then go up again to douse the other side of the airplane.

''The icing tests went as programmed,'' Hal said, then smiled suddenly. ''Except when we got a new top dog in the outfit, an obnoxious, overbearing know-it-all. I was still doing the preflight when he shouted for me to knock it off and get in the airplane. I told him the preflight wasn't done. He shouted louder this time. 'Let the damned mechanic finish that. You get inside and get ready to crank it up. And that's an *order*!'

''You know the answer. 'Yessir!' all in one clipped word. Well, turns out the mechanic had screwed up one of the fuel drains. We went upstairs and the Caribou dumped its yellow water on us, and very quickly I discovered the Beech was getting *very* heavy on one wing. I told the colonel we had a problem and I was using almost full aileron just to keep the wings level.''

Hal landed with the aileron control at its maximum deflection. Five or ten more minutes and the airplane would have whipped out of control. The colonel ranted at him and ordered Hal to keep flying, but this time Hal ignored shouts and threats and landed, and ''I made damn sure that birdbrain checked what was wrong, and showed him that *all* fuel had drained from one wing, and we were almost dead meat if I'd followed his orders. Well, the colonel sure as hell could have had me written up for insubordination and a few unkind things I'd said about him and his family ancestry, but then, *his* stupidity would have been exposed. Nothing further was said.

''But let me emphasize that when you're dealing with top dogs, rank will sometimes speak without the aid of the speaker's brain. Before I finished the complete tests on this airplane I had told a whole bunch of superior officers who questioned my findings that they didn't know what the hell they were talking about, and it was the *airplane* that always had the final say-so.

''I had some beautiful moments of standing at a stiff brace while a higher-ranking officer turned red in the face and threatened a court-martial. Finally I got so fed up with this nonsense, I simply told whoever had his nose out of joint to just go ahead and file charges. I was not the most popular pilot on the team, maybe because every time they argued with me, and someone took up the airplane to check out my reports, the airplane vindicated everything I'd reported.

''Not to be unfair and suggest that all the top dogs were of this same ilk, we had a Lieutenant Colonel Douglas F. Parham who came in to help run the outfit. Parham questioned me thoroughly about the great disputes that were going on, and I laid it right on the line. He told me to take a seat and relax. 'Silver, let me tell you something. I've been in this business a long time. I graduated West Point high in my class. I went through flight school in a way I don't think anyone ever matched. You see, my instructor wrote on my reports that I had managed something no one had ever done before. He said I had made *every* mistake in the book, but I was smart enough not to make any of them twice. Mister, you go fly that airplane just the way you've been doing. It's *your* test program.'

"Hell of a guy. Let me add something else here. Testing the NU-8F with the freedom I had was the experience of a lifetime. We didn't have any manuals to rely on. It was *testing*. Innovation was the name of the game. There was no time to be afraid or to hesitate. You decided how you were going to master the aircraft and you hung on for dear life when things got nasty, and then you landed and wrote it all down.

"When I completed the program and wrote that exhaustive report, my conclusions and recommendations were examined by I don't know how many review boards. This airplane in its civilian version was going to be a world-beater, and the companies that contributed to it took some serious umbrage with some of my findings. God bless that Colonel Parham. He called in the industry reps, told them to get the hell in the airplane, and that Silver would *show* them which way was up.

"Five of them climbed aboard and I gave them the best demonstration I've ever flown. I made that airplane talk and dance. I turned it every which way but loose, and when I landed I knew that those industry reps had a sort of real thrilling ride. The Army accepted all *my* reports, but the industry reps apparently were still wobbly from their flight with me. As it turned out, and this is what counts, every recommendation I made was accepted as a requirement before the Army would buy the airplane. At that point, I was finished with this flight test program. I'd come through it all in fine fettle and with a perfect record."

I nodded and paused for a moment. "What happened after that?" I asked.

Hal held my gaze. "What do you think happened? I shipped off to Vietnam!"

It's a Cutlass! Run for Your Life!

John Moore doesn't *look* like a test pilot. And if he did, he ought to be wearing a long white silk scarf, a hat tilted at a rakish angle, and a blazer. He's the epitome of an English gentleman. He was in his time one of the best test pilots in the United States Navy, which of course, contemplating John's exemplary skills in the cockpit, gave him one of the most cantankerous jet fighters ever built to wring out and tame, a beast that was called Cutlass.

John Moore was commissioned as a naval pilot with shiny gold wings in 1944 and quickly moved up into progressively more demanding airplanes and programs that included training as a night-fighter pilot in the classic Grumman F6F-5N Hellcat. He later joined VBF-20 and VF-10A outfits of our Navy, where he advanced to the Grumman F8F-1 Bearcat, unquestionably the hottest piston-engine fighter plane ever built. He became a flight instructor at Pensacola Naval Air Station in Florida. A flight instructor is then ready for anything, and John went halfway around the world with VF-51 to fly two full combat tours in Korea. Since he had managed to move silkily through all the foregoing, the Navy judged him to be prime test-pilot material and sent John to the U.S. Navy test pilots' school at Patuxent River, Maryland. After graduation he moved on to even more demanding flying— two years as a test pilot in the Aircraft Carrier Suitability Branch. By the time he "hung up his hook" he had flown

Grumman Hellcat

more than four hundred aircraft carrier landings in more than twenty-two different types of aircraft.

John finally left the Navy to become an engineering test pilot with North American Aviation, where he participated in development of the T-2C Buckeye jet trainer and a massive brute of an attack bomber, the RA-5C Vigilante. Moving from engineering test flying, he established and maintained the Apollo Test Operations team for Rockwell International, which sent a barrage of the Apollo manned spacecraft to the moon aboard the monstrous Saturn V rocket booster. After retiring from Rockwell International, John became the mayor of Cocoa Beach, Florida, just south of Cape Canaveral and the Kennedy Space Center, where, long ago, we met one another at the start of a long friendship. John just doesn't know when to quit and for some years now he has been an outstanding teacher at Brevard Community College in Cocoa, Florida.

Now, an introductory note about the Chance-Vought F7U-3 Cutlass, a brawling jet fighter designed for carrier service. But let John Moore make his own introduction. . . .

The Cutlass was one of the more memorable airplanes I flew in my years as a hooker. In fact, it was unforgettable. As my friend Ed Gillespie, fellow Cutlass driver, used to say—periods of excitement interspersed with moments of stark terror. At the gray-hair stage in my life, my recollections of details may be fuzzy but not so of events in surviving the Cutlass. Unfortunately, I seem to be touched by that memory disease, the name of which escapes me at the moment, so I respectfully ask the indulgence of those few surviving, heroic Cutlass drivers if my statistics are suspect.

And now in his own inimitable style:

In the summer of 1953, after two hours with VF-51 [VF-51 is the designation of Moore's combat organization] in the Korean War, Bob Rostine and I were dispatched to Pax River at the instigation of our great skipper, George Duncan, who, as it turned out, seemed to be punishing us for something. Rostine, one of the finest stick and throttle jocks who ever lived, went straight to the carrier suitability branch of flight tests where they needed a pilot with his skills to take the F7U-3 *Cutlass* carrier trial tests. I went to test pilot school, class 11.

Rostine could make any airplane, in fact any moving vehicle, look good. He could have saved the Edsel. If anyone could make the Cutlass look good, he could. He did. Bob was a reserve officer who had applied a number of times for regular Navy. Why he had not been accepted, no one knew. But he made the Cutlass look so good aboard ship that Chance Vought hired him away from the Navy. Probably the brightest move Vought ever made.

Rostine's boss, Paul Thayer, a former Cutlass pilot, had put on one of the best air shows ever at Pax [Patuxtent] River flying the F7U-1. He had roared in low over the field during a scheduled air show and pulled up into a vertical climb to the cheers of thousands. Toward the top of his ascent the entire aft end of the Cutlass burst into flames, followed by Thayer ejecting safely to the field below while the Cutlass roman-candled into Chesapeake Bay. That was Thayer's last flight in the Cutlass, which showed how smart he was and why he made president of LTV [Ling-Temco-Vought]. Rostine went on to become chief test pilot of LTV and was, until the day he died of cancer, one of the very best.

I made it through test pilot school and, in spite of being low man on the scrotum pole, was assigned to the carrier suitability branch of flight test, joining a small if innocuous group that included the likes of Nick Smith III, Al Shepard, and Rostine, under the tutelage of our skipper, Bob Calland, with John Shepherd providing vast quantities of empirical data to which no one paid any attention.

While Al Shepard and Smith were frolicking about in A4Ds, F4Ds, F9F-8s, F3Hs, and the like, I was assigned two other rather diverse programs. One was backing up Rostine in the Cutlass, since he would soon be joining Chance Vought. The other was the flex-deck program, which involved making wheels-up arrested landings into a rubber deck after John Norris of Grumman had demonstrated it could be done, for whatever reason. The air force had made two arrested landings onto a rubber deck using a straight-wing F-84 as a test vehicle. The first one had caused serious injury to the pilot's back, so they got another pilot for the second landing, which caused serious injury to the pilot's back. With the admirable wisdom of a tailhookless air force, they abandoned the project. The Navy, however, persevered, believing that with their superior pilots in fold, naval aviators could do on the pitching deck of an aircraft carrier what air-force pilots could not do on a stationary airfield.

While I was roaring around the carrier pattern in AD-5Ns during carrier suit [suitability] trials on USS *Coral Sea* (CVA-43), Rostine was completing the Cutlass carrier suit tests. That's when Chance Vought hired him and I was assigned the F7U project as Smith and Shepherd busied themselves out of sight until the deed was done. No wonder Al became an astronaut and Nick Smith head of the test pilot school—they were smarter than I was, by a bunch.

In the carrier suit stable was a collection of airplanes instrumented to measure stress parameters associated with catapult and arrested landing operations. Thus the carrier suit pilots, seven or eight of us, would frequently be dispatched in the instrumented flying machines to calibrate newly installed launch and landing equipment on various aircraft carriers.

That made for a lot of diverse carrier operations, such as Project Steam, aboard *Hancock* (CVA-19), based in San Diego. For Project Steam, we took all our instrumented carrier suit planes from Pax to North Island to evaluate and help calibrate *Hancock's* new steam catapults. I was first to depart in F7U-3 BuNo 128475, and last to arrive by several days, after lots of hydraulic fluid and JP-5 [jet fuel]. But I got there nonetheless. Supplementing our stable were a few other uninstrumented flying machines and pilots, including Floyd Nugent in another Cutlass.

One of Floyd's F7U flights was impressive. As he was catapulted, the landing gear oleos extended one of the mains to the bottom of the Pacific, about six thousand feet deep at that point. Landing the Cutlass on land or sea was normally a memorable event under the best of circumstances, but without a main landing gear or wheels up, was dicey at best. So Floyd trimmed up at eight thousand feet under the watchful eye of Nick Smith in an FJ-3, or something, and punched out some thirty miles offshore San Diego. Good parachute, good water landing, good helo pickup, and Floyd was deposited at North Island. Meanwhile, the Cutlass did not seem to miss Floyd one whit, and just kept on going. Soon it headed east toward San Diego, pursued by Nick Smith, who had discovered that this Cutlass had exceptional perseverance. Nick made several valiant attempts to tip the wayward airplane seaward by putting his wing under the stubborn F7U, gaining for his efforts only smashed-up landing lights. The Cutlass could care less.

Floyd looked up from the helo pad at North Island only to see a Cutlass, sans canopy, flying by. He wondered who was flying it, and the answer was—no one. In fact, it seemed to fly as well without Floyd as with him. Finally, after a simulated rocket attack on Point Loma and an exciting simulated strafing run on the Hotel Del Coronado, the Cutlass hung ten on a wave just south of the Hotel Del, coming to rest about fifty feet offshore among the startled abalone, many of which had never before seen a Cutlass.

Fortunately, the call for more wheels-up rubber deck landings at Pax was loud enough for me to S2F it across country with Bob Feliton, marine type, ending my F7U venture on *Hancock*.

Shortly afterward, when old No. 475 was returned to Pax, our skipper decided that at least one of our LSOs should be checked out in the Cutlass—familiarity and all that. Bill Tobin of the handlebar mustache was selected—no volunteer he—and after adequate briefings, we went down to the Cutlass for "Tobe's" first fam hop. Following yet another cockpit tour, Bill, strapped in and ready, started both engines. As they idled he observed that two of the four flight-control-system warning lights were blinking on and off—mostly on. "Why," he asked, "are these lights on?" I assured him there was nothing to be concerned about, just a peculiarity of this particular airplane. "How," he asked, "does one shut the engines off?" I showed him, whereupon he shut down both engines, unbuckled, pushed me and himself down the access ladder, and walked away. He never again got in the Cutlass, or under it, for that matter.

Most of us agreed that the Cutlass could be made into a pretty good flying machine with a few mods, like adding a conventional tail, tripling the thrust, cutting the nosewheel strut in half, completely redoing the flight control system, and getting someone else to fly it. It was, indeed, one of the first fighters with a complete irreversible flight control system—it actually had four separate hydraulic systems to power the flight controls. But it was really an unreliable, unforgiving airplane, and was helped none at all by Westinghouse's J46 engines, which generated about the same amount of heat as their toasters. From the flying standpoint, for example, Bob Rostine, briefing me early on, explained that if you approached the stall in clean configuration, the Cutlass felt as if it were slicing to the left through the air, and suggested that I become familiar with the sensation, which I did. Sure enough, a discernible slice. One of the other indomitable F7U drivers at Pax pursued the slice one day and suddenly found himself in a poststall gyration from which he could not recover. He leaped out safely at about five thousand feet into the chilly Chesapeake as his Cutlass splashed below.

How could this be? thought Bud Sickle (I think it was), a fine pilot with a bunch of F7U hours, flying with a RAG unit out of Moffett or somewhere. "I'll take a look at it," sez he. Sure enough, the slice, the poststall gyration, the ejection, the parachute blossoming out above. Two for two.

Chance-Vought sez, "Wait a minute, we'll look at this." They instrumented one of their F7Us at Dallas for the test, put a camera in the cockpit focused on the pilot, somehow found one of their pilots who would fly the mission (not Rostine, you can bet), and off they went. Well-documented flight test. Approach to stall, camera on, data on, the slice, the poststall gyration, excellent movies of great activity in the cockpit—right stick, back stick, forward stick, then both hands up on the face curtain. A firm pull and there was no one in the cockpit. Three for three.

Cutlass pilots, those who were left, were admonished to avoid the poststall gyration.

At PAX we were advised to prepare for the arrival of a new model of the Cutlass, the F7U-3M, configured to carry four Sparrow missiles, with more fuel, much more gross weight, but no more thrust. Same Westinghouse windmills, two J46s, each supposedly generating six thousand pounds of thrust in afterburner, and about 3,500 pounds in military rated thrust (MRT). Of course there was no modulation in the afterburners—either on or off. Full-up gross weight with the four Sparrows was in excess of thirty-two thousand pounds, with landing weight ranges of twenty-four thousand to twenty-five-thousand pounds when returning aboard with the four missiles and a reasonable fuel reserve.

I managed somehow to convince our skipper that I had served my time in the Cutlass and that some other lucky lad should have the opportunity to share the exhilaration I had known. Sure enough, a new and unsuspecting graduate of TPS, class 13, I think, named Johnny Long was assigned the 3M. Johnny was a neat guy, always smiling, always eager. I never flew the F7U03M while Johnny was preparing for carrier trials on *Shangri-la* (CVA-38) out of San Diego, but bid him well as he departed in his 3M for the West Coast, via Marietta, Dallas, and El Paso. Unfortunately, as Johnny landed at Dallas next to the Chance Vought plant, he lost it after touchdown. The airplane rotated counterclockwise and slid to the left off the runway, shearing all three landing gear. Johnny managed to get out safely—the plane did not burn—but he was badly incapacitated with a broken back.

My exhilaration at knowing that Johnny was alive, if bent, was short-lived as I was advised of my newest assignment, the F7U-3M project. I do believe that in my flying career, that was my first "oh shit."

When the replacement 3M was ready at Vought, I was dispatched via commercial airliner to Dallas, dressed in my clean uniform. The pall of the event was only assuaged by the adulation of the stewardii and their admiration for both my ribbons. Arriving in Dallas, first things first—a visit to the hospital to see Johnny Long. I found him lying on a curved slab, bent backward pretzellike, with his stomach at least a foot above his head and feet. The medics were trying to reposition a bunch of vertebrae before encasing him in plaster from head to toe. Ever-smiling Johnny—God, I don't know how he did it. Nice but brief visit (always be brief in hospitals). He did not know what happened or how he lost it. "You look great, Johnny." (He didn't.) "Bye."

After some briefings by the Chance Vought pilots (they had some great pilots, along with Rostine) I prepared for my first visit with the 3M. "We always take off in afterburner," they said. It did not take long to find out why. After getting airborne and checking systems—it seemed like just another Cutlass, if sluggish—and I came in to shoot my first anomaly. (Chance Vought used that word frequently.) While making my approach from the 180 about a hundred feet over the rooftops, and at an acceptable approach speed, i.e., 135 knots, I found that I was at full MRT trying to maintain airspeed. It was not enough. At the ninety in a lovely approach, my airspeed was rapidly decreasing to the extent I went into afterburner to accelerate out of the Dallas Econo Lodge. Once up to 150 knots I resumed the simulated carrier approach, finding myself at MRT again just trying to stay airborne. The landing was uneventful, it turned out. I made four more approaches and landings, according to my logbook, each time having to use afterburner to make it around the pattern. It was troubling.

Lengthy discussions of this problem with Chance Vought types, including the pilots, resulted in two things: (a) yes, the plane had a thrust problem which the Vought pilots accommodated with a faster, descending approach, and usually at lighter gross weights than I was going to be required to use, and (b) they agreed to engine calibration runs to assure the J46s were properly set. From the latter there was bad news. The first bad news was that, indeed, the right engine temps were incorrect, and the other bad news was that the temps were too high and in resetting them downward to correct limits I lost another couple hundred pounds of thrust at MRT.

Another anomaly evolved that would ultimately throw fear into the hearts of crash crews nationwide, to wit—the left engine on shutdown exuded great clouds of grayish smoke for about thirty seconds as the engine wound down. "Not to worry, John, it is a peculiarity of that engine and is no problem." Try telling that to the crash crews in Albuquerque.

Next trip was to see U-shaped Johnny Long who was about to be plastered in the hospital. He allowed as how he'd had the same problem at heavier gross weights but had not done much work in the approach regime with Sparrows and ammo aboard. Hoo boy!

Several days and some misgivings later I departed in F7U-3M BuNo 129736 for San Diego with a fueling stop at El Paso International, where the Vought reps would greet me and service the airplane. The trip was not without its headaches.

I received clearance from the tower to land in El Paso, made a sterling, if speedy approach and a stellar landing. taxied behind the follow-me jeep to a VIP location by the ops building and was greeted by three jeeps full of uniformed men with machine guns, the lead jeep being commanded by a guy with eagles on his collar and a .45 on his hip. In order to ascertain the reasons for the nice welcome I shut down the machine and you can imagine what the clouds of smoke emanating from the left engine did to stimulate the crash crew. With much arm waving I persuaded them not to fill the engine with foam, but then the colonel wanted to know who I was and what the hell I was doing there. It was then that the thought crossed my mind that there might be another field nearby. I wondered where the Vought guys were.

In the ops building I explained to yet another colonel that I was Lieutenant John Moore, USN, flying a highly instrumented new navy fighter to San Diego and that I could not understand why his command had not received my clearance. I wisely did not ask what was with all the B-47s and B-52s parked around. It was apparent that being an uninvited navy lieutenant on a SAC base made one less than welcome. But finally the Vought gang came up from El Paso International Airport ten miles to the south where they had been waiting for me, talked their way through the gates, serviced the machine, and off I went westward, hopefully leaving the SAC personnel with the thought that maybe they had just seen the navy's first stealth fighter, what with the no tail and all. Later, I arrived safely at Miramar.

After some FLCP at Miramar and further evaluation of the thrust problem, I learned that in an approach turn the bottom of the thrust-vs-airspeed curve was about 155 knots at these weights and the backside of the curve was Mount Everest–like, quickly exceeding whatever thrust was being generated at MRT. LSOs, of course, are not fond of those abnormally high approach speeds. But ever onward.

To assure the beginning of the tests and to eliminate me from the decision-making loop, 3M No. 7 was hoisted aboard *Shangri-la* at North Island, and I had the ship all to myself for three days of carrier trials with this wonderous machine. Almost every approach required afterburner to stay aloft at gross weights of over twenty-five thousand pounds with all ammo and missiles aboard. I became fairly adept at cycling in and out of just the left engine afterburner instead of both to sustain an acceptable approach speed, but there was little question in this pilot's mind that you could never send this airplane to the fleet under these circumstances. Fleet pilots deserved better, besides the fact that such performance would surely take a heavy toll in men and machines.

And so it was in June of 1955 that the F7U-3M and I arrived back at Pax after stops at Miramar, Albuquerque, Dallas, and Marietta. I avoided El Paso.

My debriefing with our skipper Bob Calland attracted a crowd of disbelievers, even drawing Tom Gallagher from the flying qualities branch, whose pilots had not done any FCLP in the 3M at the heavier gross weights. Calland promptly got in No. 736 for the fam and FCLP and, after one flight, vowed he would never fly it again. But he did, enough to be convinced the 3M could not go to the fleet where pilots would be required to return aboard ship with *Sparrows* and ammo, as required by NuAer, or BuWeps, or whatever it was called then. Gallagher and J. Lynn Helms each drove the plane under these circumstances and our opinions were identical. For sure, the Bureau troops needed opinions from more than a lowly lieutenant, and they were about to get them.

The Bureau-crats were unanimous in being horrified—they had ordered ninety-eight of these mothers and were being told they could not go aboard ship. Chance Vought was horrified that the Bureau was horrified. The world's largest conference outside the UN was thereby convened at Flight Test, Pax River, with ever-smooth Duke Windson deftly moderating this menagerie.

Under the Bureau premise that "we have to find a way," discussions finally focused on the new mirror landing system that no U.S. carrier had at that time. The hypothesis was that thrust would not be so critical in a descending approach as was provided by the mirror. As luck would have it, I was to press onward. The Bureau would provide a fixed mirror landing system in a few weeks, mounted on a forklift, and we would try that. Meanwhile John Shepherd in one afternoon developed and manufactured his POMOLAS (Poor Man's Optical Landing Aid System), made of painted cardboard boxes mounted on stakes in the ground alongside Runway 31, at Pax, set to give a glide slope in the manner of the mirror system. It worked surprisingly well until it got rained on and warped, but lasted long enough for us to determine that the gliding approach was somewhat of an improvement but still allowed the 3M pilot to get on the backside of the curve at heavy approach weights which required afterburner for survival.

Soon the mirror arrived mounted on its forklift and was similar to Shepherd's POMOLAS, if brighter and warp-proof. Unfortunately, the Bureau's folks latched onto my feeling that there was some improvement (less hairy) and dispatched the forklift, mirror system, the 3M, and me back to San Diego and *Shangri-la* for further evaluation of this potential. There was complete unison in San Diego—the *Shangri-la* crew did not want me there and I did not want to be there.

As it turned out, the mirror-on-the-forklift was of little use on the pitching deck given to us by the Pacific Ocean. In two days I made twenty-five approaches and landings in the 3M including fifteen touch-and-goes and ten traps, using the mirror as a glide-slope starting point, since with the deck going up and down the mirror might as well have been in the wardroom. Results were about the same as with Shepherd's POMOLAS, in that one could sustain an acceptable approach speed at about MRT, but if you got a little slow, you were on the back of the curve and into afterburner. At the lighter weights, however, with no *Sparrows,* no ammo, low fuel state, it really was quite pleasant.

The trip back to Pax was not uneventful. I filed for Albuquerque and was catapulted from *Shangri-la* for the voyage to Albuquerque. Cruising along at twenty-five thousand feet off the coast, I was busy computing the time at which the BM and I would penetrate the ADIZ, a Defense Department control zone that could not be entered without clearance, with the further requirement that penetration must be within plus or minus ten minutes from filed estimates. My attention to this matter was distracted by the distinct feeling that we were flying sideways. A glance at the utility system hydraulic pressure gauge showed zero. The first clue, of course, was the yawing, since the yaw damper system now had retired. Final calculations showed I would enter ADIZ as filed, so I set my mind to the unsavory task of evaluating the condition of No. 736 with zero hydraulic pressure. It was unsettling to contemplate.

It was mandatory to have the slats out for landing—hydraulic. It was mandatory to have the gear down—hydraulic. (No slats-in or wheels-up landings in the F7U.) Nosewheel steering, important—hydraulic. Brakes—hydraulic. Canopy—hydraulic. Not knowing where the hydraulic fluid had gone or what was to happen next, I decided to do something electronic—I switched IFF [Identification Friend or Foe] from squawk one to emergency, then advised the world I was about to crash. All this did was attract some air-force bastard in an F-86 who came alongside, got all the dope he needed, wrote me up for missing my ADIZ estimate by two minutes, waved good-bye, and flew away.

The trip into Albuquerque was not comfortable. Advising approach control of my proclaimed emergency, I requested lots of fire trucks and meat wagons, remembering Johnny Long bent backward like a pretzel after he had run off the runway at Dallas.

Approaching at ten thousand feet and about two hundred

F-86 Sabre

knots, I made some decisions. I was not going to land th mother with the canopy closed, or the slats in, or the whee up. First the canopy. I moved the lever to open, and su enough, it unlocked, and with the help of the breeze I w able to push it fully open. Whether it would stay open event of a crash was another matter. But, one down. Next selected the slats out—nothing. Actuation of the emergenc air bottle blew them out and locked. Two down. Then put the landing gear handle down—nothing. Actuating th emergency gear air bottle blew the gear down and locke Three for three!

I was truly worried about being able to keep 3M on th runway, with no nosewheel steering and iffy brakes. I w aware that without hydraulic pressure there should still b three or four brake applications from the brake reservoir bla der, and there was the emergency brake air bottle as a la resort.

The touchdown at about 125 knots (must have been 13 knots or so at Albuquerque) was smooth, and I busily g the nose over and did a lot of steering with the rudders we decelerated. At near seventy knots I'd guess I lost rudder effectiveness and started drifting off the runway to the left. Time for the first brake application. Nothing. No brakes. Heading off the runway, I actuated the emergency brake air bottle. Immediately the right tire blew as the right wheel locked, but nothing on the left brake. The 3M and I started into a wild skid to the right (thank God to the right), the airplane rotating clockwise as it skidded down and across the runway, coming to a stop on the right edge facing the direction from which we had approached. Shutting down the engines again caused grave consternation with the crash crews who really did not understand Cutlasses or smoke pouring therefrom, but I persuaded them not to flood the port engine with foam, though frankly, my dear, I didn't give a damn at that point.

It turned out that during the cat shot from *Shangri-la* the catapult bridle had bounced up into the left main gear brake assembly, destroying it and mangling hydraulic lines there in the process. Bad day at Black Rock.

A few days later, after the Voughters had flown in needed parts, the 3M was ready to press onward. So back to Pax via St. Louis and a new round of talks with the Bureau folks and their ninety-eight F7U-3Ms we said they couldn't fly aboard ship. They were inclined not to take no for an answer.

Whilst the Bureaus, BIS, NATC, and other muck-a-mucks ranker than this lieutenant tried to resolve the 3M puzzle, there was other work to be done involving ''my'' bird—namely, using its mass and instrumentation to help calibrate the newly installed constant-runout arresting gear in place on PAX's runway 31.

Of a bright summer morning two of us, an A3D with Bud Nance driving, I think, and my 3M taxied out for some arrested landings in the new gear as part of the evaluation process. It was to be 736's last flight.

I was first, scheduled to arrest as close to ninety-five knots as possible, with 736 weighing in at twenty-six thousand pounds. I concluded I would have better speed control if I taxied in rather than flew in, since there was a ten-to-fifteen-knot thirty-degree crosswind and all that I had was the airspeed indicator as a measure. John Shepherd and Jerry Vaverek were the masterminds on hand as we were to evaluate a new arresting gear metering valve during runout following arrestment. The LSO, Tommy Thompson, stood majestically by his jeep as LSOs do, and at 0700 I started my run from the end of runway 31.

I reached about 103 indicated, hopefully the ninety-five-knot engaging speed (actual speed proved to be ninety-eight knots), and just before reaching the wire I throttled back, turned on the instrumentation, and dropped the hook. Cameras ground, oscillographs whirred, and the hook snagged the arresting cable. Though things happened pretty fast for the next few minutes, I do recall many of the events that followed hook engagement. First, it was apparent to me that I was not slowing down very much—it seemed that the new metering valve was not metering—then suddenly there was a terrific impact. The arresting cable, a two-inch behemoth, had fully paid out and was two-blocked. The Cutlass, still traveling at an estimated seventy-five knots, was stopped within less than thirty feet by the stretch of the cable alone! The impact failed the nose gear strut, ramming it up through the fuselage just behind the seat, and the Cutlass nose section slammed to the concrete, fracturing the fuselage almost in two. The ejection seat firing mechanism was actuated, went to a top dead-center prefire position, and stopped. Though my shoulder straps were tight, I was propelled forward and downward so hard that I smashed my face on the top of the control stick (good old oxygen mask). The deceleration was so profound that, though my hand was on the power control levers at idle, it shot forward, putting both engines in afterburner and bending the power control levers all to hell. It was about to get messy.

I was dazed by the blow to the chops, which loosened teeth and cut lips, but was quickly aware that the Cutlass was still moving, but backward, and a sizable fire had started below the cockpit. The recoil from the stretched arresting cable had pulled the 3M backward and rotated it ninety degrees to the left. Unfortunately, the hook had released the wire, for the Cutlass in afterburner started across the runway toward the weeds.

Pilot reaction was instinctive—I pulled the bent power levers back, but they were no longer connected to anything. Full afterburner. Depressing the brake pedals produced nothing—they were also sheared. The airplane was accelerating and the fire was roaring. Oh, yes, the emergency brake air bottle, duly actuated, was no longer connected. As the Cutlass left the runway, accelerating, I realized I could not stay in the cockpit because the fire was engulfing it from below. The escape route was arduous at best. The main gear were at least eight feet out from each side of the cockpit, yet I had no choice that I could think of but to dive out of the airplane, now doing about thirty knots, and try to roll clear of the main landing gear. And so I unbuckled and stood on the edge of the cockpit, right side, and dove as hard as I could at a forty-five-degree angle away from the angry machine, hitting the ground rolling, rolling, rolling. Though I did not see the Cutlass pass over me, I found my seat pack inside the right main tire track and me on the outside of it, scraped and bloody, but intact.

Standing in the weeds, I saw the Cutlass, sliding on its nose in a ball of fire, slowing to a halt because of an encounter with rough terrain. The cockpit was now completely engulfed in flames and the engines still roaring away in afterburner. No one had seen me get out!

As the fire trucks and a meat wagon raced across the field to the crash site I walked out of the weeds, across the runway to the LSO jeep, where Tommy was busy shouting instructions into the radio mike to anyone who would listen.

Thompson looked up as I stood there looking like I had been run over by something, but hadn't, and said, "What in the hell are *you* doing here?" I wondered where he thought I should be. Meanwhile, the fire trucks were pouring foam into the cockpit in hopes of saving enough of the pilot for an open-casket burial, at the same time pouring foam into the intakes of both engines in an effort to flame them out. In moments the engines were quiet and the fire out, and from the LSO jeep we watched John Shepherd and Jerry Varek along with the corpsmen peer into the cockpit in astonishment—there was nobody home. Vaverek thought I had been completely incinerated, and Shepherd figured there had to be a body somewhere. There was; at the LSO jeep.

Thompson finally got word to the meat wagon, which roared over, picked me up, and made way to the PAX hospital. It was now 0715. At this point I really was not sure I would survive the Cutlass.

At sick bay it took the surgeon only a few minutes to determine I would live, whereupon he produced two minibottles of brandy with instructions to consume the stuff immediately. I generally did not drink brandy at that hour, but you have to listen to your doctor. Shortly thereafter, as the X-ray machine was touring my back, another flight surgeon came in, took one look, and said to the corpsman, "Get that son of a bitch some brandy." Eight ounces later I was smashed— it was now 0800.

Other than a bunch of loose teeth, sore mouth, lots of scrapes and bruises (and a hangover), I was fine. F7U-3M No. 736 was fatally injured. Johnny Long's 3M, with mine, made it two down and ninety-six to go.

Unfortunately, BuAer, or whoever, provided carrier suit with yet another F7U-3M—good old BuNo 139868. In the next few months I had the privilege of flying 868 off three more carriers, trying to convince the buyer that the 3M Cutlass should never be flown off aircraft carriers. Well, off maybe, but not *onto*. The Bureau folks, logically, asked that we define an acceptable gross weight at which the airplane could be flown safely onto carriers by fleet units, since they would soon be up to their derrieres in F7Us. There probably was none, but I seem to remember that we stipulated twenty-three thousand pounds max, where there was a small margin of error thrust-wise, but which meant to BuAer a lot of weight reduction in armament and the like, since empty (fuel) gross weight with *Sparrows* was more than twenty-three thousand pounds.

Anyway, I did not participate in the final decision-making process, having, for my valiant efforts, been assigned as *Yorktown*'s (CVA-10) handling officer.

Not long after, on a clear day somewhere in the Pacific, *Yorktown* was joined by another carrier sporting a squadron of F7U-3Ms. During our first day of joint ops I watched from my perch under an AD-6 on the flight deck as a 3M was catapulted from our sister carrier. Immediately after becoming airborne, long streaks of flame came pouring out of the starboard engine as the pilot tried to gain some altitude. Sadly, at less than a thousand feet, the Cutlass nosed over, trailing black smoke, and splashed into the blue water, taking its pilot with it.

Shortly afterward that squadron was offloaded to Atsugi and spent its WestPac [Western Pacific] tour with the pilots flying CAP [Carrier Air Patrol] over Mount Fuji during the day while chasing sashimi with Asashi beru at night.

The Cutlass took many lives before it was retired. Yet as maturity sculptures the mind, one tends to remember the good things, the happy things, and forget the unpleasant ones. So it is with most of us who survived the Cutlass—we remember it as fun to fly.

But would I do it again? Are you kidding? Of course.

It's the Little Things That Bite You in the Butt

He's lanky. Sort of, that is. He only seems that way because he moves without any visible effort, an ambling glide. His clothes, either an old flight suit or mechanic's overalls, have the unmistakable sign of a man who peers into airplane innards and then crawls his way in after whatever it is he's seen and doesn't like. He's got a lopsided grin that makes you want to grin back despite your mood. His laugh hangs in the air like musical notes left over from that point when they should have vanished. He talks in a drawl, but it's not country or even the back forty. It's *himself*—Frank Quentin Ray.

One of a kind. Or at least one of a rare breed in the huge, chrome-plated electronic world of modern aviation. Frank Q. Ray is a paradox. No clipped tones of the company executive (which he is, among other things), but that drawl is catchy. You hear it and it draws you in because you have just got to hear what this man says when he's talking about airplanes or about flying. It's like climbing the high mountain to see the wise old man at the top so you can ask the ultimate questions. Frank's more than a walking, talking encyclopedia of aviation—he *is* aviation. *Mister* Aviation, that is.

Other pilots, mechanics, crew chiefs, and company officers lose no opportunity to hear what Frank has to say. He has an intrinsic grasp of things that have wings and knows how they should behave. Many more major decisions have been made on the basis of a gentle conversation with this man, who's got grease and oil and jet fumes about him, and spits tobacco juice with dead-eye accuracy, than have come out of all the board meetings you can count.

Frank Ray wears many hats, and you'll always find oil and grease somewhere on every one of them. Among other things, Frank is one of the busiest test pilots in the flying business. He tests new airplanes, rebuilt airplanes, and airplanes that are modified, reconstructed, adapted to special conditions, or are plain suspect when they come out of the modification or maintenance hangars.

You won't read about Frank in any of the magazines with marvelous color pictures and shiny paper, because Frank is what I call an unhero. He does his test piloting and other work day in and day out and there's just no fuss to it. When you think of test pilots and the billion-dollar programs sending all sorts of weird machines into the high sky, you've got to recognize a huge force of men and women on the ground and extraordinarily complex and costly instrumentation. You'd never recognize Frank Ray in that kind of setting or in that crowd, yet to his peers his superb ability as a pilot is unquestioned. Those of us who've flown with Frank feel comfortable with him. There's no furtive glances at instruments or controls or what the man might be doing at any moment because if you know the man you know what he can do with an airplane. *Any* airplane.

It would be great to present one of those heartwarming stories of the farm boy who rested his elbows on a rail and watched with awe as barnstormers cavorted about the fields just beyond the fence. But as hard as you look, you have an ordinary kid going to school, doing what teenagers do, except that he always leaned more to the side of things with wings than the average kid. He would also be found—more often than not—with his hands buried deep in auto engines and other things mechanical. He started flying in 1956 at a small field, Parkaire Field, outside Marietta, Georgia. Like so many other youngsters of his time and era, Frank took to flying like the proverbial duck takes to water. He was always at home behind the control stick and throttle of the common taildraggers of the time, the fabric-covered Aeronca 7AC, a potbellied, gasoline-smelling taildragger with some nasty tricks that sorrowed many a newcomer (and some old hands as well).

Frank went through the flying drill with all the fuss and bother of an old coon hound sound asleep on a dusty road. He just *did* it. He kept building up his time and working his way up to bigger, more powerful, more demanding airplanes. He learned to fly in weather that was severe to clear, and when thunderstorms rolled in and battered the countryside, why, he could fly through those as well. He paid for his training out of his own pocket, working day and night as a mechanic, when he wasn't flying, so that he *could* fly. And soon he was being paid to fly, but this kind of flying was tough, and it was demanding, and it was rough on the people and the airplanes, and the accident statistics were the kind you didn't write home about.

"It was the old system of building time," Frank explains in that laid-back drawl. "You know, flying the usual types of junk. Ferrying flights, work flights, odd jobs, even testing this airplane or that when it came out of a shop and they tapped you on the shoulder and pointed to the airplane and told you those familiar words to 'check it out.' That meant the people who owned or operated those airplanes and maintained them had doubts about their own work and their own machinery, and when I flew those things, I didn't even know I was *testing* them. I just took them up and checked out how they flew, how they were rigged, if the engine or engines worked fined, and how the propellers did, and you noticed everything—the oil temperatures and pressures, the cylinder head temps, working the fuel mixture and the carburetor heat and the cowl flaps and the wing flaps and the landing gear and the brakes. You went up looking for things that were wrong, and if they were *very* wrong, you came downstairs in a hurry because that bird was about to do bad things to your hide. After a while I got more and more of those kinds of flying jobs. Sort of gravitated toward it, you might say.

"But the *real* flying was the night mail. Most of the time we flew the Twin Beech, that ubiquitous old honker you could find all over the country. Whole bunches of them were ex-military types that once were C-45 cargo ships or AT-11 bombardier trainers, with do-it-quick modifications to make them acceptable for civilian work. A lot of those mods were paint and slapdash stuff, some new radio equipment and an airplane gutted of everything inside except the pilot seat because you needed all the volume inside the cabin for hauling the mail. Well, it was more than mail. You delivered anything that needed delivering that somebody was paying for. The Twin Beech was a tough, tough machine. It was supposed to fly in a pretty sedate manner but you could do aerobatics in it and roll it and beat hell out of it. She was like a bulldozer with wings, and that made you feel comfortable when you went upstairs at night and the weather was like a boiling caldron.

"And would you believe we also flew a machine with only one engine up front. But *what* a machine! The old Fairchild 24 with the Ranger engine. Damn airplane was absolutely great. When they built that thing, they strengthened the wings with big struts, but before they closed up those struts, they poured hot linseed oil into them and did some other special design work on the bird, so you ended up with an airplane that could take just about anything you might ever run into. That old Fairchild was stressed so strong it could take fourteen g's positive and nine g's negative, and there are still people who won't believe that. But I'll tell you what. That Fairchild would keep right on flying in tough times and under forces so great they'd rip the wings right off a Mustang or some other iron bird that had such a great reputation. It was a hell of a lot stronger than many of the planes built especially for aerobatic routines. At night, I always liked that second engine, of course, but I got to admit that the Fairchild never let us down.

"We flew the same mail runs most of the time, so we got to know the routes real well. We flew them so often that after a while we'd memorized all the radio frequencies and we knew all the headings to fly and how long each one would take and it became habit. Our usual run was from Atlanta on up to Knoxville, and then on to Chattanooga, and then we'd drop mail and pick up some more and launch off to Birmingham for the last stop before heading back to Atlanta. Sometimes there were pilots who found the going real lonely. You were alone up there, but that's only if that was your kind of thinking. Why, you were up there *with your airplane,* and that's great company. You were way up above the rest of the world and flying at night sort of made you feel you were sailing along just under that dark ocean of space that went up forever. I loved every minute of it."

Frank chuckled. "Of course, there are rules in this kind of flying, and the first rule was that sure as God made green apples you were going to bust a whole bunch of them rules. Today if a pilot takes off without checking the weather—and some guys stagger away from the telephone with enough paper for a telephone directory—they're judged as shredded in the head, and the FAA will jump all over them, because they're not exercising good judgment and proper precautions. Checking weather is one thing; paranoia is another."

Did Frank Quentin Ray and his coterie of nocturnal wanderers check weather before they flew? "Well, maybe at first," Frank allowed. "A little, I guess. but it didn't take long to find out that it didn't matter. Seem sort of indifferent or uncaring to you? Well, it wasn't that way at all. You see, we were flying the *mail*. And if anybody cares to remember, the post office said their mail always got through. Despite storms and rain and sleet and snow and ice and heat and dogs *and* flying regulations, the mail *had* to get through. So it finally dawned on us that since we were going anyway, no matter what was the weather, why bother with all that forecasting blather? We'd find out about the weather en route or when we got to where we were going. Did some detouring here and there, but we went. The rule was you put on whatever mail and cargo a truck dumped by your airplane and you pumped in enough gas to hopefully get to where you were going, and you *went*."

That was also the time when most pilots were superb mechanics. They *had* to be if they wished to have a decent shot at enjoying the aches of old age. They learned to trust *themselves* to take care of their airplanes. The companies running the cargo planes weren't averse to installing rebuilt plugs, many of them rebuilt by blind people working under water while they wore mittens, as Frank was quick to tell one and all. They learned to check their exhaust manifold systems when they got cranky and wobbled and shook, because a messed-up exhaust manifold could mean a beauty of an in-flight fire, and you didn't have time for some mechanic to show up in a freezing rain to work on your machine. "Besides, they were plain lazy," explains Frank Ray. "Lazy, and to a considerable degree, they had a marvelous level of incompetence. *They* weren't going to fly, so what did they care? There were lots of old planes around and a mob of pilots trying to do just what we were doing—build time, build time, get better and better at flying."

Frank Ray then took a long, hard look at the United States Air Force. It was 1960 and the Korean War was some years behind and Vietnam still seemed to rhyme with France. Not that he minded going to Vietnam or anywhere else there was in the world, so long as he *flew* there. But the government was real hot on slashing military budgets and the people who wore Air Force blue weren't exempt from the anemic dribble of money to bring in new pilots.

Frank preferred not to wait. There was, he figured, about umpteen ways to skin a cat even if the cat didn't like it, so he enlisted, made sure they guaranteed him a slot in aircraft mechanics and went off to military schools. The Air Force was delighted to have him because Frank, who lacked all the proper degrees and certificates, had something the Air Force needed badly. He knew how to find out what was wrong with an airplane and how to fix it. People like Frank are in screaming demand at any military outfit, and Frank snatched at the brass ring and signed up for flight engineers school and went through their drill. At times it was amusing. He'd climb aboard an Air Force transport or bomber or whatever was going to leap off, and compared with many of the crew he was already a grizzled old-timer. It's the grease and the oil; it works its way into and beneath the skin on a man's face and forms lines and ridges, and boy, you look like someone who spent your whole life flying open-cockpit biplanes.

But what amused Frank—and the crews who came to know him so well—was that often he had more time as a pilot than the Air Force jocks up in the front seats of their aircraft. Little matter; there were more good pilots than there were *great* flight engineers, and the airplane crews came to regard Frank Ray as having huge feathery pinions tied tightly to his back. He knew his airplanes with a sense and feel that defied description. He'd listen to an engine and it talked to him, told him of bellyaches and pains and grumbles, and when he peeled off the cowlings, most of the time he already knew what was wrong. He could listen to hydraulic lines and tell you what kind of music those gurgles meant.

What Frank recalls most is all the hollering and dire predictions that once attended the night mail and cargo runs in the old Twin Beeches and sometimes that cast-iron Fairchild 24, because the pilots so overloaded their airplanes. Judging by what the feds would say and what the regulations pronounced in dire terms, those old airplanes should never have flown so consistently with tires squashed from the weight above them.

"But *that* was nothing to what we did with the real heavy iron in the Air Force," he remembers, laughing at the insanities of everyday military flight. "I was flight engineer on a KC-97, the big Boeing C-97 cargo ship modified into an aerial tanker, so we could refuel fighters and bombers in the air—usually over the middle of the ocean. Now you can talk about overgross all you want, but you really didn't know what it meant until you got into the KC-97. First of all, that airplane had a wild reputation as one of the best three-engine ships ever built.

"That's because while it took off on four engines, it usually came back with only three of them still running. Anyway, we used to fly those bastards at ten thousand pounds overgross! And that was the *old* model, before they hung some jet engines on pods beneath the wings to extend the life expectancy of the crews.

"At Hunter Air Force Base in Savannah, Georgia, they've got a beautiful long runway. Twelve thousand feet. You could land the space shuttle there and it will come to a stop with a couple thousand feet still in front of you. But in that KC-97, with all that extra weight, you needed everything you could get. More times than I want to remember I've seen the nosewheel crossing the numbers on the opposite end of the runway from where we started, nearly two and a half miles *behind* us, before the pilot rotated. And then you didn't climb. You couldn't. The guy with the yoke in his hand would head straight for anyplace that was level, preferably the ocean, and keep that big old bird down real low to stay in ground effect, which gives you a free cushioning dividend when otherwise your airplane might decide it was time to become a submarine. You stayed like that, engines wide open, watching the temps very carefully, until you burned off enough fuel to be meaningfully lighter in weight, and not until then did that old sloughbelly start to climb.

"And as for engine reliability and durability in those days, I guess the less said, the better. Usually you expect a minimum of 1,200 hours out of a piston engine before it's time to put it through the shop for an overhaul. On many of the big radial engines you get about two thousand hours or so. But on those R4360s we thought we had a good engine if the thing would just hold together for 250 hours."

For three years Frank flew as flight engineer on the KC-97s and the huge Douglas C-124 Globemaster IIs, more affectionately known as Old Shaky. He figured then he'd join the reserves and keep his hand in. But in the meantime, there was that chance of a lifetime.

It's called Outlaw Time. You can fly the hell out of anything but you're not a *rated* Air Force pilot, so legally you do not take up any of those iron birds on your own. To keep everything legal there's got to be a commissioned officer on deck. Well, that's not really too much of a problem, because so long as everybody could squeeze within those regulations, Frank could fly the hell out of everything from the big transports to the hot fighters. He put in a few hundred hours in the T-33, and then in the TF-102, and he flew the two-seat sizzler, the Lockheed F-104 Starfighter, and got in a bunch of time at Mach 2. and maybe just a bit more than that.

He was at home in anything with wings on it.

Frank Ray had always had a plan. He wanted to work on airplanes, but he also wanted to fly them as much as he could. So he put all his skills together, knuckled down to some hard work, and set himself up for what he figures is the perfect way to go. Master mechanic *and* the pilot who tests everything that comes out of his shop. Down at Miami International, where his office is in the midst of Tropical Aviation, he moved through a succession of growing aircraft groups from Aero Facilities to Page Aerojet and right on up to where he is today. He's been president of a bunch of these outfits but he's always been the number-one man on the totem pole in maintenance, rebuilding, and flying what his hands have wrought.

First there was the matter of pilot tickets and ratings. He ascended the ladder from private pilot in the little honkers with one grumbler up front to multiengine with two, three, four, or more engines, including piston, turboprop, and pure jet. Okay, that took care of how many engines might be on something. He already had his commerical license and his instrument ticket, so he figured he should embellish on these a bit. He hied off to the waterways and got his single-engine and multiengine seaplane ratings, and he tacked on his CFI (Certified Flight Instructor) rating and then became a CFII (Certified Flight Instructor Instrument) as well.

What was left? Why, the ATP—the Air Transport Rating— so he became qualified as an airline pilot as well. Anything else? Sure. If you get type-rated or authorized to fly in at least three completely different types of heavy iron—the heavy planes that fly on piston power and thrashing props— you can get ticketed so that you are authorized to fly *any* such airplane, of any kind, from any part of the world. Frank added that little di-do to his tickets.

Then there was the other side of the coin. He already had his A&P (Airframe and Powerplant) license as a mechanic. He was already a ticketed flight engineer, so he went on to become an AI—Aircraft Inspector—for the things with wings and the powerplants that move them through the air. After *that* came his DME ticket, the Designated Mechanic Examiner, which means he checks out other mechanics and runs them through the mill to see if they qualify for their tickets as certified mechanics. Then came one of the crown jewels of aviation, the DAR—the Designated Airworthiness Representative.

Which meant that by now, he could do airworthiness certifications for standard category and experimental category airplanes of any kind or size, and he could fly and test anything with wings on it, and had the authority after test and inspection to grant it whatever certificate he judged the rules said it fit. That meant everything from the little honkers to the huge four-engined jetliners.

He *still* wasn't through! He went off to England to get his British commercial pilot license, and also his British AME— Aircraft Maintenance Engineer—so that he could work both sides of the ocean with equal authority.

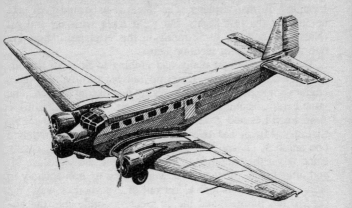

Junkers Ju-52/3m-g8e

Then he got rated in the one-of-a-kind airplane in the whole country that he really wanted to fly as captain from the left seat. That wasn't too difficult to arrange. I owned the airplane, the legendary Junkers Ju-52/3m-g8e, best known as Iron Annie or Tante Ju, and my ship (N52JU was the official registration) was the *only* German-built machine of its kind available in the country. I had the great pleasure (as the official examiner on my bird) to put Frank Ray through the wringer for him to qualify in the airplane, and he had a great time tap-dancing and singing his way down the runway and cavorting in the air.

Well, why not? He'd helped rebuild that machine from its scabrous, sagging ill health after it came out of that high jungle country in South America, and for years afterward he did the annual inspections on the airplane, and fed it and soothed its corrugated-metal brow, and for years we flew air shows together and did things in that airplane that even the Germans said were flatly impossible.

Remember Nick Silverio? Well, Nick, Frank, and I spent a lot of time together in that Ju-52, especially since Nick was the mastermind along with Frank in a bunch of modifications I wanted on that airplane. The three of us would then take her up for the test flights and we'd trade seats on and off (Nick also had his Ju-52 rating in this airplane). There are two flights that earn mention here.

The first test flight really had nothing to do with the airplane. Per se, that is. The ship ran beautifully, the three engines smooth, props synchronizing just like advertised. The issue here is Miami International Airport. We taxied out from Aero Facilities and ground control cleared us to Runway 9L (9 Left). Miami has two huge runways running parallel to one another, 9L and 9R, and the big airline jobbies usually came in on their long finals to land on 9R. So we'd use 9L and after lifting off the tower would clear us immediately to start a climbing left turn to get out of everybody's way. We cobbed the throttles and the Ju went smoothly into the air, and on this flight I was in the left seat while Frank and Nick were studying everything to be sure the clocks were working and the gear was still welded beneath the airplane. At that moment I knew this was not going to be like your everyday test hop.

Without time to tell anyone in the airplane, I thumbed my mike button, at the same time hauling the Ju into a climbing right turn that was taking us into the traffic on the 9R runway. It took Frank and Nick about the blink of an eye to size up things, but the tower controller was ready to bust a gut when he ordered us back to our former position over 9L.

"Negative that, Miami," I called back. "Advise you break off all traffic *now*." There was a strange silence and I think the strangled sounds of an angry man in the tower when I added: "Miami Tower, take a look at the east end of the field, please."

Dark clouds had been hanging fairly low over the eastern side of the field—oceanside, that is—and as we'd lifted off in the Ju this incredible, humongous, utterly black and angry funnel cloud had speared downward into a full-blown tornado. Timber, cement blocks, automobiles, trucks, rooftops, signs, and all kinds of debris whirled madly where the funnel was gouging the ground and the tornado was marching majestically toward the airfield. The next thing we heard was some really rapid-fire orders from the tower to continue our right urn and everybody else was told to "Break right! Break right! All aircraft break right!" Which sort of made good sense, since airplanes and their pilots, and even their passengers, do not do well in a huge tornado.

The obvious question was why we—I—hadn't simply hauled over to the left. That way I wouldn't have interfered with anyone. Frank looked up at Nick and said, "See? I told you these things follow this guy around." Sure enough, *another* funnel cloud rumbling parallel to and moving west, just north of 9L, and eating trees with a ferocious appetite.

Everything worked out nicely and we flew off to the area by Homestead Air Force Base to do our air work and start writing down numbers and such. We had a good view of the long air-force runway, and saw an F-100 jet fighter on its long final to land.

Well, they say things like to come in threes, and I dialed in the Homestead frequency. "Homestead Tower, advise you have your incoming traffic break off its approach." Before the tower could answer, a third tornado speared suddenly to the ground directly between the F-100 and the Homestead runway. It tore up some farmland, gave a few cows and other assorted barnyard denizens some flights of their own, but we didn't stay to watch, preferring to find air without dark clouds directly over us. It made for an interesting flight.

In running these test and checkout flights you never really know what's going to come out of nowhere and sink its teeth into your backside. On another flight the airplane had passed all its own tests, but we were testing a new windscreen for the open rear gun turret on the top aft end of the fuselage, just before the vertical fin. Nothing could be simpler than a windscreen (it says here and there), but that's not the way it works. It's always the little things that catch you unawares.

Here we were in this German bomber that we already knew inside out. Between Frank Ray and Nick Silverio we had the talents of a dozen top mechanics and test pilots. Between the three of us we'd flown all manner of military aircraft (count me out as a mechanic). The forward fuselage of the Ju-52, especially the cockpit area, looks like it was made to fly in a vacuum. No smooth, curving, sleek, streamlined lines. Flat surfaces, crazy angles, flat windscreen—made to order for maximum drag. So we built our own gunner's windscreen, flat in the middle, and angled sharply and cleanly to each side and said, "Let's see how it flies." Simplest thing in the world.

Frank took the right seat and I was flying captain and Nick just wanted to get the hell away from his office. We took off, and at ninety miles per hour we got bit in the butt. don't know what that sharp-angled windscreen was doing back behind us, but suddenly the entire airplane buffeted sharply, we felt a steady vibration, and the rudder reversed. Normally when you make a left turn, you use your left foot on the left rudder pedal and you roll the yoke to the left, and if you're even fairly coordinated the bird banks into a left turn. Now, when I used left rudder, that big vertical surface turned sharply to the right and the Ju wallowed like a pregnant pig trying to climb a slippery slope. We flew around like this and at another ten miles an hour the rudder control was back to its usual manner, but the airplane was vibrating as though people were using air hammers out on the wings.

Time to go home. We played the approach steep and high so we'd have extra airspeed. Sure enough, at a hundred miles per hour the rudder got antsy again, at ninety the rudder pedals kicked back at our feet, we went through the crazy rumble. The speed dropped below ninety and everything was normal again. None of us had ever run into anything like this before. So we called Munich, Germany, to talk with Kurt Streit, who's *the* master Ju-52 pilot from his old Luftwaffe days. He roared with laughter and said put a curved windshield back there by the turret and everything would be fine. Nick called Miami Plastics. They had some B-29 gunner sighting blisters and we cut one to shape and installed it back by the turret and that old Ju flew as smooth as glass.

For Frank Ray, every flight is a test flight. For example:

"I took a Turbo Commander out of Miami to test and check a double-engine change and a major overhaul on all components to the airframe. The typical thing we do. Rebuild them from nose to tail and wing tip to wing tip. These are often planes from South America that have been so abused for years it's a miracle they ever make it up to Miami and our shop. We refurbish them completely and the book calls for a thorough test flight to iron out the wrinkles. I climbed through eighteen thousand feet when all of a sudden the pressurization system of this airplane fails completely. It *always* gets your attention because I was running a max internal pressure test, and in just about two seconds the cabin pressure went from sea level to eighteen thousand feet in a dramatic explosive decompression. Of course the inside of the cabin was like being in a thick cloud because of the sudden condensation; it *was* thick fog.

"It also blew the hell out of my right eardrum. Someone stuck an ice pick in my ear, or at least it felt that way, and I was already nosing over and diving like Hogan's goat to get to lower altitude. I've got a lifetime of skinned knuckles and scrapes and head bangs and I'm used to this sort of thing, but this time the pain in the right ear was so severe that streams of water were coming out of my eyes like garden hoses on full. It's funny trying to see the runway through two glasses full of water, but I got her down and as soon as I stopped they hauled me off to the emergency room. I still can't hear very well out of that ear, but at least it's still where it belongs. Interesting.

"I took up another Turbo Commander which had gone through the same kind of overhaul that we did on the Ear Buster, but this one had me sitting close to the edge of the seat. It was an old model and that means it had time to build fatigue in its metal structure and you can't always detect that. So I went up to see how it all worked. It was the middle of summer, something over a hundred degrees Fahrenheit on the ramp. I got the air-conditioning system going full blast as I climbed out. When you get upstairs the outside air is cold and you don't need air-conditioning. In fact, it got downright cold in that airplane. I turned off the AC and switched to cabin heat. It didn't come on too swift, so I turned it up to max output. It got *very* warm. I turned it down and it got *much* warmer. In fact, no matter what I did from then on, that cabin was turning into a furnace. There's raw air, hotter than Hades, pouring from the engine system straight into the cabin. That's when I remembered that on this airplane there aren't any bleed-air shutoff valves, so you can't shut off the heat.

"The only option you have is to keep the engines running and you fry, or you shut off the engines and you don't fly very well, even if things cool down. By now I'm clawing my way around to get back as fast as I can to the airport and I've already declared an emergency. The longer we're in the air and the lower we get, the worse it gets. The vinyl around the heat vents is now blistering and smoking and it's a race between frying and flying. Well, we got back in and I was sort of gasping. Hit that runway and threw open the doors.

"Immediately the crash trucks rolled because thick smoke poured out the doors and billowed all about and behind the airplane and I let that ship come to a stop and I hung out the door because I was on the edge of passing out. I didn't even dare taxi. I've been in the Sahara and Death Valley and they're like cold compared to the heat that built up in the Commander. We had to replace all the interior furnishings, panel mounts—well, more than half the inside of that ship. Not any fun.

"The Turbo Commanders seemed to collect trouble. I took a refurbished model out of Fort Lauderdale Executive Airport after a new avionics installation by the Bendix people, and I'm just over Fort Lauderdale International, going south, when smoke starts coming out from behind the panel. A wisp of smoke. It was like magic. While I stared at the wisp it changed to a thick billowing cloud. By good fortune I was talking to the control tower below us and I lost no time in telling them I have a cockpit thick with smoke, we're either on fire or about to be on fire, and I'm shutting down *all* electrical power and here I come. Just before I shut down the radio panel I heard him telling me I was number one and I dumped that mother on the ground. With the electrical system off, the smoke diminished. I turned on power, left off everything except one radio, and flew back to the Bendix shop at Exec. We pulled their brand-new, latest-model transponder out of the panel. You'd never believe what we saw. What you'd find in a bed of coals after you've burned your way through dinner in your backyard barbecue. The damn thing had fire-eaten itself, metal and all."

One day a pilot flies in to Frank's shop in a hot turboprop, a Mitsubishi MU-2, which has a reputation of always being "on the edge," and demanding *very* accomplished pilots to keep out of the obit pages. The order was for everything in that airplane to be changed. Even every actuator had to be replaced. This time the pilot who regularly flew the airplane told Frank to call him when the ship was ready and they'd do the first test flight together. They took off with the owner in the left seat and Frank riding copilot in the right. To Frank's surprise everything worked beautifully. Thirty minutes of pulling, turning, twisting, shoving, and working everything the MU-2 had, and they rolled back on their way to Miami. After they landed, Frank and his crew would crawl through the airplane looking for leaks and any other problems. But since everything had worked so well he didn't expect more than a glitch here and there.

"Until we were on final approach," Frank said. "We've got approach flaps down, and on the MU-2 these are full-span flaps. No ailerons. This monkey airplane uses spoilers instead that bang up from the wings. The guy in the left seat is about three hundred feet above the ground and he reached over to put in another notch of flaps and when he did I *sensed* something wrong. He was having trouble keeping that right wing up. So I looked outside best I could, but you don't see much with a wing on top of the airplane. Look at the controls *inside* the airplane, dummy, I told myself. The guy had full left spoiler working, but the airplane was still trying to roll to the right and he wasn't doing anything about it.

"Time to go to work and take over. Immediately I put the flaps to full up and took the controls. The pilot didn't like that and made rude noises and told me to get the hell off the controls. Well, I just ignored him. I determined a long time ago never to sit still and let some idiot kill me in an airplane. I can do that quite well myself if that's what its all about. He complained but I left the flaps in full-up position and I plastered that thing onto the runway doing about 180 miles per hour, coming down like a rock. I was amazed the gear didn't collapse; that is one very tough bird.

"What happened was enough to make you pull out your hair. The mechanics had rigged the full-span flaps on one side of the airplane just the opposite of what they should have been. When the pilot brought the flaps down on that side, *they went up*, and those full-span flaps just turned into a massive aileron. Those little spoilers didn't have the capacity to overcome that kind of effect, and if I hadn't put the flaps back up, we'd have rolled right into the ground. That sort of thing makes a lovely fireball, but this wasn't the Fourth of July and I preferred the hard landing instead. There's a lesson here. Its always these sudden little things at *low* altitude that will do you in."

Frank nailed some sort of flying pest with a blast of tobacco juice and scratched his head. "You've flown the Cessna 340 with me. An airplane that keeps you on your toes. Well, some years ago that thing developed so many problems with its tail feathers Cessna ordered the horizontal stabilizers replaced on *all* the 340s flying. The stabilizers on the airplanes were cracking. Sometimes they cracked a bit *too* much. One of the prototypes was on a certification flight and a chase pilot called him by radio and hollered that some pieces were flying off his tail. All they heard from the 340 test pilot was that 'Something's terribly wrong,' and boy, was he right. About that time the tail wrenched completely off the airplane and it somersaulted all the way to the ground and exploded.

"Even the first time I flew the 340 I could *feel* something *wrong* with the tail. I could feel the elevators vibrate. So subtle the average pilot might never notice it, but to me it was like shooting off flares, and I said to hell with it and slowed down and brought it back to the field and I wouldn't fly it anymore. Then Cessna came out with the big stabilizer replacement program. As luck would have it they called me late on Friday and said, 'We need a test flight right away. How about taking up that 340 you just finished and do a dive test on it?'

"What that meant was diving that mother all the way to redline, right to the max allowable. You go over redline and anything can happen. 'We want to see if the tail will stay on at redline,' they added. Gee thanks, fellas. But I got in the airplane and a young pilot, new to the game, really wanted to come along, so I said sure, jump in. Off we got from Miami and we're still just above the runway, everything down and dirty yet, and suddenly the left wing feels heavy. *Real* heavy. I don't like this at high altitude and I like it a lot less down on the deck. I rolled in trim and then the airplane tries to roll *hard* to the left. I'm all of a hundred feet in the air and now this thing is going real crazy on me, I've got full right rudder, and I'm trying like crazy to bring this thing around to the right. I've already been hollering to the tower that I've got problems and I'm going to try to come around. They say to land on *any* runway I can reach and they break off all incoming flights so I won't be distracted (or run into someone else).

"I tried to turn to land on runway 30, but my right leg was now shaking so hard from effort, the muscles starting to spasm, that I yelled to the kid with me to 'get your foot on that right rudder pedal and push as hard as you can!' He does just that and, hey! We're starting to turn! That gave me a moment to ask myself the question you've got to always ask yourself when the drums are beating: What's the last thing you did? Immediately, remembering, I'm cranking trim like mad in the direction opposite to what I'd used before and like magic all my problems go away and that airplane is flying fine and dandy.

"Shall I say I was steamed? You could have done clams and mussels with the steam coming out of my ears. I was going to give my mechanics absolute hell for not checking the trim—which they had reversed—but then I shut up, because the fact of the matter was that neither did I check that trim before even starting the engines. Who could ever have expected that a top crew and a real smart-ass like me could make such a stupid mistake of not checking? It's always the little things that bite you in the butt."

There are always occasions when the man who tests airplanes day in and day out learns a new lesson. . . .

Frank took up a Cessna 421 after a double engine change. Everything forward of the firewalls had been replaced with new equipment. To give the engines a good run he set out for Vero Beach from Miami. On takeoff the engines acted as if their fuel mixture was a bit too rich. He leaned the mixture controls manually and everything seemed okay and he continued up the coast. Always pay attention to the little things. They landed at Vero, checked out the ship, everything looked fine, and they fired up and punched out back for Miami. They got as far south as Stuart and the engines began to run rough. *Both* engines. It might be bad fuel. "Nope," Franks says, "the fuel was fine. But the engines kept getting rougher and rougher and I have one eyeball locked onto the field at Stuart. By now the whole plane is vibrating like a cocktail mixer. Time to go down, baby! I lean, I try everything, nothing helps, but I'm already heading for the field. I come back on power for the descent and the engines smooth out. Seems crazy to *limp* back to Miami, but that's what we do. Low power, rumbling along like a kid's go-cart, and we land and pull the engine cowls.

"The automatic fuel-feed systems for both engines were *loose*. The nuts that held them on to at least one bank of cylinders on each engine were gone. This destroys the sensing system and turns fuel flow from smooth to turbulent. On each engine I had three cylinders running extremely lean, and three that were extremely rich. So it didn't matter if I leaned or enriched. Like going full to the floor in a car with the gas pedal and holding full brake. Lots of steam and noise and smoke and nothing seems to work right.

"Put it down to one more notch on the learning curve."

It's always the unexpected. Frank launches out of Miami in a Piper Cheyenne III, a pleasant ferry flight from Miami to Lakeland. Vacation time, like. He settles down for cruise and looks around to check out the airplane. What he calls "to see if my nacelles are bleeding." No bleeding, but smoke is sort of sneaking out from one engine nacelle. Wispy gray that, well, it *looked* like smoke. "So," Frank goes on, "I kept looking and looking and then I studied the other engine and it's doing the same thing, and I don't understand what's going on and *that* scares me. I'm halfway to Lakeland, so I go on; besides, it's all swamp beneath me, and I wanted the factory rep to look at things. I land okay and taxi in and the rep is waiting for me and his eyes are like saucers and getting bigger and bigger as I park. Now he's actually backing away from the airplane. That's hint enough for me. I shut down and get the hell out of there and immediately I know what's wrong. The smell of jet fuel was enough to almost knock me down.

"Jet fuel is running out of both nacelles. The line crew runs up with fire bottles and they pull the cowlings and there's the problem. The main fuel supply line for each engine had never been tightened. They looked okay before starting, but as it turned out the vibration from flight had loosened everything and the lines were being held by a whisker. The jet fuel was being sucked right through the generator of each engine.

"It was hot on the ramp and I was ice cold. Because the pressures on each engine had held steady. They didn't spark. I knew that without looking any further. If even one of them *had* sparked, that airplane and me would have looked like we'd been hit by a SAM. Fireball time."

And then there was Venezuela: "This time we got into it when we went into the mountains near Maracaibo in Venezuela. We got a call from the man who owned a cattle ranch. Neat little place, about a half-million acres, and the place had forty families living on it and umpteen thousand deer cattle. He also had a small airstrip there and his own Cheyenne for travel. Sometime in the past he'd driven a massive steel rail into the ground at one end of his field and in a couple of months it was covered with weeds.

"One day he's in a big hurry to go somewhere and he wheels that Cheyenne around, and with power on almost to full bore, he runs the prop on one engine smack into the steel rail. That kind of dinged things up a bit. They sent the engine and prop up to us in Miami for the fix, we did the job and sent it back, and he had the locals put Humpty Dumpty back together again. Then we get another call. 'Come down and test the airplane for me,' he says. Okay, that's how I earn my living. I ask if he's had the plane rigged properly and he's impatient and says everything's been done.

"I flew down there commercial, somebody gave me a lift to his field, and I didn't waste any time climbing aboard the Cheyenne and cranking it up. Change 'everything' to 'almost nothing.' I couldn't get the left engine out of idle. Everything under the panel was a rat's nest. I didn't have the proper tools with me, just what they had at the field to fix tractors and bulldozers and cars. So I uncowled the other engine and started measuring the control rods and fuel control and other gidgets and finally got that repaired engine to where I had full power. Of course, it had a tremendous throttle spread. When both engines were at full power, one throttle was a couple of inches away from the other, instead of their being lined up evenly. And with this Mickey Mouse rig I had no reverse thrust with the props. If I had to abort from this field, it would be with brakes only and there wouldn't be enough room for a safe stop. We'd go charging off into the boonies. And the more I thought of the field at Maracaibo, the lack of reverse thrust *there* for stopping made me hate myself. I wanted to wait for morning, but there was severe weather coming in. I calculated everything the best I could and figured if I could get through the mountain pass on my first crack, we'd get into Maracaibo.

"Well, it was an insane decision. I took off with a plane full of Venezuelans and tools and baggage. And you know what? Nothing went wrong. We hit the rough weather, but I was going full bore to beat the storm and I threaded that mountain pass, even though I was working the throttles all the time to keep even power. At Maracaibo it was dicey. No reverse thrust, but the brakes stopped us at the far end of the runway. Everything had been so dumb on my part I swore I'd never go back to that field again. And I never did."

"This has happened to me only once. I didn't understand it then and I don't understand it now, and it doesn't make any sense because by all the rules and the logic and the sense and experience I've had in a lifetime of flying, it just cannot happen. But it did.

"We'd installed a global navigation unit in a new Turbo Commander. God, what a change! A *new* airplane. It even smelled new. It was terrific. We brought the tech rep from the Britton company with us for the navigation test—not the airplane on a test flight—and the man wanted to see his own equipment in action, so to speak. That way he could be certain the navigation gear was perfectly calibrated before the airplane went on to its customer.

"We filed an instrument flight plan, a round robin from Miami to Bimini, then to Orlando, and back to Miami. It was one of those lovely clear days—you could see forever—and we climbed up to twenty-five thousand feet and tooling along as slick as owl snot on a brass doorknob. A wonderful flight.

"Just as we were approaching Bimini the tech rep suddenly shouts: 'Quick! Look at that!' The way his voice was pitched I scanned everything immediately for fire, or whatever, I didn't see a thing and I looked back over my shoulder, and

his guy is white as a sheet. He's pointing with a shaking
and at the magnetic compass and I turned to look at it and
knew just how he felt.

"It was impossible. The compass was changing direction
hrough 180 degrees. Then it snapped to a stop, you had time
only to see that it *had* stopped, then instantly it snapped back
o 180 again. It kept doing this. Physically this is not possi-
le, but it kept doing just that.

"I studied everything again and was astonished to note
hat everything electronic in the airplane had gone belly up.
mean it was still on, power was on, but nothing worked.
The radios were absolutely silent and then disbelief got wilder,
ecause all sound faded from the cabin in that airplane. Here
we were at twenty-five thousand feet with two engines run-
ing and the props whirling away, and the wind howling
against the airplane, and you couldn't hear anything. None
of us could. It was unbelievably silent. Someone said some-
hing and he was two feet away and you couldn't even hear
is voice.

"It was what I call crushingly silent. A deafening silence
hat just could not be real. I looked down. We were directly
over Bimini and I had been ready to make my turn, and in
atter, dead silence I turned the airplane and we departed
he coast of Bimini—and like you'd snapped your fingers,
everything was back to normal. All the electronics came back
on line, all sound returned. Just like nothing had ever hap-
ened. But it had and we'd all experienced something that
vent beyond all reasoning.

"What was it? I don't know."

"I was going to ask you if you ever made a short-field
akeoff, but I figured you wouldn't stop laughing for a week
with all the things you'd done in that Ju-52. Well, that will
elp you understand—and maybe you'll even appreciate *this*
akeoff. Remember when I was living down in the islands?
t was marvelous down there. Nearby was a little airstrip. I'd
ever flown into it but had driven there to marvel at the
nsanity some people call airstrips. It was on the north side
of Jamaica in a place called Discovery Bay.

"One day I get a call to take an Aero Commander 500S,
he Shrike model, out of there. At first I figured it was a

joke, because the people who owned the strip had said it was 1,800 feet long, but I would gladly eat every foot over 1,500. You know the old saw—nothing stretches the length of an airstrip like imagination.

"This thing started out by running uphill. Then it crested a mound and it ran downhill. On the other side of the crest there was maybe three hundred feet of turf left when the airstrip ended suddenly. I mean that. At the end of the strip there was a dropoff of about a hundred feet into the sea. And this is where they wanted me to fly that Shrike, with seven people aboard! *And* the baggage bin crammed to the top. At least I knew I could remove half the fuel.

"I was studying the whole thing and figured the smartest thing I could do was to go home and drink a case of beer. But it *was* an interesting challenge. Some fellow ambles up to me, and he looks like he's been here forever. 'You want to know the only way to fly out of here?' he asks, and in that instant my ears grow larger and work better. The more he talked, the more I realized he knew what the hell he was talking about. It *was* the only way.

"So I load everybody aboard and I check the center of gravity real carefully, and finish my fourth inspection of the airplane, and we push it back as far as it will go with the tail in the weeds and the nose pointed toward the Caribbean Sea. *That* is the only way to go. Toward the ocean. I fire her up and I do the best run-up I have ever done. I run those engines up until they're screaming and I'm checking out every gauge, and I move every knob and handle and control, and then there's no more to be done. Except to tighten my stomach and hold my breath.

"I've got everything full forward, and we're shaking like mad, and I pop the brakes and let her run. No flaps, which sounds crazy, but this whole thing was crazy. I was trying to push that airplane along *going uphill,* and we were accelerating and I wished I had rocket bottles under me or that I had been smart enough to go home and drink that beer. But there we were, pounding along up that crazy hill.

"Right at the top of the hill, a few feet over it, and we're starting downhill and there's maybe 250 feet or less left in front of us, and I raise the nosewheel up so it's free of the ground and instantly I reach over and punch in half flaps and we're going like hell and we reach the end of the runway and we do not have flying speed.

"But this is a normal takeoff from this idiotic field! I ran her right off the edge of the runway and I'm yanking up the gear as fast as I can and the airplane drops sickeningly toward the water and it's still stall time, sweetheart, because we do *not* have flying speed yet. But the gear is up, and that helps because we have less drag now, and I let her drop (I have no choice) until we fall into the ground effect, that cushion of air, and we wallow a bit, but the descent stops and the water skims by terrifyingly close beneath us. Now, if not even one spark plug in each engine doesn't miss a beat, soon we'll have enough speed to climb out of that ground effect and we'll be on our way.

"But if one spark plug skips, even for a moment, you're in a bathtub with wings and you take up swimming real fast.

"It was interesting. You can't win 'em all, but we did win that one."

Frank grins. "Because you know, it's the *little* things that bite you in the butt. . . ."

A NOTE ABOUT THE BANTAM AIR & SPACE SERIES

This is the era of flight—the century which has seen man soar, not only into the skies of Earth but beyond the gravity of his home planet and out into the blank void of space. An incredible accomplishment achieved in an incredibly short time.

How did it happen?

The AIR & SPACE series is dedicated to the men and women who brought this fantastic accomplishment about, often at the cost of their lives—a library of books which will tell the grand story of man's indomitable determination to seek the new, to explore the farthest frontier.

The driving theme of the series is the skill of *piloting,* for without this, not even the first step would have been possible. Like the Wright brothers and those who, for some 35 years, followed in their erratic flight path, the early flyers had to be designer, engineer, and inventor. Of necessity, they were the pilots of the crazy machines they dreamt up and strung together.

Even when the technology became slightly more sophisticated, and piloting became a separate skill, the quality of a flyer's ability remained rooted in a sound working knowledge of his machine. World War I, with its spurt of development in aircraft, made little change in the role of the flyer who remained, basically, pilot-navigator-engineer.

Various individuals, like Charles Lindbergh, risked their lives and made high drama of the new dimension they were

arving in the air. But still, until 1939, flying was a romantic,
evil-may-care wonder, confined to a relative handful of
ardy individuals. Commercial flight on a large scale was a
mere gleam in the eye of men like Howard Hughes.

It took a second major conflict, World War II, from 1939
to 1945, to provoke the imperative that required new concepts
from the designers—and created the arena where hundreds of
young men and women would learn the expertise demanded
by high-speed, high-tech aircraft.

From the start of flight, death has taken its toll. Flying has
always been a high-risk adventure. Never, since men first
launched themselves into the air, has the new element given
up its sacrifice of stolen lives, just as men have never given
up the driving urge to go farther, higher, faster. Despite only
a fifty-fifty chance of any mission succeeding, *still* the dream
draws many more men and women to spaceflight than any
program can accommodate. And still, in 1969, when Mike
Collins, Buzz Aldrin and Neil Armstrong first took man to
the Moon, the skill of piloting, sheer flying ability, was what
actually landed the "Eagle" on the Moon's surface. And
still, despite technological sophistication undreamed of 30 or
40 years earlier, despite demands on any flyer for levels of
performance and competence and the new understanding of
computer science not necessary in early aircraft, it is piloting,
human control of the aircraft—sometimes, indeed, inspired
control—that remains the major factor in getting there and
back safely. From this rugged breed of individualists came
the bush pilots and the astronauts of today.

After America first landed men on the Moon, the Russian
space program pushed ahead with plans for eventually creating a permanent space station where men could live. And in
1982 they sent up two men—Valentin Lebedev and Anatoly
Berezovoy—to live on Solyut-7 for seven months. This extraordinary feat has been recorded in the diaries of pilot
Lebedev, *Diary of a Cosmonaut: 211 Days in Space*.

The Bantam AIR & SPACE series will include several
titles by or about flyers from all over the world—and about
the planes they flew, including World War II, the postwar
era of barnstorming and into the jet age, plus the personal
histories of many of the world's greatest pilots. Man is still
the most important element in flying.

Index

Page numbers of illustrations appear in italics

ABOUT THE AUTHOR

The author of over 140 books, several dozen technical and flight manuals, and several thousand magazine and newspaper articles and series, Martin Strasser Caidin is one of the outstanding aeronautics and aviation authorities in the world. The National War College, the Air University, and many international educational and training institutions use his books and other writings as strategy guides, historical references, and textbooks. He has several times won the Aviation/Space Writers Association top awards as the outstanding author in the world in the field of aviation. He is the recipient of the honored Brewer Trophy Award for aviation education programs. Martin Caidin is also the recipient of the Pioneer Aviator and Master Aviator awards from the Silver Wings pilot organization, and has been honored with special awards from the U.S. Air Force, NASA, the U.S. Navy, and other top government groups. He is the only civilian to have lived and flown with the USAF Thunderbirds jet aerobatic team and won high honors for his book on that experience). He is a member of the Ten-Ton Club of England for his supersonic flying in the earlier days of "Mach-Busting," and is as well known for his stunt flying and airshow performances as for his writing.

Martin Caidin is the former Consultant to the Commander of the Air Force Missile Test Center and was involved in rocket, missile, and spacecraft development from its earliest days. For years he worked with Dr. Wernher von Braun and a select team working secretly on a rocket to be launched to the moon. He is a former Consultant to the Flight Surgeon, the Office of Flight Safety, and to the Administrator of the Federal Aviation Administration. He has ridden in centrifuges, dived vertically at high supersonic speeds, undergone explosive decompression for flight research, has been a parachutist, and has witnessed and been involved in the firing of literally hundreds of missiles, rockets, and space vehicles.

Martin Caidin is married to Dee Dee M. Caidin, and they are well known for their joint activities in airshow, movie and research work in flying. They have flown together in rebuilt warbirds, flying boats, bombers, and other aircraft and work as a tightly knit professional team.

Martin Caidin, in addition to his writing, flying, teaching and guest appearances throughout the country and in universities, is also engaged in several research programs of a "highly provocative" nature.